D0933972

EINSTEIN
IN THE
BOARDROOM

Moving Beyond Intellectual
Capital to I-Stuff

SUZANNE S. HARRISON
AND
PATRICK H. SULLIVAN

WILEY

John Wiley & Sons, Inc.

For general information on our other products and services, or technical support, please contact our Customer Care Department within the United States at 800-762-2974, outside the United States at 317-572-3993 or fax 317-572-4002.

Wiley also publishes its books in a variety of electronic formats. Some content that appears in print may not be available in electronic books.

For more information about Wiley products, visit our Web site at http://www.wiley.com.

Library of Congress Cataloging-in-Publication Data:
Harrison, Suzanne S.
  Einstein in the boardroom : moving beyond intellectual capital to I-stuff / Suzanne S. Harrison and Patrick H. Sullivan.
    p. cm.
  Includes bibliographical references and index.
  ISBN-13: 978-0-471-70332-7 (cloth)
  ISBN-10: 0-471-70332-X (cloth)
  1. Intellectual capital—Management. I. Sullivan, Patrick H. II. Title.
  HD53.H376 2006
  658.4′038—dc22

                                                      2005031932

Printed in the United States of America
10 9 8 7 6 5 4 3 2 1

To Sandra, Juan, Derek, and Alana.
Without them there would be nothing of value.

CONTENTS

ACKNOWLEDGMENTS

A S ANY AUTHOR can attest, a book is a complex and interacting set of activities. Good ideas have many parents, and this was certainly the case with *Einstein in the Boardroom*. *Einstein* is the fifth book the authors have written about getting value from intangibles. This book is the result of collaboration with a number of people who provided the inspiration guidance, support, and ideas that have made it possible. For these people and their willingness to share company stories with us, we are deeply grateful. Although we conceived the original framework of ideas, many people spent hours helping us shape the concepts, and countless others donated their time and insights to animate the ideas further.

We are particularly indebted to the Executives and Thought Leaders who contributed their stories: Charles Armstrong, Steve Baggott, Carol Beckham, Alphaeus Bingham, Debra Charlynn Clayton, Scott Frank, Tony Frencham, Vince Grassi, Karen Gullett, Harry Gwinnell, Theresa Kotanchek, Henri Linde, Celine Monette, Robert Nelson, Anne Ness, Sharon Oriel, Jim O'Shaughnessy, Michael Pierantozzi, John Raley, Hubert Saint-Onge, Mark Radcliffe, Aaron Schachtt, Nancy Schrock, Rob Smith, Jonathan Spier, Bruce Story, Jeanne Suchodolski, Karl-Erik Sveiby, Bill Swirsky, John Tao, Jeff Weedman, Stewart Witzeman, and David VandenEinde.

The authors would like to express their special appreciation to Sharon Oriel, of Talisker & Associates, and to John Raley, of Cargill, Inc. Their many hours reviewing and critiquing drafts and helping us to clarify our thinking contributed significantly to this endeavor. Sharon and John—we are truly grateful for your insights, wisdom, and tenacity. This book could not have been written without your contributions.

We would also like to acknowledge the help of Efrat Kasznik and Naheed Hasnat of ICMG. Their assistance and support, both professional and personal, was given freely and often at a moment's notice. We greatly appreciate everything you do for us. And finally we would like to say thank you to our editor Susan McDermott for her guidance and support in making *Einstein* happen as well as for her continuing efforts to promote the management of intangibles for value.

Einstein was created by marrying the experiences and views of the ICM Gathering with the consulting experiences of the authors. We are especially grateful to the companies of the ICM Gathering for sharing their knowledge, experiences, successes, and failures with us. We would also like to thank the companies in the IP Forum and AU Gathering for their insights into our evolving thinking about I-stuff.

AUTHORS' FOREWORD

THE ICM GATHERING

In the Autumn of 1994, several of us in the then nascent IC management community realized that we had very different perspectives on the thing called "Intellectual Capital," as well as on how it should be managed. Wanting to explore these differences further, we decided it could be a good idea to bring together all of the companies in the world that actively managed their intellectual capital. That would allow us a way to define and perhaps to delve into active approaches to managing intellectual capital.

We were able to bring seven companies together, in Berkeley, California, in January 1995 to share what we knew on the topic. The participating companies included Dow, DuPont, Hewlett-Packard, Hughes Space and Communications, Hoffman LaRoche, Skandia, and the Law & Economics Consulting Group.

The participants set as their purpose to define the term intellectual capital and to determine how it is managed, at least for those companies attending the meeting. We realized early in the proceedings that we were having difficulty communicating because, while we used similar terms to define elements of intellectual capital, we each defined them differently. As a result, we had to create a language and to agree on common terms and definitions in order to communicate with one another; and so we did. By noon of the second day the excitement level in the room was almost electric; no one wanted the meeting to end. We agreed to meet again, and four months later we reconvened to continue the conversation. The group has continued to meet three times each year for, now, over ten years.

Before each meeting, the members agree on the "hot topics" to be featured at the forthcoming meeting. Sometimes outside speakers are invited but, after long experience, the group has learned that more is learned from the sophisticated membership than from outside speakers. For that reason, most of the meetings involve only the participating companies.

Meetings usually begin slowly, with show-and-tell around the table on the agreed hot topic. Often one or more companies are asked to prepare a report to the group about some aspect of a hot topic: what they have been doing about it at their firm, what they would like to do about it, or requesting assistance in thinking through how to tackle the hot topic at their firm. At the beginning of the second day, a list of potential topics for focused discussion has been created from the first day's proceedings. The list is quickly winnowed down to the two or three "hottest." The discussions that follow take on a life and an energy of their own. In the room are people who are among the most knowledgeable in the world about the practices of managing intangibles. They share a collective knowledge that is probably unequaled. When this collective knowledge is focused on topics of mutual interest and importance, the result represents the very best thinking possible.

ICM Gathering members are perhaps three to five years ahead of others in their thinking about the ways to extract value from IP and I-stuff. This book contains many of the lessons these companies have learned, from themselves and from one another. These are not proprietary or secret. The Gathering companies realize it is in their self-interest to have more companies learning and sharing how to manage and profit from intangibles. As Einstein once said, "The only source of knowledge is experience." So we invite you to read this book and to use the companies' experiences to help shape and grow your own knowledge. In so doing, you become a part of the process of creating a world where the ultimate source of value is limited only by our imagination and the creation of new ideas.

1

INTRODUCTION: THE EINSTEIN LEGACY

HUMANS ARE CREATIVE beings. They think and are the source of all knowledge for society, whether in the form of new sources of power (draft animals, water wheels, hydroelectric turbines, nuclear power), new methods of communication, faster and cheaper personal transportation, or an improved method for irrigating crops. We continue to create new ideas that add to the world's storehouse of knowledge. Humans have been adding to their total knowledge steadily over the centuries, and the amount of knowledge we create is multiplying at an incredible rate. Beginning with the amount of knowledge in the known world at the time of Christ, studies have estimated that the first doubling of that knowledge took place about 1700 A.D.. The second doubling occurred around the year 1900. It is estimated today that the world's knowledge base will double again by 2010 and again after that by 2013.

The pace of change that was dramatically brought to public attention in 1970 by author Alvin Toffler in *Future Shock* continues to accelerate. Our benign acceptance of this astonishing rate of change of knowledge, innovation, and information would be staggering to anyone who had not experienced its development. Were we able to transport someone from the early 1900s forward in time to observe our society today, doubtless they would be amazed by the amount of knowledge, innovation, and information that we often blithely take for granted.

Intangibles such as knowledge and know-how, as well as products based on those intangibles, have come to play a dominant role in our society. Although their effects can be seen everywhere around us, we rarely give them notice. To illustrate the point, think of just one intangible: *information*; it is all around us. We seek it out, and we pay for access to it, yet we rarely mention how useful it has become in daily life. In an average day, we wake up in the morning and turn on the radio or television for the news, weather, and traffic reports (all types of information). We want the latest information about stock movements and interest rates, or the long-term forecast for the Dow Jones Industrial Average.

1

We pay for broadband capabilities for our computers in order to search quickly for information on the World Wide Web. We go to movies (which provide information in the form of entertainment), as well as rent and buy entertainment to enjoy at home. Cell phone use has exploded around the globe, providing us with instant access to friends, relatives, and business contacts, all of whom may exchange information and pictures with us over the phone. Our automobiles are filled with technologies that keep us in touch, entertain us, and provide up-to-the-minute news. Rather than seeking out the solitude of distant vacation retreats, many of us grumble if we are even briefly out of touch with the information-providing networks that feed our PDAs.

INTANGIBLES IN THE EINSTEIN CONTEXT

Albert Einstein's greatest contribution to our society was to think about an everyday phenomenon (light) in new ways and to develop a framework within which one could think about and describe better what was happening all around us. In addition, Einstein came to understand the relationship between an intangible (light) and tangibles (mass) in his famous equation $E = MC^2$. We chose Einstein as a symbol for this book because here we discuss the management of intangibles, something that many firms have been doing for quite some time but without a framework or way of discussing or describing it fully.

In the business context, we have learned that from the perspective of people managing intangibles, there are really only two kinds. There is intellectual property (IP), which companies have used to "cut their teeth" on how intangibles may be managed. The second kind that managers define is the "non-IP" intangibles, or "everything else." The "Edison" book was about Best Practices in managing IP. "Einstein", the obvious next book was to reveal Best Practices in managing the firm's non-IP intangibles. But, defining the intangibles of interest in terms of what they are not; (i.e., the non-IP intangibles) is not very satisfying. So we asked companies in the Gathering, clients, and colleagues to suggest a better term. We explained that we wanted a term capable of encompassing all tacit knowledge, know-how, relationships as well as the non-legally protected and codified knowledge of the firm. In addition, the term should not contain financial or accounting overtones. Discussions raged over the course of a full year; with many ideas and terms proposed. In the end, we found that we had eliminated all alternatives but one. While I-stuff is not a term we all embrace, it was the only term we could identify that matched the criteria with a minimum of baggage. We are open to alternatives, but for purposes of this book, we will use I-stuff.

Issues Surrounding the Management of Intangibles

The discipline of managing intangibles continues to evolve as new lessons are learned and new practices and methods replace older, no longer adequate ones. Still in its infancy, the movement has a number of challenges:

1. *No agreed definition of what comprises intangibles and no common set of measures or measurements for them developed by the community.* Using an old management saw: "If you can't measure it, you can't manage it." Until an adequate and broad-based set of measures of intangibles and intangibles value is agreed, it will be difficult to manage fully this important component of the organization's value.

2. *Confusion about disciplinary frameworks.* During the early development of knowledge about intangibles, a series of "disciplinary" frameworks were developed to provide a better understanding and description of the phenomena of intangibles. These frameworks were formed within the context of several different disciplines or schools of thought. Examples include knowledge management, innovation, human resources, IP (legal), and IP (business). Each disciplinary framework was helpful in the development of ideas and concepts within its own confines, but intangibles management has now grown so large that it can no longer be contained within any one disciplinary view. The different views espoused by proponents of each discipline are often difficult to rationalize, often represent insular thinking, and are no longer as helpful as they once were.

3. *No generally agreed-on management framework for intangibles management.* Although the framework described and illustrated in this book outlines how the ICM Gathering companies think about and manage their intangibles, previously we had not seen a comprehensive and well-practiced framework for describing, defining, and managing the entire set of the organization's intangibles.

4. *Inadequate information on best practices for managing the full set of the firm's intangibles.*

5. *Lack of a practical financial framework to aid accountants, regulators, investors, and managers in measuring, valuing, and disclosing intangibles.*

6. *Lack of effective tools for intangibles management.*

In the pages that follow, the authors and the ICM Gathering companies provide some illumination on most of the foregoing issues. Intangibles management is an evolving discipline. The Intangibles management community continues its journey to understand and to capitalize on the full range of the firm's intangibles. For firms who began their intangibles journey with intellectual property, the shift to I-stuff is the obvious next stop. Although no claims are made that the methods, processes, and frameworks that follow are "the answer," we believe that they will be helpful for practitioners, managers, stakeholders, and the financial community in understanding how firms can manage and extract value from their intangibles on a regular and sustained basis.

The Increasing Importance of Intangibles

In recent years the number of companies whose value lies largely with their intangibles has increased dramatically. In a study of thousands of nonfinancial companies over a 20-year period, Dr. Margaret Blair, then of the Brookings Institution, reported a significant shift in the makeup of company assets. She studied all the nonfinancial publicly traded firms in the Compustat database. In 1978, her study showed, 80 percent of the average firm's value could be attributable to the value of the tangible assets on its balance sheet, with 20 percent of the company's value due to other factors. In 10 years, by 1988, the makeup had shifted to 45 percent tangible assets and 55 percent other factors. By 1998, only 30 percent of the value of the firms studied was attributable to the value of their tangible assets, whereas a stunning 70 percent was attributable to other factors. What are these other factors? Why have they become so important?

It was originally suggested that the "other factors" were the firm's intangible assets. The hypothesis was that the value of the company is the sum of its assets, both tangible and intangible. On closer examination, this theory has generally been discarded, in favor of the more widely held belief that a firm's market capitalization includes investors' expectations of future revenue in addition to any value they might attribute to the firm's intangibles.

An Accenture study written in 2004 found similar patterns in the evolving size of the "other factors" component of market capitalization but explained it differently. The Accenture study concluded that the amount of a firm's market capitalization less the value of its tangible assets represented that portion of the firm's assets and activities *not under active management*.[1]

---

[1] J. Bellow, R. Burgman, G. Roos and M. Molnar, A New Paradigm for Managing Shareholder Value, Accenture Institute for High Performance Business, www.accenture.com, July 2004.

What Are Intangibles?

Over time, the intellectual capital community has defined the elements that constitute both tacit knowledge and nonprotected codified knowledge. Companies managing their intangibles on a full-time basis categorize their intangibles using a listing such as that shown in Exhibit 1.1.

In the simplest terms, intangibles represent the knowledge, know-how, and relationships that may be used to create value for their owner or owning organization. Intangibles may be tacit or codified. When they are tacit, they reside within the mind(s) of company employees and other stakeholders. When they are codified, they have been committed to some form of media—typed into a computer, drawn on a blueprint, written on a piece of paper, or painted on a canvas. In an attempt to make the definition of intangibles more understandable, the U.S. Financial Accounting Standards Board, whose interests include developing standards for measuring and reporting on intangibles, has created a list of what it considers to be a firm's intangibles (see Exhibit 1.2).

Different sources produce different lists of what may be included under the heading of "intangibles." No one list is definitive. and all are illustrative. We believe this makes the point that the elements constituting the set called "intangibles" are not entirely known; there is no one comprehensive list of intangibles.

EXHIBIT 1.1   Elements of Intellectual Capital from the Perspective of the Intangibles Community

- Knowledge
    - Tacit
    - Codified
- Relationships
    - Individuals
    - Groups
- Processes (including combinations of tacit and codified knowledge)
- People
    - Knowledge-laden people
    - Relationship-laden people
    - Customers
        - Individuals
        - Defined entities (including combinations of tacit and codified knowledge)

EXHIBIT 1.2   Intangibles from the Perspective of the U.S. Financial Accounting Standards Board

Market-related
Trademarks, trade names
Service marks
Trade dress
Newspaper mastheads
Internet domain names

Customer-related
Customer lists
Customer contracts
Customer relationships

Artistic-related
Plays, operas, ballets
Books, other literary works
Musical works
Pictures, photographs
Video and audiovisual material

Contract-based
Licensing agreements
Advertising or service contracts
Lease agreements
Construction permits
Operating and broadcast rights
Employment contracts

Technology-based
Patented technology
Computer software
Unpatented technology
Databases
Trade secrets, secret formulas

Nevertheless, there *is* substantial agreement as to the elements that constitute "intangibles": tacit and codified knowledge and relationships in all of their many forms. Of particular relevance to the topic of this book, however, is the set of intangibles *that can be converted into profits.*

How Intangibles Differ from Tangibles

The characteristics that differentiate intangibles from tangibles are of particular importance to anyone who wants to measure them or extract value from them. Professor Baruch Lev of New York University's Stern School of Business provided an early identification and discussion of some of the major differences. In his book *Intangibles*, he lists the primary differentiating characteristics (see Exhibit 1.3).

From the value extraction and valuation perspectives, however, there are two characteristics of particular importance:

1. *Context dependency:* The value potential of intangibles depends on the context in which that value will be realized. Each company or organi-

EXHIBIT 1.3   Characteristics of Tangibles and Intangibles

Characteristics	Tangibles	Intangibles
Rivalry	Deployment for one use precludes other.	May be deployed simultaneously for many uses.
Excludability	Benefits may be enjoyed by the owner exclusively.	Both owners and nonowners may benefit from their use; excludability is difficult.
Marketability	Markets exist; market value is relatively easy to determine.	Markets either do not exist or are thin; market value is difficult to determine unambiguously.
Value	Fair market value (FMV) is a good measure of value to the owner.	FMV is usually different from value to owner; FMV may be determinable for only one use, but one intangible may have more than one use; value-in-use (VIU) may be a more accurate measure of value to the owner.

Source: Adapted from B. Lev, *Intangibles: Management, Measurement, and Reporting* (Washington, D.C.: Brookings Institution Press, 2001), pp. 21–47.

zation has a unique set of strategies, strengths, weaknesses, assets, internal champions, stakeholders, shareholders, and so on. Because of these and other factors, an intangible may have a specific value in the context of one organization and an entirely different value in the context of another.

2. *Multiple simultaneous value streams:* Intangibles are capable of generating more than one value stream simultaneously. Tangible assets are almost always capable of generating only one value stream. If a firm owns a building, it cannot generate revenue from its use as an office building during the day and, for example, another value stream for its use as an apartment house at night. Tangible assets have only one use and generate only one value stream for their owner. Intangibles are different, however. They may be used in many ways simultaneously without interfering with one another. (There are, of course, circumstances in which one use of an intangible precludes some of its other possible uses. In such a case, the highest and best use for the owner should be the major consideration in deploying such an intangible.)

A major difference between intangibles and tangibles is the way in which they may be valued. Accounting rules call for valuing tangibles according to their cost or current market value, whichever is *lower*; intangibles, however, may be valued according to the sum of the discounted value of their multiple value streams, or the amount offered for them by a party outside of the firm, whichever is *higher*.

The Importance of Context

Context determines the value of an intangible. Several years ago, for example, Coca-Cola had a business unit that developed and sold home vending devices, whereas long-time competitor Pepsi-Cola did not. With this in mind, it should be obvious that someone with a new innovation in home vending could have expected a much more interested response from Coke than from Pepsi. Here we see two companies, the same industry, similar products, but different contexts.

Context may be thought of on two levels. The first is the level of the organization. The example of Coca-Cola and Pepsi-Cola demonstrates organizational context. Organizational context typically is determined by long-term direction, corporate strategy, corporate resources, stakeholders, shareholders, and other "big picture" factors. Value stream context, on the other hand, is determined by the many factors that firms consider in deciding how to extract value from their intangibles. Factors in the value stream context include:

- *The kind of intangible:* Knowledge, know-how (know-how is knowledge that is actionable), relationship, IP, and so on.
- *The kind of value sought:* Firms may seek defensive value, such as protection or freedom to operate, or offensive value, such as revenue, cost avoidance, or positioning (see Appendix B for a discussion of the different kinds of value available from intangibles).
- *How the innovation will be applied:* Often an innovation will have a number of potential applications. For example, several years ago Xerox developed a new intermediate chemical for use in making toner for its copying machines. This chemical could also be used as an intermediate in five other chemical processes for different kinds of plastics. The company had to decide whether to commercialize only one application of the chemical or one or more of the others as well.
- *The cash conversion mechanism:* For value extraction when revenue is the desired outcome, a fixed set of mechanisms is available for converting an innovation into cash: sale, licensing, joint venturing, strategic alliance, or integration in company activities.

- *Market segments:* For each application selected, define the markets into which it will be marketed. Some applications may be capable of commercialization in a range of market segments, whereas the commercialization of others may be more focused on one or only a few segments.
- *Perspective:* This element of context identifies from whose perspective the value stream is to be developed. Possible perspectives for valuation include those of the owner, an internal decision-maker, a potential buyer, shareholders and investors, and outside stakeholders.
- *Dimensions of measurement:* The dimensions of measurement for an intangible may include qualitative measures using words (e.g., "a little" or "a lot") or quantitative measures using measures such as vectors, ranges, or points. Quantitative measurement may be stated in monetary terms (dollars, yen, euros) or in nonmonetary terms (percentage, size, rate of change).

Understanding and defining the context for intangibles is an important step in understanding the potential value of an intangible to the organization. Whether at the strategic or value stream level, context is a fundamental contributor to the usefulness and value of an intangible.

PERSPECTIVES ON INTANGIBLES

The intangibles management community began and evolved from separate perspectives or schools of thought. Although these schools of thought tend to agree on the elements of intangibles, they do not agree on which of those elements are most important.

To illustrate this point, suppose one made a pile of colored balloons in the middle of the floor, with each balloon representing one element of intangibles. The pile of balloons might look like Exhibit 1.4.

Someone looking at the pile from the top would see a different configuration than someone looking at it from the side. For purposes of illustration, let us say there are four different perspectives on an organization's intangibles: the knowledge view, the value extraction view, the financial reporting view, and the investor view, as demonstrated in Exhibit 1.5. There can, of course, be many more perspectives on the firm's intangibles, but four will suffice to make our point.

From each vantage point, the viewer sees some balloons in the foreground and others in the background. Different balloons are in the foreground from the knowledge view compared with the value extraction view. From the perspective

EXHIBIT 1.4   The Elements of Intangibles

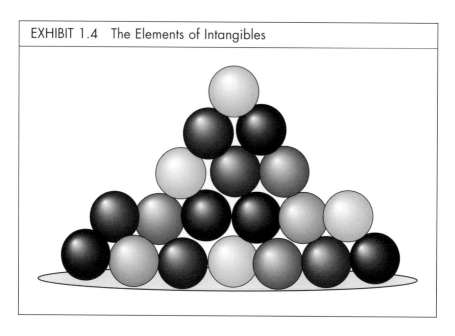

EXHIBIT 1.5   Different Perspectives on Intangibles

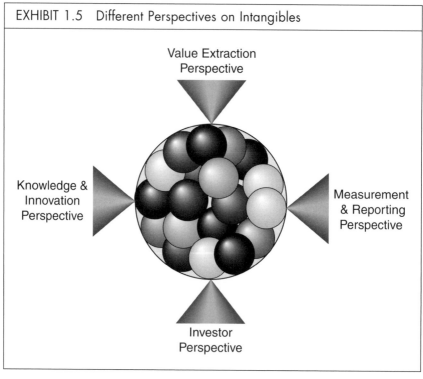

EXHIBIT 1.6   The Firm's Intangibles from a Knowledge Perspective

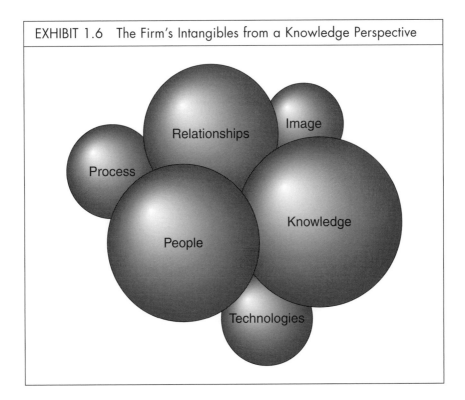

of someone interested in managing the firm's knowledge, the pile might look like Exhibit 1.6. From this perspective, relationships and people are most important, with image, technologies, and processes being of interest as well but slightly less so.

When the perspective shifts to extracting value, tacit and codified knowledge and complementary business assets become important, with measurement, people, processes, and image of somewhat less importance (see Exhibit 1.7).

The perspective of the CFO, the person responsible for reporting on the firm's assets to external parties, is constrained by the reporting requirements outlined by the profession and by law. The CFO's view of intangibles is concerned with the things that can be stated in accounting terms (see Exhibit 1.8).

Finally, to complete this illustration, consider the investor perspective. From the investor perspective, the pile of balloons might look like Exhibit 1.9. Because investors are interested in financial measurement, products and services, and the firm's ability to leverage its offerings in the marketplace, those balloons appear in the foreground. Of almost equal interest to investors are the roles for IP in

EXHIBIT 1.7 The Firm's Intangibles from a Value Extraction Perspective

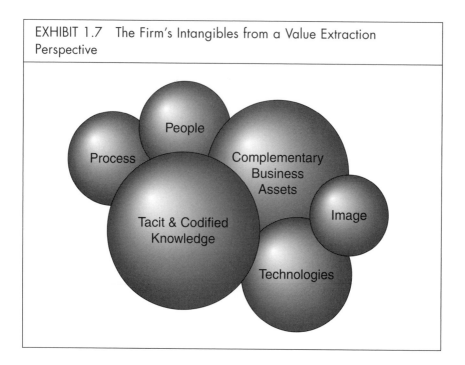

the business, the alignment of the company's IP with the business strategy, and the firm's customers.

The Hegemony of Perspective

It is clear that there is no one "right" view of intangibles (or intellectual capital). In fact, one's own preferred view *along with* one or more different views may be helpful in resolving an issue or problem associated with intangibles.

Just as there are many perspectives on intangibles, so too are there a number of popular models of intangibles and intangibles management. Each has its uses, and each is helpful for understanding or resolving some recurring issues. No one model is "correct" or complete.

For example, the ICM Gathering, concerned as it was with extracting value from intangibles, created a model of intellectual capital (intangibles) and knowledge-based companies (see Exhibit 1.10). This model was particularly useful for thinking about how organizations might extract value from their intangibles.[2]

---

[2]ICM Gathering description

EXHIBIT 1.8   The Measurement and Reporting Perspective on Intangibles

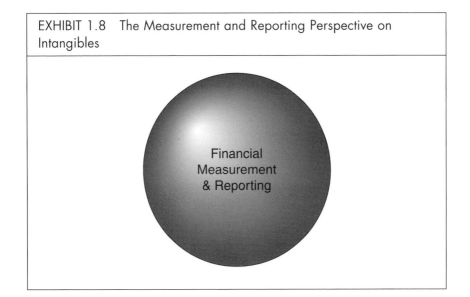

EXHIBIT 1.9   The Firm's Intangibles from the Investor's Perspective

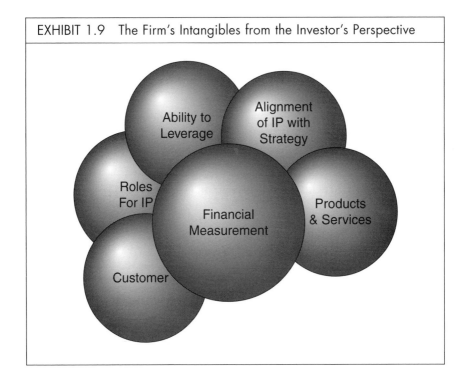

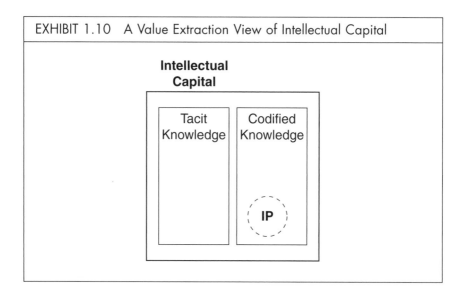

EXHIBIT 1.10   A Value Extraction View of Intellectual Capital

Although the "box" model of Exhibit 1.10 has proved quite useful for visualizing key elements of the value extraction process, it is not particularly helpful for managers who want to create value through intangibles. For this purpose, the "three-ring" model of intellectual capital is more useful (see Exhibit 1.11).

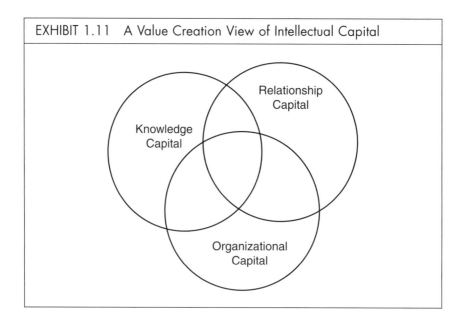

EXHIBIT 1.11   A Value Creation View of Intellectual Capital

The "So What" of Perspective

One's perspective on a topic as complex as intangibles management may be both helpful and limiting, for three reasons:

1. All perspectives on intangibles are correct from where the viewer stands. From wherever the viewer is positioned around the pile of colored balloons, he or she sees the pile of balloons accurately.
2. Each perspective on intangibles is incomplete, that is, no one perspective is able to comprehend or incorporate all the elements of intangibles.
3. To understand fully what constitutes an organization's intangibles, the different views must be considered together. Each view of intangibles is valid; the views are complementary rather than competitive. The more we can combine and expand our individual and narrow perspectives on intangibles, the more easily we will be able to identify the portions of the firm's intangibles that we were not aware of previously.

THE IMPACT OF INTANGIBLES ON ORGANIZATIONS

The evolution of intangibles management, as a discipline, followed a pattern that is detectable in hindsight but was not discernable at the time. What has become the intangibles management movement had three distinct origins. The first was the groundbreaking work in Japan of Hiroyuki Itami, who studied the effect of invisible assets on the management of Japanese corporations.[3] The second was the work of a disparate set of economists (Penrose, Rumelt, Wernerfelt, and Teece) seeking a different view or theory of the firm. Professor David Teece of the University of California at Berkeley, synthesized and expanded on their work in his seminal 1986 article on technology commercialization.[4] Finally, the work of Karl-Eric Sveiby in Sweden, published originally in Swedish, addressed the human capital dimension of intangibles, providing a rich and tantalizing view of the potential for valuing the enterprise based on the competencies and knowledge of its employees.

---

[3]H. Itami, and T.W. Roehl, *Mobilizing Invisible Assets*, Harvard University Press, Boston, MA. 1987.

[4]D. Teece, "Profiting from Technological Innovation: Implications for Integration, Collaboration, Licensing and Public Policy," *Research Policy* 15 (1986): 285–305.

One cannot dismiss the effect that the accounting profession had, unknowingly hindering the recognition of intangibles as "real" items of value for the firm. Accountants, concerned as they are with the accurate reporting of finances for businesses, follow the Generally Accepted Accounting Principles (GAAP) in identifying and reporting on firms' "assets." Justifiably conservative, the accounting community sought to use the then-standard methods for valuing and reporting on a firm's assets. The accepted methods proved difficult to apply to intangibles. With hindsight, we now realize that this is because intangibles have different characteristics than tangibles. These differences significantly affect the degree to which traditional valuations methods apply to intangibles (See Appendix E). But as intangibles came to represent more and more of the value of businesses, and the need for accurate valuation of intangibles became more pressing, financial scandals of stunning significance exploded onto the front pages of newspapers around the world. The accounting community found itself embroiled in a series of very public issues (e.g., the Enron and WorldCom accounting scandals) that consumed their time and energy. As a lasting result of these scandals, and the inevitable reforms that followed, accountants found themselves heavily focused on the reporting aspect of financial activities, with the measurement aspect (particularly as it relates to intangibles) receiving little attention.

In the United States, as a result of the "reporting" legislation spawned in the wake of the accounting scandals, chief financial officers had no incentive to spend time with company I-stuff managers who dealt with the particulars of the firm's intangibles. "Can we put your intangibles on the balance sheet?" they would often ask. Or, "If we can't put it into 'real' financial terms, I can't afford the time to deal with it!"

Although more and more of the value of the firm was becoming associated with its intangibles, paradoxically less and less of the financial value reported to investors contained information about those very same intangibles.

In the early 1980s, while the business world was slowly coming to realize the value that intangibles provided, a series of events in the United States propelled one dimension of intangibles into business prominence. The three-year period 1983 to 1985 saw several key changes in U.S. international and legal policy that presaged the importance of IP intangibles to the United States. The President's Commission on Industrial Competitiveness identified IP as critical to achieving and maintaining competitiveness in American industry. At the same time, the new Court of Appeals for the Federal Circuit became active and began to unify legal precedent in patent cases that previously had been scattered among the 11 Circuit Courts of Appeal. Antitrust restrictions were by the passage of the National Cooperative Research Act (1984), which permitted competitors to do joint research more freely. Finally, the U.S. Department of Justice decided that the incentive of a patent is pro- rather than anticompetitive and began to change its long-held antimonopoly perspective, at least as it related to patents. As a result, the importance of patents in the United States has dramatically increased.

The events of the early 1980s put teeth into patents as never before. Their value as barriers to competitive entry or as competitive blocks suddenly became significant. United States courts saw a surge of IP infringement cases in the decades following. The primary focus of many firms, particularly those in North America, moved to IP. After all, now it was true that one claim by an adversary, in one patent, could put your firm out of business.

New firms sprang up to help businesses deal with the new reality surrounding the value of IP. These firms provided assistance in screening new ideas for patentability, with valuation of patents, with patent searches, with sophisticated software for managing a firm's patents, and with tools and advice for analyzing one's own as well as one's competitors' portfolios.

In addition, traditional firms are now offering products or services from a different perspective than they did in the past. FedEx sells time; restaurants no longer sell food, they sell a dining experience; mobile phones no longer sell phone service, they sell mobility or connectivity. New firms provide products or services that were unheard of only a few years ago. Entire cities are offering wireless Internet hook-ups for citizens and visitors. Telephone, cable, and satellite companies are vying to be the access point to homes for all their information, communications, and entertainment needs. Telephone-based support services are now often outsourced to companies in Bangalore, India; so, whenever you call up a company for some form of customer support, you may find yourself talking with a pleasant, well-trained, and helpful person whose English is flavored with an Indian accent.

The impact of the shift toward intangibles has had as significant an effect on business as it has on individuals. The effect has been felt in several areas of business:

1. What businesses are now able to sell to meet new needs in their marketplace
2. How products and services are sold
3. How businesses have to think differently about the ways in which they create new products and services

Companies are replacing tangible business assets with intangibles. Consider Amazon.com, one of the most successful booksellers in the world. Amazon has an intangible sales channel that merely requires customers to have access to the Internet. From a customer perspective, the store is open 24 hours a day, and interactions with the firm's customer service activity are almost always capable of being handled online.

Some Outcomes of the Rising Importance of Intangibles

As intangibles grew in importance and contributed to a greater proportion of the value of organizations, it became apparent that harnessing that value usually required a coordinated effort from many perspectives. Those different perspectives reveal the elements necessary to understand the latent value of intangibles fully. For example, the value of a firm's tacit knowledge can be made explicit when one approaches it from the value extraction perspective and brings into play skills not considered from the knowledge perspective. Attorneys, licensing officers, financial experts, and marketing people may all be required to extract value fully from the firm's tacit knowledge.

As firms become more complex they find they cannot create by themselves all the intangibles their organization needs. They must turn to "friendly" parties, often the firm's stakeholders. Stakeholders include suppliers, local governments, investors, customers, and others. The importance of stakeholders to the organization tends to increase with increasing organizational size and complexity.

Why Manage the Organization's Intangibles?

We think the answer to the question "Why manage the organization's intangibles?" should be obvious, but we will enumerate what we believe to be the principal reasons. First, intangibles of all kinds represent the fundamental sources of value for an organization. Because the purpose of organizations is to provide value to their constituents, they must be able to create the value they promise. Value comes from the ideas, knowledge, know-how, expertise, and relationships of the firm's employees and stakeholders. Finding ways to focus employee and stakeholder energies around the promised areas of value involves managing the firm's intangibles.

The second principal reason for organizations to manage their intangibles is that in business organizations (particularly publicly traded ones), approximately 75 percent of their value is not attributable to tangibles. The business and financial communities agree that the remainder of the market value of a firm is constituted, in part, by the value of the firm's intangibles. No one can say how much of the nontangible value is associated directly with intangibles, but we suspect that collectively it is a significant percentage.

The third and final reason for managing the organization's intangibles is a paradoxical one: For most firms, intangibles are not under active management. Although there is agreement that intangibles are important, and there is agreement that they constitute a significant portion of the firm's value, few companies have actually identified, much less inventoried, their intangibles. Still fewer have developed any capability for managing their intangibles.

EINSTEIN IN THE BOARDROOM

Albert Einstein was a man filled with questions about the world around him. He became fascinated by intangibles in the everyday things the rest of us take for granted. For example, he realized that what was understood about the physics of light helped to explain its basic constitution, whether it moves in straight lines or curves, and how fast it travels. He wondered what happened to light as it proceeded beyond the limits of planet Earth. Did its properties change? Did it matter what light did when you looked at it from a perspective other than a terrestrial one? He wondered about the relationship between light (an apparent intangible) and mass (tangibles). He wondered what would happen to tangibles if they were able to travel at the same speed as light. This persistent and intense musing about an intangible that exists all around us led him to realize that one could identify universal truths by looking at everyday objects from a new or different perspective.

Like Einstein, all of us observe aspects of the things we call intangibles that are not explainable using currently available frameworks and methods of measurement. We observe that the basic value residing in organizations is intangible, but we find we have no way to define, describe, or rationalize adequately what we observe. We need a new way of looking at intangibles.

To date the intangibles community has developed along disciplinary lines. The legal discipline views intangibles as intellectual property; the knowledge discipline views them as knowledge; the R&D management community views them as innovation; the measurement and reporting community views intangibles as a new kind of asset; and so forth. However, none of these views, by itself, fully describes intangibles and their value. What is needed in the long term is a new perspective on intangibles, one like Einstein's $E = MC^2$, which encapsulates their fundamental essence.

Until such a new view emerges, the intangibles community must find ways to combine their silo-like disciplinary views and to expand their collective understanding of what intangibles are and how to manage them best for the benefit of the organization, the business, and the community.

This book is a move in that direction. The ideas contained herein represent a multidisciplinary view of intangibles and their management. The ideas and best practices about intangibles outlined in the chapters that follow have been developed by practitioners in the legal, knowledge, financial, R&D, human resources, measurement and reporting, economics, social, and environmental communities. Also represented are industry views: pharmaceuticals, industrial gases, chemicals, computing, aerospace, automotive, venture capital, insurance, entertainment, beverages, consumer electronics, paper products, office products, and telecommunications.

We believe that the framework developed by the ICM Gathering and the stories of each company's best practices demonstrating the management of their I-stuff will be helpful to companies on two fronts: First, to define and describe the current efforts toward managing intangibles in a manner that makes business sense; and second, to learn from the examples of Gathering companies what the management of the firm's I-stuff intangibles makes possible.

2

THE EINSTEIN VALUE CONTINUUM

THE I-STUFF VIEW of intangibles emerged from discussions among the Intellectual Capital Management (ICM) Gathering firms and from our work with other companies around the world. From the perspective of managers within the organization, there are only two kinds of intangibles management: the management of intellectual property (IP) and the management of the rest of the company's intangibles, its I-stuff. We came to understand that the path to sophistication in I-stuff management is different from that for IP management.

IP management blossomed dramatically from 1995 to 2005 as court-driven damage awards made it clear that IP was both valuable and strategic. The development of IP management as a new discipline transcended the legal function of the organization. Real IP management brought researchers, lawyers, marketers, and business people together to find more ways of extracting value from the organization's IP. Companies that use IP management to extract business value from the firm's IP have succeeded in part for two reasons: They have focused on IP from the perspective of the business (as opposed to the law), and they have brought together people from throughout the firm—legal, marketing, business development, and innovation—to make decisions about how to use their IP.

THE DIFFERENCE BETWEEN I-STUFF AND IP

I-stuff differs significantly from IP, and these distinctions require different approaches to its management. There are at least three key differences between IP and I-stuff: (1) degree of definition, (2) degree of focus, and (3) capability for leverage.

- *Degree of definition:* All intellectual property is codified, following a strict set of legally mandated requirements defining what may be codified, in what form, the processes for obtaining status as IP, and how protection may be pursued. I-stuff has no such codification requirements. In fact, the bulk of I-stuff is not codified, but tacit. As such, it is difficult to define as precisely as codified knowledge. In addition, it includes more components than are found in codified information. I-stuff includes relationships and know-how, which encompass both values and intuition as well as physical skills and capabilities. It may be individual pieces of knowledge or know-how; it may be a community of practice within the organization; or it may be an organization-wide capability.

- *Degree of focus:* It is relatively easy to determine the possible business purpose or role for each piece of IP. Often a simple inventory spreadsheet will suffice, listing each piece of IP and the business purpose(s) it fulfills for the organization. In contrast, I-stuff is usually dispersed across the organization and located in the minds of employees.
- *Capability of leverage:* Codified intangibles are more capable of benefiting from network effects than are tacit intangibles. Networks can be physical (like telephone wiring) or virtual (like the Internet). The more people there are on the network, the greater the potential benefits of membership. Also, the more pathways a network provides to its members, the more potential there is for leveraging information on the network. Telephone networks, for example, provide a method for sharing information between individuals. However, telephone networks have not proved successful in providing communications between one person and groups or between two groups. (Conference calls may be an exception, but even though the one-to-many communications that teleconferences provide are a step in the right direction, teleconferencing is still not considered satisfactory.) Radio has long provided networks that are very good at leveraging one-way communications from a single source to large numbers or receivers in homes or automobiles (collectively, a large group). The Internet has proved astonishingly successful at communicating codified information from person to person, or person to a group or groups, encompassing millions of participants. Through the Net, we are learning more about two-way communications with the possible involvement of thousands of participants.

It is difficult to leverage most tacit knowledge fully because of the difficulty in connecting the right people at the right time in a manner that is actionable. Knowledge is most often communicated from one person to one other person, or to a relatively small group of people. Communicating tacit information to large groups in an actionable manner is still problematic (although television and radio are currently the most successful mediums for such one-way communications). However, the Internet is making significant inroads into expanding the possibilities.

I-Stuff Management Thought Leaders

As the four areas of I-stuff management activity began to become apparent, so too did their roots. We noticed that each of the four areas, while now an inter-disciplinary approach to I-stuff management, nevertheless had roots in one or more of the traditional intellectual capital management silos. We thought it would be interesting to add the perspectives of well-known thought leaders about each of the identified management activity areas.

For example, the Building path involves the identification of the organiza-tion's sustainable I-stuff, the creation of a knowledge culture, and the creation of an internal network. These activities are well known in the knowledge man-agement community, but in this case, they are performed with an eye toward value extraction. The person we indentified as making the greatest intellectual contribution to managment in these areas is Karl-Erik Sveiby. Sveiby has at dif-ferent times been a senior executive of a publishing firm, an academic, and a con-sultant. In 1986 he published his first book (in Swedish) exploring how to manage the rapidly growing field of service organizations having no production, but only the knowledge and creativity of their employees. In 1990 he published the first book on knowledge management. He is the creator of a number of practical tools and methods for extracting value from both tacit and codified knowledge.

The underpinnings of the Leveraging path are drawn from the communi-ty of managers whose focus is on the extraction vlaue from their intangibles. For most corporations wishing to routinely extract value, the ability to create processes, methods and organizational capabilities are key to the ability to lever-age their intangibles. Leveraging also requires the flexibility to modify and change business models as necessary and the ability to use the company's brands effectively for the generation of profits. We identified Sharon Oriel, recently retired as the Director of Dow Chemical's Global Intellectual Capital Manage-ment Tech Center, as a thought leader in this area of management activity. At Dow she provided the leadership for the company's world-renowned capabili-ty for managing and extracting value from its intangibles. Oriel has a demon-strated ability to create new approaches to value extraction and to implement them in a large diverse organization. Very highly regarded in the intangibles management community, she is a frequent speaker and advisor to companies and groups aspiring to excellence in their ability to profit from intangibles.

The Integrating path involves an in-depth understanding of how to align the organization with the business strategy; to break down the barriers to cross-organizational sharing, cooperation, and mutual support within the company;

and the ability to integrate with stakeholders and customers outside of the organization. Integrating may be one of the most difficult of the paths to navigate, but also one whose benefits can be immeasurable. We identified Hubert Saint Onge as a major thought leader in this field of management activity. His work for the past twenty-five years has focused on developing the full potential of organizations and their human assets to optimize performance. He has spearheaded the creation of methods for completely aligning businesses, business strategies, brands and employee-customer interactions. He is widely acknowledged as one of the most respected thought leaders and practitioners in integrating and transforming organiations to optimize performance and profits.

I-Stuff Management Activities

Recognizing the differences between IP and I-stuff, the authors asked the ICM Gathering companies to share their respective I-stuff management activities to help us define these differences in terms of management. We noted the terminology used and whether and how the company's I-stuff management activity focused on value, value extraction, or some other goal. We then developed a list of umbrella activities that captures all the members' I-stuff management activities. We identified four major categories:

1. Building the Portfolio of I-Stuff
2. Leveraging the Portfolio of I-Stuff
3. Integrating the Portfolio of I-Stuff
4. Sustaining the Corporation through the Use of I-Stuff

Each of these is a unique grouping of activities and, for each, the Gathering identified what individual companies were doing, and which of these activities seemed to fit into the "Best Practice" category. The four chapters that follow deal with each of these activity groupings in detail; the following is an overview of the Einstein Value Continuum activity groupings.

Building the Portfolio of I-Stuff

Gathering companies did not create their I-stuff portfolios with similar types of intangibles; rather, each company's mix of intangibles was unique, and each managed its portfolio for different purposes. Nevertheless, all companies tended to practice these activities in building their I-stuff portfolio:

- *Creating a knowledge culture.* In order for a company to leverage knowledge successfully, it must have a culture that fosters knowledge sharing. Unlike tangible assets that can be owned and controlled by one person or entity, knowledge may have many owners and may be used in many ways simultaneously. The degree to which a company culture recognizes, encourages, and rewards knowledge sharing is key to its ability to maximize the value of the firm's knowledge.
- *Determining what I-stuff is sustainable.* For most companies, the knowledge that has the greatest business impact is knowledge that differentiates the company and provides a nontransitory competitive advantage. We call this I-stuff "sustainable knowledge." Sustainable knowledge is the knowledge that should be codified and actively managed.
- *Creating a network.* Once codified, knowledge becomes more powerful within the firm when it can be shared. Sharing knowledge effectively usually requires defined IT structures and systems, as well as an understanding of the firm's knowledge-sharing objectives and routine.

Leveraging the Portfolio of I-Stuff

Companies are interested in finding I-stuff that can produce meaningful returns for the firm. Leveraging I-stuff usually requires the following kinds of activities:

- *Developing routine processes for extracting value from I-Stuff.* There are as many ways to commercialize I-Stuff as there are companies. Some companies commercialize their I-Stuff directly by selling their knowledge (professional service firms, doctors, and so on). Other companies look for opportunities to add value to existing revenue-generating activity through the addition of I-Stuff to the revenue equation. However you choose to monetize I-Stuff, it will require formalized processes and compliance requirements for the entire firm.
- *Being prepared to challenge your business model.* As a company begins to comprehend the magnitude of I-Stuff and its value potential, the question will inevitably arise: What business are we really in? Selling knowledge, whether directly or via a partnering model, requires profound changes in the infrastructure of an organization. Until companies are comfortable understanding and questioning the business model, I-Stuff commercialization will remain an ad hoc activity.

- *Brand management.* The art of creating and maintaining product brands has been around for quite awhile. As intangibles have evolved, we find more companies worrying about corporate identity, branding and the beginnings of branding metrics and methodologies. The creation and management of brands in these new business environments involves a detailed understanding of several dimensions of I-Stuff management.

Integrating I-Stuff across Business and Organizational Lines

As with IP, companies that integrate their I-stuff management practices across business and organizational lines can produce profitable results for all concerned:

- *Linking I-stuff strategies with the overall corporate strategy and objectives.* The value of I-stuff to an organization depends, in large part, on the degree to which it supports or permits company business strategies and activities. Companies on the Integrating Path focus on identifying the kinds of value they want to obtain from their I-Stuff and the role it will play. (The various paths will be explained at the end of this chapter.) Once those are known, they can develop an I-Stuff strategy for producing the desired value.
- *Measuring I-stuff.* Firms on the Integrating Path need to define and describe their I-Stuff in terms that are meaningful to the company, its business strategy, and its business activities. Because the traditional accounting framework is not able to measure intangibles adequately, firms must create new ways to measure their I-Stuff, ways that relate their intangibles to the company's business activities.
- *Leveraging and expanding the management of I-Stuff outside the corporation.* A company's I-Stuff often extends outside the corporation, in the form of "customer capital" and the I-Stuff used to interact with suppliers, customers, and competitors. Likewise, a company may benefit from using another company's I-Stuff. Companies on this path are seeking ways to leverage their own externally focused I-Stuff as well as the I-Stuff of others.

Sustaining the Company through the Use of I-Stuff

Tactically, companies aspire to create sustainable revenue streams for their individual businesses. Strategically, they aspire to create sustainability for the firm. (We define sustainable I-stuff as including, but not limited to, such things as the corporate brand, reputation, relevance to the consumer, knowledge regeneration, and overall competitive appeal.)

- *Using I-stuff as a catalyst for corporate sustainability.* Corporations recognize that they can no longer rely on nonrenewable tangible assets to sustain growth. A strategic focus on renewable "I-stuff" catalyzes economic growth that can be sustained.
- *Using values to enable employee and corporate sustainability.* Companies must define their corporate values and accurately balance the relationship between corporate values and employee values, between corporate values and the corporate business strategy, and between corporate values and sustainability. For example, when a corporation has a vision of itself that is measured in months or a few years, it is difficult to inculcate a "sustainability" value into employees. On the other hand, a corporation whose vision timeframe is measured in decades will find it easier for employees to include a long-term or sustainability perspective into their personal value-set.
- *I-stuff reporting.* U.S. corporations operate under a set of quarterly financial disclosure requirements. Such periodic short-term reporting rarely takes the long-term nature of intangibles into account. In contrast, the triple-bottom-line reports put out by companies like Shell and Dow are prototypes of principles-based reporting. Companies must develop a reporting method that is reflective of the value intangibles provide for the corporation.

THE EINSTEIN VALUE CONTINUUM

One of the things we learned from *Edison in the Boardroom* was that the Value Hierarchy pyramid is a very powerful visual and practical framework that enables corporate management to "see" how their company can increase their IP sophistication in a manner consistent with the corporate strategy and objectives of the firm. However, central to the pyramid's success was the need to build a solid foundation of best practices and then move up as necessary. We have learned that firms progress from one level of IP management sophistication to the next through a sequential process. In managing IP, the best practices at each level must be mastered in order to create the foundation necessary to proceed to the next level of sophistication: Defense precedes cost control, defense and cost control precede profit-making, and so on.

The same is not true for I-stuff management. Companies may begin managing their I-stuff through any of the four activities described above and can move from one grouping of I-stuff management activity to any other activity grouping directly, without having to pass through another on the way.

We wanted to develop a graphic that would capture this unique quality of I-stuff management. It would need to have some unusual characteristics. First, it would have to depict direct access between an organization working in one

EXHIBIT 2.1   The Einstein Value Continuum Showing the Best
Practice Paths

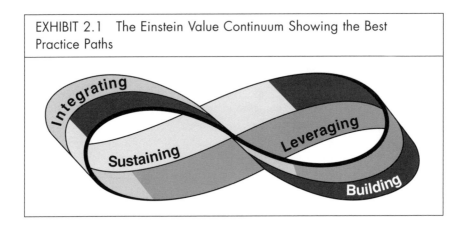

activity grouping and any other activity grouping. Furthermore, it could not suggest that any one path toward sophistication in I-stuff management is more
desirable than any other.

The Sustaining path is concerned with the long-term viability of the organization. It is concerned with the understanding and use of values to strengthen
organizational unity, the use of I-stuff as a catalyst for long-term growth, and
the use of reports to keep the organization's stakeholders aware of company
direction and activity. We identified Bill Swirsky, Vice President of the Canadian Institute of Chartered Accountants (CICA) as a significant thought leader in
the area of sustainability. Swirsky was an early visionary about the potential of
intangibles to contribute to the organization's profitability and long-term
growth. In the course of his responsibilities at the CICA, he initiated a number
of early projects and studies to learn more about this new form of "asset" and
issues surrounding its management. He has been instrumental in the development of and creative approaches to measuring and managing intangibles, particularly for long-term viability. Swirsky has been the driving force behind the
founding of the Value Measurement and Reporting Collaborative, a multi-
national accounting task force examining the issues associated with the measur-
ment of value, particulary as it relates to intangibles.

In the chapters that follow, each of the thought leaders will provide their
view of the Einstein Value Continuum path under discussion, its importance.

We settled on symbolizing the fact that movement from one activity
grouping is possible. It also shows that there is no defined starting or ending
point for the practice of I-stuff management, or any implied progression of
sophistication.

With that in mind, we can begin our journey though the Einstein Value Continuum and see how to utilize I-stuff for increased value!

3

BUILDING THE PORTFOLIO OF I-STUFF

THE EINSTEIN VALUE Continuum has multiple "gateways or entry points," with the first being through the Building Path (see Exhibit 3.1). Companies entering I-stuff management at the Building Path have often been influenced by the "knowledge view" of intangibles. They believe that knowledge is valuable to the firm and seek to learn more about the knowledge they have and how their firms are using it. In their exploration, these firms come to realize that, in addition to knowledge, other kinds of intangibles reside within the organization, which also fall under the heading of I-stuff. The first step in managing I-stuff is to create a knowledge infrastructure. This entails identifying the knowledge and other intangibles (e.g., know-how, relationships) that reside in their organization and then creating an infrastructure that facilitates knowledge sharing across the company.

EXHIBIT 3.1 The Einstein Value Continuum, Highlighting the Building Path

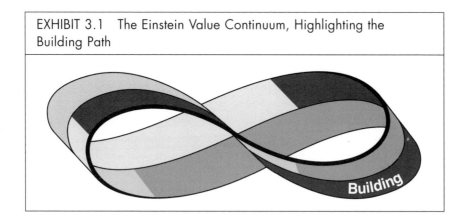

Thought Leader Comments

Intangibles: Uncover the Hidden Value!

When a Viking berserker died in battle, he was secured a place at the table in Valhalla, where he could feast on the roasted hog Särimmer all day. The hog was recreated every night and then roasted again and again and again. For a society in which one summer of bad weather could mean famine, Heaven was a place with an infinite abundance of food.

Should a place like that exist, it must surely be Heaven, because the Vikings could not fathom a society on Earth in which the most valuable resource was infinite. However, this is exactly what knowledge and other intangibles could be to a business. People's brains have a never-ending capacity to create knowledge, but, our corporations and public organizations are only able to exploit a fraction of it. How can we release this infinite resource?

The Vikings knew that when they shared their gold or food with someone it was a zero-sum game; their loss was the other party's win. A wise man kept his gold and did not readily share what was rightly his. Sharing knowledge, however, is not a zero-sum game and it never has been. Unlike financial assets, intangibles such as knowledge tend to grow when they are shared. So—how can we improve sharing of knowledge in the organization?

Creating new knowledge and sharing knowledge are the two best ways to generate value from intangibles. The questions are simple and eternal, but the implications of the answers mean a revolution in the way businesses create value—and we have only just begun!

The knowledge management "movement" had a window of opportunity in the late 1980s and early 1990s, but then "knowledge management" as a term was highjacked by the big consulting firms and the IT industry. They promised cost reductions by converting knowledge held in the brains of individuals to information and storing it in databases.

Promises of cost reductions immediately got the attention of chief executives, of course. They poured billions of dollars into oxymorons like "knowledge systems," "knowledge databases," "knowledge technology," and "knowledge engineers." IT systems surveys in the last decade generally report that some 60 to 70 percent of the knowledge management initiatives have been internal cost cutting related to information storage and transfer. Less than 20 percent typically respond that their knowledge management efforts have had to do with innovation, customer knowledge, and revenue growth.

To create new knowledge and to increase revenues, managers must think differently; they must think in a way that is *knowledge focused*. They must learn to deal with issues like: What knowledge do we give our customers? And what do we receive from them? How must we change our internal collaborative climate to make our knowledge workers more effective? These issues are more complex than buying an IT system to save costs, but they create infinitely more value. After all, you can only save 100 percent of the costs, but the sky is the limit when it comes to increasing revenues.

The trouble with the first two ways of creating value is that the solutions for value creation are *revenue oriented* and that the revenues tend to be intangible and hidden because currently they are not measured. Customers bring more than financial revenues; they also bring knowledge that is *intangible revenue*: product ideas, competitive intelligence, feedback, referrals, and so on. If you are a manager you know this, of course. But do you know how large the intangible revenues are? Whether they are growing or reducing in value? Have you put the intangible revenues into the strategic plan?

An example is the call center of the successful South African mobile phone company, MTN, which was originally set up to deal with customer complaints. The department was dominated by low-paid staff, encumbered by high staff turnover, and generally regarded as inefficient. Management applied knowledge focus and taught the call operators to elicit ideas for service improvements from the customers. In only two weeks this gave them ideas for more than ten new products and services, which they implemented. A simple system was also developed to relay real-time information about connection problems to the network monitoring unit, which previously had relied on technical data only. This information was found to be a valuable complement. The call center is now strategically regarded as MTN's "sensitive skin." With a minor investment in people and skills, new intangible revenues were created.

Intangible revenues tend to be hidden; a knowledge focus can reveal them. An example is the nursing staff in the Norwegian private hospital Lovisenberg, who performed an experiment to reduce the anxiety of patients going into surgery: They invited ex-patients to meet the new patients and share their knowledge. They found that patients' anxiety was indeed reduced—which would normally have been sufficient to regard the experiment a success. However, the knowledge manager also asked *how* the staff had noticed the lower anxiety among the patients. Both doctors and nurses answered that the patients asked fewer questions (= time savings), and the nurses added that they did not have to administer as many relaxation drugs as before (= cost savings). The ex-patients were alive (!); hence they were "experts" that the new patients could trust (more so than the doctors in this case), so they successfully replaced the doctors. The hospital had gained additional hidden intangible revenues by tapping into the unique knowledge of the ex-patients.

Intangible revenues exist whether you measure them or not and whether you are aware of them or not. It is a management decision either to convert them to money or to ignore them. The MTN managers chose to convert the intangible revenues to new service offerings and financial revenues, and the Lovisenberg Hospital doctors chose to allocate the time they gained to more valuable issues.

Knowledge-focused organisations maximize total revenues from customers, both tangible and intangible, not just sales volumes in dollars. The selection of customers becomes a decision of high strategic significance because customer interfaces can literally be regarded as knowledge gateways. Some customers bring many intangible revenues; others only bring money. Which do you prefer? Products and services are developed with a focus on the knowledge they bring to the customers and how they enhance a company's ability to serve their customers.

Generally, we can distinguish between three types of intangible revenues, those that:

- *Improve external relations:* the relationship with the external environment including all stakeholders such as suppliers, society in general, the natural environment, and so on.
- *Improve internal structure:* all the systems, flows, cultures, and spaces that make up the organization internally. It is a broadening of the bandwidth through improved collaboration.
- *Improve the competence of employees:* individual learning from customers and other stakeholders.

I cannot predict the future, but this book is a sign that we might be approaching a paradigm shift. More and more business people are beginning to realize that human beings are the value creators, not the IT systems. Knowledge management is tainted by an IT stigma, so it is not an ideal term to use—but what this period will be called is perhaps not up to us. After all, the dramatic changes in the world economy experienced by those living in the late 18th century were not labeled "The Industrial Revolution" by those living through it. It took us another hundred years to come up with the label.

Karl-Erik Sveiby, Professor of Knowledge Management, Hanken Business School, Helsinki, Finland

What Building Path Companies Are Trying to Accomplish

In any organization or company, individuals have bits and pieces of information that could allow the creation of new value streams if they were combined. In other words, merely by connecting its I-stuff, a company could create new sources of value. The concept of knowledge sharing as a way to increase value is a new one for many executives and may require a shift in corporate thinking. Most senior executives "grew up" in the tangibles world, in which tangibles (e.g., a building, a piece of machinery, and so on) had value. In the world of tangibles, one could benefit from the laws of supply and demand. Companies could sometimes increase the value of their tangibles by withholding them from the marketplace (thereby creating an increase in demand for a fixed amount of supply). However, the value of *in*tangibles does not increase when they are withheld; on the contrary, value increases when they are shared.

There are many examples of organizations with dysfunctional behavior in terms of information and knowledge sharing. For example, some companies reward outstanding individual employee performance. Employees who develop specific knowledge or who are adept at utilizing it to improve capabilities or decision making may be compensated or rewarded. However, such a system sometimes leads people to withhold knowledge or information from their co-workers in order to create an advantage for themselves. When it is practiced by individuals, this phenomenon is sometimes called the "knowledge is power" effect. On an organizational level, we sometimes observe entire units that encourage the flow of information up and down but restrict the information from flowing across organizational boundaries. This so-called silo effect sometimes pervades entire organizations.

The "knowledge is power" and "silo" effects, with their negative consequences for information flow, can be minimized by the creation of a positive knowledge-friendly culture and infrastructure.

Companies building their portfolio of I-stuff are looking for ways to identify their knowledge and link it to the company's bottom line. Having realized that knowledge is a fundamental driver of value, they are interested in creating a knowledge culture that will foster the concept of sharing and collaborating, determining what knowledge and I-stuff they possess that provides differentiable value to the firm, and how it can be best accessed and shared. Most importantly, companies understand the value of knowledge and culture and are looking for ways to allow connections, conversations, and/or interactions to produce additional value for the firm.

BEST PRACTICES FOR THE BUILDING PATH

Companies on the Building Path are looking for ways to encourage and foster the use of knowledge and I-stuff in their organizations. For example, companies need to create a culture that recognizes the importance of knowledge and I-stuff and maximizes its utility within the firm. In addition, companies on the Building Path are also identifying the I-stuff that has the greatest business

EXHIBIT 3.2   Building Path: Best Practices
Best Practice 1: Creating an I-stuff culture
Best Practice 2: Identifying sustainable I-stuff
Best Practice 3: Creating a network

impact or that differentiates their firm or otherwise provides them with a competitive advantage. Finally, the best practices on this path involve activities that align the company's I-stuff with its business strategy in order to leverage the firm's business activity more fully (see Exhibit 3.2).

Best Practice 1: Creating an I-Stuff Culture

There are many definitions of the term "culture" in the business environment. In our experience, many of the companies we work with define organizational culture as ". . . a set of accepted ideas, behaviors, values, and expectations for interacting within the corporation." These provide employees with guidelines that help them determine:

- How things are done in the company
- Rules for sharing knowledge and information internally (among and between employees and groups) and externally (with customers, suppliers, competitors, and other third parties)
- That the fundamental values of the organization are in alignment with the corporate strategy and objectives

As we evaluated the best practices around creating an I-stuff culture, several patterns became apparent. First, every company has a culture, whether it is created formally or informally. How companies ensure that their cultures embrace knowledge, knowledge sharing, and collaboration to meet the corporate strategy and objectives varies. In some cases, the culture is created with sharing and collaboration in mind; in others it is added after the fact; and others purposefully alter the culture to highlight knowledge and collaboration. Let us take a look at these patterns in more detail.

Hewlett-Packard has long been known for its strong corporate culture, referred to as "the HP Way." The HP Way is, at its core, the codification of the values of HP's founders, William Hewlett and David Packard (see Exhibit 3.3).

EXHIBIT 3.3 Principles of the Hewlett-Packard Way

1. **Profit.** To recognize that profit is the best single measure of our contribution to society and the ultimate source of our corporate strength. We should attempt to achieve the maximum possible profit consistent with our other objectives.

2. **Customers.** To strive for continual improvement in the quality, usefulness, and value of the products and services we offer our customers.

3. **Field of Interest.** To concentrate our efforts, continually seeking new opportunities for growth but limiting our involvement to fields in which we have capability and can make a contribution.

4. **Growth.** To emphasize growth as a measure of strength and a requirement for survival.

5. **Employees.** To provide employment opportunities for HP people that include the opportunity to share in the company's success, which they help make possible. To provide for them job security based on performance and to provide the opportunity for personal satisfaction that comes from a sense of accomplishment in their work.

6. **Organization.** To maintain an organizational environment that fosters individual motivation, initiative, and creativity and a wide latitude of freedom in working toward established objectives and goals.

7. **Citizenship.** To meet the obligations of good citizenship by making contributions to the community and to the institutions in our society that generate the environment in which we operate.

Any organization or group of people who have worked together for some time develops a philosophy, a set of values, a series of traditions and customs. These, in total, are unique to the organization. So it is with Hewlett-Packard. We have a set of values—deeply held beliefs that guide us in meeting our objectives, in working with one another, and in dealing with customers, shareholders, and others. Our corporate objectives are built upon these values. The objectives serve as a day-to-day guide for decision making. To help us meet our objectives, we employ various plans and practices. It is the combination of these elements—our values, corporate objectives, plans and practices—that forms the HP Way.

Excerpted from David Packard, *The HP Way—How Bill Hewlett and I Built Our Company.* Harper Business, NY, pp. 80–81.

HP's founders were able to create and instill a set of values into the organization that set the stage for a sharing of knowledge across all elements of the organization. Not every company has forward-thinking founders who are able to instill long-lasting values in the organization. Are there other approaches to setting the stage for an intangibles-friendly culture to be established? Our research has shown that for most companies the awareness of the need to establish a knowledge infrastructure results from a major corporate event or shift in business focus.

For example, the breakup of the AT&T telecommunications monopoly had a profound effect on all aspects of the surviving "Baby Bells," including how they thought about knowledge and I-stuff. Carol Beckham, Vice-President of BellSouth Intellectual Property Management and Marketing Corporations, tells how her company built a knowledge culture capable of responding to significant changes in the company's environment:

> When what is now BellSouth was part of the AT&T monopoly, employees felt free to share their knowledge and ideas with anyone who asked for it. After all, when you are in a regulated monopoly environment, there is no need to worry about competitors stealing your knowledge or your innovative ideas. It is only in a competitive environment that organizations feel compelled to withhold knowledge or innovations in order to maintain their competitive differentiation. When your company moves toward a less regulated environment where there is competition, then distinguishing yourself becomes important.
>
> As BellSouth made the shift from one environment to the other, the organization's culture had to change from one where any and all knowledge was shared freely to one where protecting company knowledge was important.
>
> BellSouth sought ways to rapidly change employee views on proprietary knowledge through an education program. A one-day mandatory training class was developed for all employees. It focused on explaining proprietary knowledge, what's important, why it's important, what to keep confidential, and under what circumstances employees could share knowledge. It covered how employees could share knowledge within the corporation itself and how the company would protect such information.
>
> Interestingly, at that time BellSouth employees put a premium on what others (like our suppliers) knew, and saw it as more valuable than what individuals within the company knew. They didn't realize that our suppliers get much of their new product knowledge from their relationship with BellSouth. As a consequence, our employees didn't realize that what we had was valuable. It took only a few examples in the training class to demonstrate where a company, especially a start-up company, having received a new contract with BellSouth, found its stock rising dramatically, fueled by the BellSouth name and the expectation that we were going to teach them how their product should work in our network.

For employees participating in the training program, the change in attitude and understanding of the value of company knowledge was immediate. It took nearly a year and a half, however, to complete the training company-wide and to begin realizing the benefits of the changes in employee behavior. We had the added benefit of seeing our employees start to recognize the importance of their inventions. As a result, our IP portfolio started to grow.

The initial focus of our education program was on defining what was proprietary and how it was to be protected. At BellSouth we use the initials "IP" to refer to all information and knowledge that other companies may call "proprietary." Our focus on the importance of "IP" has now grown to a company-wide belief that if you don't protect it, you have nothing to sell or license, because you may already have given it away!

Working with a corporate culture has often been seen as a "touchy-feely" activity best left to the Human Resources Department or the "Knowledge" people. A company's culture and the underlying values can be a crucial building block for a successful I-stuff management program. So, companies need to understand (1) what the fundamental drivers of their culture are and (2) whether they are consistent with knowledge sharing, collaboration, and I-stuff. If the culture needs to be tweaked, management may need to do so through education, process realignment, or a more fundamental values assessment. We have discussed ways companies can create or alter their cultures to be more knowledge friendly, but companies can also inadvertently affect their culture in a negative fashion as well. With the bust of the dot.com era and the impact of 9/11, the U.S. economy experienced an economic downturn. Historically, whenever that has happened, companies begin to focus on cutting costs and reining in spending. Thus we typically see companies laying off employees and cutting back on "non-core" activities. This can create serious consequences to a company's I-stuff. John Raley, Intellectual Asset Manager at Cargill, explains:

> Managing IP, as discussed in *Edison in the Boardroom*, has both tactical and strategic elements; tactically, the generation of IP, managing its costs, etc., and strategically, leveraging IP to grow the company and to guide future efforts. In contrast, managing I-stuff is a totally strategic effort. Creating an I-stuff culture is not done in just a few days. Rather, it is an ongoing and accumulative effort to impart an enduring change upon an organization and how it works. A consistency of focus and effort is needed to build the new reality. But, in reverse, it doesn't take much to impair, retard, or reverse the creation of an I-stuff culture. One of the implications of creating an I-stuff culture is that the effort has to transcend and be immune from short-term issues or concerns. It has to be an unusual set of circumstances for a company to ignore the needed maintenance to keep its equipment in proper operating order. Likewise, for an I-stuff culture, the needed nurturing and maintenance

of the intellect of the organization cannot be put off or ignored. For creating and sustaining an I-stuff culture, cost cannot supersede culture. I am aware of one Fortune 500 Company in which for many, many years, the organization's library circulated journals and periodicals throughout the organization. Personnel only needed to sign up on distribution lists to have items they were interested in routed to their offices or workstations. In this way people could easily keep up to date in areas of their expertise, work responsibilities, and interests. However, in a cost-cutting move, the company stopped this practice. This by itself is not that unusual. Many companies have gone the electronic route with on-line access via the company's intranet and have benefited not only from the cost savings of eliminating hard copy circulation but also from their people having access to an even larger world of information and knowledge. However, at this one company, this was not the case. Just the cost savings of eliminating hard copy circulation was put in place. If people wanted to read work-related journals and periodicals they would have to take time away from where they were working and go to the organization's library. Not only is the main facility quite large, but this company also has many other facilities in the area. For a variety of reasons, many people have chosen not to take the time to leave their offices or workstations and go to the organization's library. The result has been a cost savings, but at what cost to the intellect of the organization? Are personnel not keeping up to date in important subject areas? What impacts will this have on future innovativeness and even the long-term sustainability of the organization in its present (or former) form?

Unlike other assets, I-stuff needs constant replenishment or it stagnates. If cost cutting or other activities interfere with an employee's ability to be creative, or affects their learning, or their ability to communicate and share knowledge inside the company, then it has serious implications for maintaining corporate I-stuff. This view is directly at odds with the accounting view of value, which we will discuss in more detail later.

Best Practice 2: Identifying Differentiable I-Stuff

As consultants we are often called into companies to help identify pockets of value in their respective portfolios of I-stuff. One of the first things we ask is whether the company knows which I-stuff provides differentiable value or competitive advantage for their firm. It is not uncommon to hear one of the following responses: "Everything we know is valuable" or "We have no idea." Both answers highlight the need to understand which I-stuff drives the value of the business.

Prior to *Edison in the Boardroom* in 2001, only a few of the companies we interviewed had a know-how inventory or understood which know-how was really valuable. Today more companies are beginning to recognize the value of their differentiable knowledge and that all knowledge is not created equal. Cargill is one company that has only recently realized this.

Traditionally a producer of agricultural and food products, Cargill is transitioning from a commodity producer to an international provider of food, agricultural, and financial services products and services. It has come to realize that I-stuff is the key to its successful transition. This transition has in turn led to the need for a set of management processes around identifying and managing their sustainable knowledge. David VandenEinde, Senior Intellectual Asset Manager, and Harry Gwinnell, Vice-President, Chief IP Counsel, discuss how Cargill has handled the transformation:

> Cargill is a privately held company with over 124,000 employees and over $70 billion in sales. The company operates in 60 countries and has 80-plus business units grouped into 11 platforms. About six years ago Cargill's Management decided to reposition Cargill from just a commodity company to a customer solutions company. That meant we were going to move beyond selling stuff by the pound and find a way to sell our knowledge as well. Of course that required us to know what knowledge we had, and what knowledge to keep proprietary and confidential. Six years ago we had almost no systems in place that would allow us to do that.
>
> A trigger event in 1997 launched Cargill on a new path. In the process of forming a joint venture with The Dow Chemical Company, each parent superimposed its controls onto the venture, saying: "Here's how we want this business to run." Cargill found itself observing the results of Dow's long experience in managing the IP and I-stuff they had contributed. In observing Dow's approach, Cargill realized it had much to learn.
>
> So the company began a three-step I-stuff improvement process. The first step was to change the culture into one that was more aware and supportive of I-stuff. To do so, we needed to develop the language and the way we were going to talk as a corporation around the fact that we had things that were valuable. But we really needed to develop a new and common language.
>
> The Intellectual Capital Management group started working on that aspect— education, training, and development—and on getting people to understand the difference between IP, which was pretty easy to inventory, and I-stuff, which Cargill had so much of and which we wanted so badly to use to create additional value for the company, but had a hard time getting people to realize was there.
>
> The second step was getting the business units to create inventories of all of their IP and I-stuff, and once a list was created, working with each business unit to prioritize their intangibles according to its importance to the business.

The third step was putting the infrastructure and compliance systems in place around that. We created policies and circulated those widely around the company and made sure that each business unit worked on the top ten compliance issues that were required. We developed an infrastructure to help people understand what's a trade secret and what's not a trade secret. Very quickly we came to the conclusion that all trade secrets are not created equal. We found there are trade secrets that drive value for the business, and there are trade secrets that don't.

So at the end of doing this inventory, we had a huge pile of I-stuff for every business unit. Those lists are maintained at the business unit level.

We then engaged in what I call "filtering" to get from the significant many to the critical few. And I want to emphasize that: critical few. These were the things that created value for the business.

Now each business unit can have a clearer understanding of their IP and I-stuff and how it is adding value to their bottom line.

The Boeing Company also has a knowledge-categorization system that evolved out of the organization's legal and military security history. Jeanne Suchodolski, IP attorney with Boeing Commercial Airplanes in Boeing's Commercial Airplane Division, explains:

The categories that exist today include trade secret information that encompasses both Boeing knowledge as well as our suppliers', customers', and other third-party knowledge with which we are entrusted. Boeing trade secrets are further subdivided into two subcategories: "limited" and "proprietary," which require different levels of authorization to share or release externally. There is also a set of defense- and military-related categories, which includes all the military security classifications and contractor intellectual property rights (e.g., unrestricted, government purpose rights, confidential, secret, top secret, etc.) And then there are sets of regulatory categories that classify technical information by degree of export control. Technical information may be uncontrolled, require an export license, or be otherwise governed by ITAR (International Traffic in Arms) regulations.

The specific schema for categorization is based entirely on what makes sense to the company and/or business. What is important, however, is that the categorization scheme is easily understood and communicated broadly to the employees and outside parties (if applicable). Only then can companies get assistance in maintaining and updating their knowledge categories and also ensure that employees know where to go for information and, most importantly, how to handle it both inside and outside the firm. (See Exhibit 3.4.) For some firms this may result in some kind of an inventory document, while for others it may be the creation of an internal lexicon that can allow knowledge groupings to be "tagged."

EXHIBIT 3.4   I-Stuff in Financial Organizations

In general the financial services industry, and particularly the insurance industry has been a late arrival to the intellectual property and intangibles arena. I was asked to help create and manage its intellectual property and intellectual assets for value. I soon realized that IP was only a very small part of the intangibles they had. The bulk of our competitive advantage is based upon our relationships, brand, ratings, price, and customer service; in other words, our I-stuff. The insurance industry has historically openly shared its innovations. At the time I began to focus on this area, the insurance industry was beginning to quietly explore the area of intellectual asset management. Our first task was to educate employees that their knowledge was valuable, and in some instances could be legally protected.

Overall the financial industries' understanding of both IP and I-stuff, while improving, is still generally low. We initially focused on patent filings and whether that was right for us and the processes for doing so. While our organization chose to file for patents on several core areas important to our business, at the same time we realized that protection of I-stuff, in the form of trade secrets, systems applications, risk analytics tools, and our innovations processes needed to be another key area of focus.

We tackled the area of educating our employees on confidentiality and created training programs for our business to create a common language and understanding of IP and I-stuff. As we progressed through this period of time, our focus was to protect these tangible and intangible assets, get them codified or digitized, and ensure these assets became a more visible and significant value to the organization. It was a huge training, education, and learning curve and cultural shift and challenge for the organization as a whole. We helped employees and the organization to better understand new terms and created an IP based vocabulary, and showed them how to identify and protect these assets as part of their daily jobs.

While we continued to learn more about the IP and I-stuff, we realized we needed to pay more attention to the areas and processes in the business where IP and I-stuff is created. In our organization, ideas are created to solve business problems usually in the form of a new product, IT system application, or customer service program. We heavily utilize outside vendors to develop the IT applications and business programs such as training programs, customer seminars, etc., and immediately realized the need to work closely with the sourcing department and other people having direct customer and vendor contacts. It was imperative we have the appropriate detection techniques and agreements in place at the point we were discussing new concepts, ideas, or putting development work out for bid or proposal to vendors and suppliers. This became the second area of focus, to ensure we were adequately identifying and protecting the creation and documentation of IP and I-stuff at it earliest point in the innovation and development cycles. When we began to examine our agreements and processes for interacting with outside vendors and

(continues)

consultants, the potential magnitude of our IP and I-stuff leakage hit home. We recognized we had the potential to hemorrhage ideas, not just worry about a little leak. We first got to work clarifying our Confidentiality Agreements (CA), then the Master Service Agreements (MSA) that we used to hire and manage vendors and consultants, and finally Request for Proposal (RFP) documents. The key change to these documents was to include specific IP/I-stuff language and markings and specific carve-outs or time bound clauses to maintain or protect new business ideas, concepts, processes, or application design techniques. The key concept is the RFP now makes it clear we will retain ownership of the resulting IP, I-stuff, system or product, and the vendor will be bound by confidentiality and non-reuse.

The majority of our RFP's are sent to IT, marketing, and consulting vendors. In essence we are structuring our thinking for someone to provide, or often create for us, a new product or service based upon our latest knowledge and thinking. If you think about what an RFP is, it is essentially reducing our best thinking and intellect about how we are going to conduct business, or build things for our use to solve a business problem. In essence, we are going to build it because we cannot buy it or license it in; does that sound like a new product to you? It did to us. We were about to give someone else detailed information about it, without proper protections. This didn't make sense to us. Lastly we focused on the Task Order (TO), which finalizes the requirements of the project, the deliverables, timelines, and costs associated with the completion of the project. We found these documents need to be more tightly integrated with Confidentiality Agreements, Master Service Agreements, Request for Proposals, and standardized across the organization as the TOs actually scope out the work to be done.

So let's look at how this worked for us. We were beginning to work on a multi-million dollar, multi-year financial reengineering project that included several outside IT vendors, service providers and consulting organizations. As we were defining our requirements, we realized we were designing improvements that neither the vendors nor consultants had seen or considered before, but that had potential value to both groups as improvements they could sell to others. Once we identified these improvements as I-stuff, we added specific carve-out clauses in our contracts that asserted our ownership and bound them to confidentiality restrictions. While our RFPs & TOs provided the context of what needed to be designed into the system, we purposely withheld the actual business rules of how the system will work and developed that specific IT application internally with interfaces to their applications. The valuable I-stuff was not disclosed. We also kept the requirements for the internally developed applications secured via password protection on our internal networks, where vendors would normally have complete access.

Robert F. Nelson, Intellectual Asset Manager for a financial services company

Best Practice 3: Creating a Network

Organizations continuously create knowledge. We have already shown how some organizations have been able to sort their knowledge to give a better understanding of the value it provides to the company. However, as Lew Platt, former CEO of Hewlett-Packard, once said, "If HP knew what HP knows we would be three times as profitable." So how do companies organize or network knowledge, documents, and people together with the business to facilitate continued value generation? The story of how the pharmaceutical manufacturer Eli Lilly and Company aligned its I-stuff resources, as told by Director of Knowledge Management Aaron Schacht, provides insight into one company's best practice:

> In early 2000 I was asked to become the Director of Knowledge Management and create a self-sustaining system to support knowledge sharing. I felt that people spent too much time in their research tracking down the source of some piece of knowledge; be it another person or a reference object, we had people spending more time looking for information than doing something with the knowledge once they found it. We wanted a method for identifying knowledge that provided searches that were robust, reliable, and accurate.
>
> The company had a fundamental issue with knowledge searching. We viewed the issue as broader than information searching, or Internet searching. We asked ourselves whether it would be possible to search through our own organization to find information and knowledge that was attached to people. We reasoned that codified information, such as that found in an e-mail or a report, did not have the richness one could find by talking directly to the author of the piece. This view caused us to explore how we could navigate Lilly's social and professional networks.
>
> We coined this phrase: *We are all about connections; connecting people to people, people to data, and people to technology.* To achieve a capability for this kind of connectivity, I created three different groups. The first was a technology group, whose function was to put in place the technology to support the tools needed for organizational knowledge management.
>
> The second group was concerned with how the company employs tools to categorize knowledge and information and data so they may be accessed. The third group focused on Lilly's people and culture, specifically how to think about business processes enabled with the right kind of knowledge-sharing inputs.
>
> The first task we set ourselves was to examine the Lilly culture. Lilly is a social culture that places a lot of emphasis on connecting people to people, through communities and/or through good expert databases. The thinking was that if we could connect people to documents then they would be able to contact the source person with additional questions.

We focused on creating a model of the cognitive nervous system of our business. We called it the "knowledge alignment backbone." For example, if I think about myself as the center of such a network, I can ask myself: What are all the connections I have? It's all the documents I've authored, it's all the documents I might have used, it's all the people I collaborate with or have collaborated with. It's all of the projects I've worked on.

Our task was to organize information in a way that allowed a searcher not only to see a source but also to understand something about the author or the person. In particular we want the searcher to be able to obtain information about the source: Does it relate to their area of interest and the kind of knowledge the source may have. If we could accomplish this, then people in the company could decide whether and how source people or their documents might impact the searcher's existing project or information needs.

Finally, we attempted to measure success by quantifying the rate of participation and use of tools that we had created. There was no corporate mandate or call for people to use these tools, yet the rate of participation rose quickly and then maintained itself. An interesting note is that people looking to hire internally will search the database first and peruse the listed experts. So people are targeting internal hires from the database, which in turn leads to more people participating, which then creates more knowledge sharing around the company.

To remain competitive in a highly competitive global marketplace, some innovative companies have created systems for the efficient transmission of valuable know-how and critical information, both internally and externally. Charles Armstrong initiated that process within S.A. Armstrong Limited, a global manufacturer and supplier of pumps and fluid-handling equipment that today holds primary market positions in North America and the United Kingdom. Charles realized that he needed a solid information backbone to enable the organization to utilize its constantly evolving and growing I-stuff quickly and efficiently. This is his account of how he achieved this:

S. A. Armstrong Limited is a privately held family company that has been in business for over 70 years providing fluid handling equipment. We operate in three continents, sell products in 43 countries, and have about 600 employees. Over the years our product offering has become incredibly complex. We have five different customer types who, to one degree or another, have different requirements of our organization. Furthermore, we have nine product categories, which result in over eight million different end products. This high degree of complexity is one of the issues that evolved in our manufacturing process. It forced us to look at how to manage complexity and develop an agile organization, or, as I'd like to call it, a "conductive organization." A conductive organization is one that has the capability to transmit quality knowledge repeatedly throughout the organization, as well as between customers and employees.

Our strategy has been to evolve from a generic product company to a customer solution provider and to become exceptionally adept at meshing the ever-growing complexity of our technical offerings and the customer's requirements. We had to achieve this against the backdrop of global geographical challenges and market fragmentation.

One of the challenges of a product organization evolving into a solution provider is the nature of the dialogue between a salesperson (or distributor, or representative, or agent) and the customer. This new dialogue must reflect our mission not to just sell products, but to actually get involved with our customer's issues and help solve them with a solutions-based offering.

That's how we came to develop "Rapids," which is product configuration software that delivers customized goods and services that meet individual customers' needs with mass-production efficiency.

This Web-based system is part of the knowledge infrastructure that captures the know-how of our product data experts and automates the entire "negotiation to order" information activity. Ultimately, it simplifies the whole process of product selection, quoting, generating 3-D drawings for our customers, and whatever technical specifications are required for an engineering bid. It completely streamlines the business process, allowing transactions to take place in real time through direct interaction with the customer. This software is an intelligent repository for the know-how of the business and puts it at the fingertips of the end-user (sales rep, engineer, customer). The end-user can work remotely and can later synchronize the data with the organization for all of the project and technical information updates. This online and offline capability is a noteworthy achievement and has made a huge difference in our ability to work remotely and globally. It has significantly increased our organization's ability to rapidly configure new products and solutions in response to changing customer needs.

When a business makes eight million configurable end products, one can imagine that the scope for application and order errors is dependent on the knowledge and skill level of the sales representative or customer. The rules-based engine in the software allows our product data experts to embed their know-how in an explicit format that can be accessed by our end-users. As a result, Rapids is our platform for organizing, building, and sharing know-how, and it has become a sustaining knowledge portal for the organization. In parallel, we created a knowledge exchange platform driven by a Livelink engine where multimedia e-learning modules support many products and applications in Rapids.

Rapids enables the organization to quickly respond to the changing marketplace. A new product can be entered into the database in less than three weeks. That was one of our specifications of the system at the outset. We also wanted people to be able to synchronize their computers to the server so that the most up-to-date information was always available. Previously, updating 50,000 consulting engineering catalogs in the United States was an enormous job, not only in printing, but also in the reliable and timely distribution of the information. We realized that the process of keeping our information current was becoming increasingly impractical and we found ourselves in a position where there were a lot of things that we weren't able to do in an agile way to support the customer. Today, enabled by Rapids, our technical updates, pricing, quotations, revisions, and customer feedback are consistently available across a global platform. Rapids also enables a new capability the sales rep had never had before: to enter into a different solutions-based conversation with the customer. Today we can say: I understand this to be the problem that you're facing, and here are some options and solutions that we can configure together, as we sit. And, if you want to receive a quotation, submittal drawing, or any technical data or place an order, we can do it together now.

So, Rapids represents embedded know-how and processes and facilitates a unique customer experience.

From an internal perspective, Rapids has both demanded and enabled us to work horizontally in the organization. Rapids touches every functional department in the organization on a global basis: finance for product costing, marketing for pricing and product configurations, engineering for technical data and 3D drawings, IT for software development, manufacturing for logistics, and service in operating and parts data.

To populate the rules-based engine, the input of people who had a specific span of know-how in the organization was required. To identify this expertise, we developed a knowledge network map (Knetmap) of the organization by querying who goes to whom for specific expertise. By making explicit all of the points of expertise by product group and by geography, we determined who had the knowledge to populate Rapids. Then we assigned product data experts and teams from different disciplines to build the product modules. The emerging product data function is concerned with not only listening to the customer requirement but also specifying the needs so the organization can configure to satisfy those needs. So, it's been a very interesting practice because when you start out, the scope of interdependencies is not always obvious. You can deliver product without a lot of interdependencies, but you can't deliver complex solutions to your customers unless the whole organization is enabled to work in a fairly seamless way together.

Vince Grassi, director of Global Learning and Knowledge Management at Air Products, discusses how the networking of people, processes, and knowledge has been beneficial for his company:

Air Products holds the distinction of being the world's only combined gases and chemicals company, which gives us a unique portfolio of businesses and a broader base of knowledge than you would find in the field of industrial gases or chemicals alone. Such a diversity of expertise has propelled Air Products to the forefront of certain industries, for example, semiconductors and flat panel displays, where we have become a critical partner to some of the world's largest and best-known electronics companies. At the same time, all of this expansive knowledge was leading to a wide diversity of businesses—until recently we had 17 independent, strategic business units with many of them following different processes and using varying tools and methods for problem solving.

Air Products' leadership recognized the need to harness the collective expertise of its organization and, in 2000, launched an internal vision called "Deliver the Difference." The main driver behind this vision is to operate as "one company" focused on our customers, working together with one common set of business processes. Within "Deliver the Difference" was the Work Process initiative that challenged employees to focus on standardizing, shortening, simplifying, and sharing work processes across groups, divisions, and global regions. The ultimate goal of these efforts is to better serve our customers and at the same time enable continuous improvement, cost reduction, and growth.

When we started converging on our one-company systems approach, we focused on knowledge management, in particular the issues of knowledge codification, sharing, and reuse.

One of the knowledge management capabilities that we developed was how to effectively solicit, collect, and manage the implementation of new ideas.

Once we defined the business outcomes that we needed from idea management, we looked across all of our line operations to understand the best practices already in place. As just one example, we discovered that we had at least four disparate systems in place that could be transitioned to one single process and tool. We put together a convergence team, mapped out the work processes that were being followed, identified the tools that were being used, and identified the cultural issues. The process we developed was called Idea Management, and the tool was called Idea Tracker.

The challenge with Idea Management is how to involve the entire company without making the process and tool overly complex. The first step was to break down the overall process into smaller project pieces. We used communities of practice to help us do that. For example, there was a community associated with business process improvement and another community focused on document management. All these communities would use the same tool so that when people entered the tool they could see a list of the communities; people could then work, deposit ideas, or work on ideas associated with the communities that were of interest to them. Having chartered the community, each community became responsible for the ideas assigned to it. Each community would solve business problems using the process and tool in a way that was best for it.

One of the benefits of this system has been our ability to reduce redundant R&D efforts taking place around the company. In addition, it has also allowed us to share ideas across very different businesses quickly and to ensure quick compliance. Idea

Tracker is integrated with our invention process. Ideas are forwarded from Idea Tracker to our invention process, which can result in intellectual property protection as a result of robust information control.

The idea management process and tool have been in place since 2001. More than 10,000 ideas have been submitted and acted upon in the system. Benefits go well beyond cost savings, as these ideas have led to new business growth and innovation across the enterprise.

The vignettes and discussion so far have focused on intranetwork management of I-stuff (the company and its internal relationships). However, company employees are increasingly networking outside of the organization for knowledge and I-stuff as well. This shift has been occurring over the past five years as companies have had to tighten their belts because of both the recession and the dot.com bust. As Jeff Weedman, Vice-President of External Business Development for Procter & Gamble, likes to say, "At P&G we have moved from *Not Invented Here* to *Proudly Found Elsewhere*." More and more companies are realizing that there is a business need to utilize knowledge and ideas outside the organization in order to maintain a competitive edge. Networking to connect people to documents is important, but firms will gain more utilization and commercialization potential by linking people to people to facilitate and permit continued ideation and invention. How do firms search for knowledge outside their organization? Although patent and IP searching tools have increased the level of sophistication, companies are not geared to searching for nonlegally protected knowledge. As companies begin to rely more on their I-stuff, there is a need for new search tools to help them find knowledge solutions or even problems (see Exhibit 3.5).

In addition to searching for markets and competitive information relating to I-stuff, companies are more and more looking for individuals with both the relevant expertise and solutions to the existing problems they may articulate. This has spawned the creation of an expertise marketplace with companies such as Innocentive (www.innocentive.com) and YourEncore (www.yourencore.com).

CONCLUSIONS: BEYOND BUILDING

Companies engaged in building their portfolio of I-stuff are following the same path as Einstein, who carefully laid the groundwork for his startling discoveries by thoroughly understanding the knowledge that already existed. When flattered about the unique nature of his discoveries Einstein is reported to have responded, "I stood on the shoulders of giants." Companies on the Building Path are engaged in the process of finding the "shoulders" upon which they will be creating future profits for their firm.

EXHIBIT 3.5   Accelovation's Story

Jonathan: Companies profit from I-stuff by identifying market opportunities, exploiting portfolios of existing inventions (in many cases, ideas that are pre-invented or pre-patented), and exploring when and how to reach beyond their companies' boundaries to bring in outside innovations. Past approaches and tools have focused on intellectual property, in particular, patents. But to innovate in the world beyond IP—the world of I-stuff—businesses need more than information on patents; they need insights about markets. The question is, where can companies go to identify insights about new market opportunities, innovations, competitors, infringers, etc.?

The fact is that with more than eight billion pages and hundreds of terabytes of information now on the World Wide Web, the "voice of the market" is now online, accessible to anyone. The true problem lies not in finding data, but in distinguishing between the billions of pages to unearth deeply buried, useful information that companies can use to expand, innovate, and grow. Traditional search tools tend to look at the popularity of pages or use keywords. This works fairly well for patent search, but not when searching for market insights. Business users commercializing I-stuff need much more focused knowledge and existing tools are simply not suited for the job. True market insights deal with real, expressed market needs that affect many people. They are authoritative. They are relevant. And they can be awfully hard to find. Accelovation, founded in 2003, delivers a revolutionary type of search solution based on intelligent mining of the internet and "deep web" to rapidly deliver high value market insights.

Stewart: For Eastman Chemical, the intriguing thing about the Accelovation system is the ability to get useful, well-organized, and rationalized information out of a diverse base of information, namely, the over eight billion pages of Internet content Jonathan mentioned. To be able to search that and organize it in a format that had previously been unavailable is tremendously valuable. We found this an extremely interesting approach since in the chemical industry we are typically one or two steps away from the final end use of our products. In other words, a chemical raw material is typically sold to another company, which then does something with it. They put it in a paint can. They put it in a consumer product like a detergent or a cosmetic, or they fabricate it into something that ultimately becomes a formed object like a bottle, a package of some sort, or a sign. So we're often at least two steps removed before it gets on the shelf where a consumer buys it. The nature of this value chain means that you're often starved for information, and so the ability to gain some insight into what might be driving these needs is both unique and highly valued. The second thing they offered is that the tool can organize the data and allow you to see some trends, relationships, and insights that are not available otherwise. This is, as I said, something quite unique and that we hadn't seen in any other system. We were skeptical at first and wanted to see if this was just what people affectionately referred to as virtual-ware, or whether it really was a functioning IT tool that accomplished what Accelovation claimed. To do this we picked a few test cases in a few very different areas.

(continues)

The first one we looked at was a new product in a totally new market. We had Accelovation do a search for us, not only to gain market insights, but also to gain some competitive information: Namely, were there other companies aimed at the same market need via a completely different solution? That search provided some interesting insights. It turned up some of what we knew, but it gave us some validation that there was a pretty limited solution set out there that people were deploying to address this need. It also confirmed that the players we thought were out there were really there, and it didn't turn up any significant additional players. There were no real "Ah-Has," but negative information is also valuable, since, as is well known in innovation, as you proceed down any innovation pipeline, the longer you're in the more you're spending. So having that confirmation was valuable.

The second project we did with Accelovation was around an existing product that's well established and offers a unique set of features. We knew Eastman was the only company offering this specific product, but we wanted additional insight regarding competitive products or combinations of products that offered the same or similar features. That search and analysis thus gave both market insight and, again, a sense of competitive position.

I would say without hesitation that Accelovation can accomplish in a few weeks what would be many months if not a year's worth of pretty tedious and detailed market studies. For some of the things they turn up, there literally would be no other way to get the information. We did a follow-up on the first case with a study around product positioning and language, specifically sales language. I can't think of any way that information would have been available by any other means.

I think at first Accelovation may have hesitated to take on our job because accomplishing our goals required a new type of search with their tool. At the end of the day, they in fact developed some extremely valuable information that would have been unattainable by any other methods. For Eastman, as we broaden our focus from IP to I-stuff, we realize we need different types of tools and an infrastructure to allow us to search and to do things around knowledge and I-stuff. Interestingly, I-stuff enables you to look more broadly at "innovation." The move from IP to I-stuff is consistent with other significant trends in industrial innovation, most notably, use of an open innovation system. The game is clearly changing from creating the best innovations,entirely internally to sourcing (whether internally or externally) the best innovations and then managing this knowledge (this I-stuff created) and marrying it with appropriate market and competitive insights. Accelovation allows you to address the conundrum of the information age: We're drowning in information but starving for knowledge. So the ability to take information, organize it, and then use it with your intangibles (in combination with other factors) is how companies of the next generation are going to succeed.

Interview conducted with Jonathan Spier, CEO and Co-Founder, Accelovation, and J. Stewart Witzeman, Director, Technology Strategy, Eastman Chemical Company.

4

LEVERAGING THE PORTFOLIO OF I-STUFF

COMPANIES ON THE Leveraging Path want to make money from their I-stuff. Companies that believe their I-stuff has business value champion the "commercialization" view of I-stuff. These companies may already have been routinely extracting value from their intellectual property, or they may have been commercializing some I-stuff serendipitously. Companies on the Leveraging Path realize that I-stuff can have a measurable effect on the bottom line and that commercializing I-stuff often requires a different perspective on sales (e.g., selling what we used to provide for free, and giving away for free things we used to sell).

Thought Leader Comments

Leveraging is unique because, unlike many business practices, it does not have to be implemented across the entire company to have a direct impact on corporate revenue and sustainability. The decision of one business unit to develop a new offering through the leveraging of its I-stuff in combination with another entity's I-stuff can result in faster time to market, faster positive cash flow, lower cost of capital, and an immediate as well as future impact at the corporate level.

As the company experiences in this chapter illustrate, the leveraging of I-stuff can lead to innovative business models, resulting in unique products or services. When companies extract value from their IP, they are starting to leverage their supporting I-stuff. It is the application of the knowledge, reports, and prototypes to the IP (patent, domain name, trademark) that creates the value. Individual business units within a firm may do this at different stages in their business or product cycle, but they have seldom defined a vocabulary or work processes or even identified employees to leverage intangibles in a consistent manner.

What vocabulary does a company need to describe leveraging? Conversations at the ICM Gathering and other conferences often quickly move from the management of IP to how you really make money using intangibles. Often, the conversations start with an organizational chart and attempts to explain the non-IP of the firm. There seems to be agreement on the importance and volume of I-stuff but little knowledge about how to leverage it. As firms seek new ways to sustain their growth in a profitable manner, they are beginning to recognize the need for both new business models and a new vocabulary.

Furthermore, as we develop the vocabulary and practices to create value from I-stuff, we must also recognize that inventions (IP) do not equal innovations. A large patent portfolio does not guarantee business success. The linkage between leveraging and innovation is powerful when innovation is understood to be bringing new products to the market, changing the rules of the game, and leveraging available I-stuff to sustain competitive advantage.

Companies seeking to move from serendipitous leveraging (brand management or casual licensing, for example) to strategic leveraging need new business models that recognize and utilize I-stuff. If a business is a products-offered business that wants to grow by leveraging its I-stuff, it must step back from its current offerings and take a broader view of what the business really is. The risk if it does not do this is that it will continue selling its products and giving away its I-stuff without increasing revenue.

Consider one example: A business determines that if it provides additional technical support for its product and trains its sales force better it will get both more sales and more profit. This approach will definitely increase its costs, and its competitors will easily be able to copy what it is doing.

The business that creates a model utilizing the I-stuff of the firm recognizes that it can create a sustainable value stream by developing unique combinations of its intangibles. In the 1990's The Dow Chemical Company recognized that it needed a new business model to quickly make money from a newly developed product line. Dow did not have the brand recognition or sales force to introduce the new products without a huge investment of money and time. DuPont possessed the brand and the sales force but had an aging product line. By combining their I-stuff, the two firms created DuPont Dow Elastomers, a profitable $1 billion entity. Profits were shared equally between the two parents.

Monsanto educates its agricultural seed sales and marketing people about the value of the patented products they are selling. As a result, the company commands both a premium on patented products and increased market share. Another illustration is committing to global customers that they will receive products designed for the countries where they do business for no premium if they sign a long-term contract. Both of these tactics, particularly if done as a first move, can be difficult for competitors to immediately duplicate immediately. The vocabulary to describe these practices may vary, but what these firms are doing is leveraging their unique intangibles to enhance profitability.

The implementation of new business models to leverage I-stuff may require an initial investment in appropriate resources and a change in employee deployment. Leveraging firms need to recognize that to deliver on their new business model, they may need to invest in new software, partners, or work processes to get a model that fully utilizes I-stuff. They may even need to create or acquire new I-stuff. This may lead to a realignment of the human resources within a business. Again, one of the dimensions of leveraging is that it can be done successfully at the business level with corporate impact.

Often the firms or business units that leverage I-stuff the best are those that have no significant capital or tangible base to manage. They are not distracted by volume variances, days of inventory, and fluctuations in raw material costs. As the biotech sector was developing, the firms parlayed their IP portfolios, the people, research results, and clinical trials (the majority being I-stuff) to attract employees, investors, and partners. Thus biotech companies were leveraging their I-stuff to create future growth. This is very different from only commercializing a firm's IP.

The opportunities for leveraging companies to both create new value streams and learn how to create competitive advantage from I-stuff are limited only by the capacity for change. The challenge for companies that succeed in leveraging intangibles on an individual business or product basis is to recognize the potential benefit if they were to integrate the same practices across the company. Until boards and stakeholders start asking questions about how intangibles are being managed across the entire company, firms remain serendipitous leveragers.

As shown in this chapter, P&G, Boeing, Cargill, Visa International, Eli Lilly and Company, and Thomson have all moved well beyond product brand management as the primary means of leveraging their intangibles. They have taken a new look at their customers and markets and harnessed the power of their intangibles to new business models.

In the future, companies that have recognized the contributions made by leveraging their I-stuff will be receptive to integrating the concepts fully across the corporation. Intangibles are very portable (which can be both a plus and a minus), and thus a company can leverage them globally, often with minimal cost of capital. While leveraging, a company can also learn what is needed to secure and protect its I-stuff corporately and then apply this knowledge as it moves on to the Integration Path.

Sharon Oriel, Talisker & Associates LLC, former Director of ICM, The Dow Chemical Company

What Companies on the Leveraging Path Are Trying to Accomplish

Companies on the Leveraging Path are already experienced in the commercialization of I-stuff, either their own or that of others. They are eager to begin extracting value from their I-stuff, particularly when it promises to add new revenue streams to the firm's existing or more traditional ones. Companies on this path seek to convert their I-stuff into revenues and profits that are greater than those produced by their traditional business activity. They have a common set of objectives (see Exhibit 4.1), as follows:

- *To extract value from the "low-hanging" I-stuff in the organization.* As with IP, companies must determine the kind(s) of value they want to obtain from their I-stuff. Does the company already have processes in place for value extraction, and if so, can these be built on or modified to suit the needs of I-stuff value extraction? Does the company have complementary business assets in place, and if so, can these be used to extract value from the firm's I-stuff?
- *To create a business model that matches their I-stuff, not the existing business.* To do this effectively, a company must differentiate its business model from its strategic plan. It must determine whether the I-stuff business model should be different from the company's existing business model. If so, why? The firm must determine which elements of an I-stuff business model will differentiate the firm's offerings in the marketplace.
- *To manage brands proactively.* Each company must identify business objectives for its brand. Does the brand contain a promise (explicit or implied)? If so, what is it? What value can be extracted from the brand(s)?

EXHIBIT 4.1   The Einstein Value Continuum Highlighting the Leveraging Path

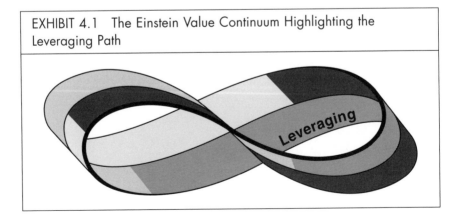

Does the firm have processes in place that can help with extracting value from brands and branding I-stuff?

How Companies Leverage Their I-Stuff

Companies entering I-stuff management on the Leveraging Path tend to begin with commercialization opportunities that are extensions of their current business activity. Usually these opportunities represent small changes to an existing business model and do not significantly tap into the full potential of the company's I-stuff. Nevertheless, this can be a great place to start.

Consider Coca-Cola and its successful Dasani bottled water product. When the company was looking for new products to introduce in its efforts to generate new growth, it focused on carbonated and flavored beverages, arguably because this was what their core business was about. When these efforts didn't seem to provide sufficient growth opportunities, Coke looked for alternatives. The result was Dasani bottled water. Because the processes the company had been using for manufacturing carbonated beverages relied on water, Coke was able to convert its existing knowledge about processing pure water into a new and successful revenue stream.

Companies operating on the Leveraging Path realize that, just as with IP, successful I-stuff management and value conversion require concentrated strategic effort. This strategy is inevitably different from, and complementary to, the firm's existing business strategy.

Generating Value from I-Stuff

Most of us think of value in dollar terms. However, firms can extract many kinds of value from their intellectual capital and I-stuff, value that is not measurable in dollar terms. We refer to dollar value as "direct value" and to other kinds of value as "indirect value." Both kinds of value may be the result of either defensive or offensive activity (see Exhibit 4.2).

- *Direct value:* Value from activities that unambiguously link the I-stuff with an identifiable cash flow. Direct value can be measured in currency terms (e.g., dollars, yen, euros).
- *Indirect value:* Identifiable value, often intuitively obvious and sometimes compelling, that is not associated with a specific transaction (such as a license or a sale).

EXHIBIT 4.2   Value Matrix*

Kinds of Value	IP	I-Stuff
Defensive	Protection Design freedom Cross-licensing (defensive) Litigation bargaining power	Cross-licensing (defensive) Litigation bargaining power
Offensive **Revenue**		
From products and services	Sale, licensing, joint ventures, strategic alliances, integration	New products or services to offer (sale, license, strategic alliance, integration)
Directly from the intangible	Sale, licensing, joint venture, co-branding, strategic alliance, litigation damages	Sale, licensing, joint venture, strategic alliance
Cost Reduction	Litigation avoidance Access to technology of others	Litigation avoidance Improved knowledge transfer Reduced knowledge gaps
Strategic Position	Reputation/image Name recognition Competitive blocking Barrier to entry Supplier control	Reputation/image Competitive blocking Barrier to entry Customer loyalty

*For more information about each entry in this table, see Appendix A.

- *Defensive value:* Prepares the firm to mitigate disruptive action by individuals or groups outside the firm. It requires preparation, and it is the development of assets or resources that will help repel or neutralize intrusive activities that threaten the firm.
- *Offensive value:* Focuses on individuals or groups outside the firm. Its purpose is to advance the organization's ability to achieve its strategic purpose or to implement its strategy. Offensive activity frequently concerns revenue or profit generation.

The Kinds of Value Intangibles Can Provide

As was initially discussed in *Edison in the Boardroom*, accounting-based meas-urement (which measures transactions occurring in the past) is not at all help-ful when one is dealing with intangibles (whose value lies in the future). Indeed, in our consulting practice we have seen many internal company methods for intangibles valuation, methods that depend on understanding the value and context that intangibles provide to the organization. Although an in-depth examination of the ways in which intangibles brought value to organizations revealed a spectrum of different kinds of business value, we found that most can be grouped under two major headings: defensive value and offensive value.[1]

Whereas the kinds of business value available under the defensive heading were small in number, the kinds of offensive values that intangibles could pro-vide was much more extensive (see Exhibit 4.2).

Using a list of the kinds of value provided, companies may identify which kinds of value are most consistent with their organization's business activity and business strategy. Knowing the kind of value sought from their intangibles, companies may measure the degree to which their intangibles provide what is sought. In addition, they can then devise methods and processes for extraction and delivery of this value. Because most companies do not know how many different kinds of value their IP and I-stuff can provide, they tend to underspec-ify (or not define at all) what they want from their intangibles.

Once a company knows the kinds of value it wishes to extract, it becomes a more straightforward task to measure the degree to which they are or could be extracting that value from individual intangibles or groups of intangibles. For this kind of valuation, the value streams method is most often used.

There are two general ways to leverage intangibles such as I-stuff. The first is to use the company's complementary business assets (CBAs); the second is to innovate in the design of company's I-Stuff business model.

Using Complementary Business Assets

Complementary Business Assets (CBAs) may be thought of as the string of assets through which the firm's innovations must be processed in order to reach the customer. They change an innovation in form and location into something a customer is interested in purchasing. In the "tangible" world, CBAs may

---

[1]For a more complete discussion of the kinds of value that intangibles can provide, see Appendix A.

include manufacturing facilities, distribution channels, and sales outlets. No matter how interesting an innovation may be, it will have little commercial interest until it is paired with or processed by the appropriate CBAs.[2]

One example of using CBAs to develop a business comes from our own backyard. Our company, ICMG, is a consulting firm that for years remained small while building a reputation in the field of intangibles management. We "advertised" by word of mouth and by publishing articles in professional journals. This produced a steady stream of consulting projects, but the stream was only sufficient in size for a small company. Our complementary business assets were quite small. We realized that we could not grow without a significant marketing outreach capability, but such a capability would require investment that was far greater than our company's resources would allow. Thus we began to search for a strategic alliance partner with the CBAs we lacked. Our search produced an alignment with Arthur Andersen, formerly one of the Big Five accounting firms, which wanted to break into the intangibles management consulting business. Although Andersen had no experience in the field, the company brought a plethora of complementary business assets to the relationship, including a large and well-tuned marketing capability. ICMG brought its knowledge and know-how in intangibles management consulting. The alliance was a growing success until other events caused Arthur Andersen to collapse.

Using Innovation in Business Models

In identifying ways to commercialize I-stuff, companies inevitably find themselves dealing with whether, and to what degree, they must make changes to their existing business model. They usually begin the leveraging process by identifying opportunities for commercializing I-stuff without significantly changing the company's existing business model. As they become more comfortable with commercializing their I-stuff, they become more willing to innovate and move away from the firm's traditional business model into what, for them, is "new territory." The path to I-stuff commercialization as it relates to adapting the company's traditional business model(s) incorporates the following steps:

> *Level One Innovation:* Commercialize I-stuff using the existing business model or using minor modifications to the existing business model. For example, the company may continue to operate within its existing business model but may begin to outlicense its I-stuff as opportunities arise.

---

[2]For a more comprehensive discussion of complementary business assets, see Appendix C.

Level Two Innovation: Commercialize I-stuff within the existing business model but with more significant changes. For example, the company may establish a formal organizational unit charged with outlicensing its I-stuff.

Level Three Innovation: Commercialize I-stuff with a new or significantly modified business model. For example, one Swedish printer that had a long-term contract with the Swedish legislature to revise and print law books opened a new business providing legal search services to lawyers, using the law book information that had been stored in their computers for printing purposes.

Level Four Innovation: Change the rules of the game. A good example here would be Amazon.com, which changed the rules of the game for selling books by building a virtual, rather than brick-and-mortar, bookstore.[3]

A business model has many possible dimensions, among them:[4]

- Architecture of the profit stream
  - Architecture of revenue streams
  - Architecture of cost streams
- Relationship sought with customer
  - Transaction relationship
  - Product solution relationship
  - Business solution relationship
  - Partnering relationship
- Kind of differentiable innovation
  - Product
  - Channel
  - Pricing mechanism
  - Technology
  - Marketing
  - Manufacturing
- Tangibility of the asset
  - The product
  - The channels (e.g., marketing, sales, distribution).

---

[3]Ideas concerning the levels of innovation were developed by Patrick Sullivan and Ian McCoull through project work done for Scottish Enterprise.

[4]Our research and experience have shown that very little is known about business models in general and specifically about how they apply to the extraction of value from I-stuff. For a more complete treatment of business models, see Appendix D. We have collected information and literature on business models and have also collected all of the Gathering's discussions about business models they have observed or used themselves.

One aspect of business models that is mentioned frequently but is not found in the literature concerns the relationship between a firm and its customers. Hubert Saint-Onge, one of the I-stuff leaders in relationship concepts, defines those relationships as follows:

Transaction relationship: At the transactions level, the customer relationship is punctuated by a one-time sale of a product/service and with relatively little invested in the relationship by either the customer or the customer, i.e., having an ATM relationship with a bank.

Product solution relationship: At the product solutions level, the supplier works with the customer to group and customize an array of products into an offering that is grounded in the business needs of the customer and creates additional value, i.e., obtaining personal banking services.

Business solution relationship: At the business solutions level, the supplier develops an in-depth understanding of the customer's business and, as a result, suggests solutions that the customer would not have thought possible. These solutions are customized and integrated in a manner that makes them fit readily into the business context of the customer to create an unprecedented level of value, i.e., utilizing banking and financial planning services.

Partnering relationship: At the partnering level, the supplier and the customer work closely together to jointly craft business opportunities that would not have been possible without a deep mutual understanding/ trust, i.e., total wealth management services.

BEST PRACTICES FOR THE LEVERAGING PATH

Companies successfully operating on the leveraging path usually use three areas of best practice: (1) they develop routine processes for extracting value from I-stuff; (2) they are prepared to change the business model; and (3) they manage their brands (see Exhibit 4.3).

EXHIBIT 4.3   Leveraging Path: Best Practices

Best Practice 1: Develop routine processes for extracting value from I-stuff.

Best Practice 2: Be prepared to challenge your business model.

Best Practice 3: Manage your brands.

Best Practice 1: Develop Routine Processes for Extracting Value from I-Stuff

There are as many ways to commercialize I-stuff as there are companies. Some companies commercialize their I-stuff directly by selling their knowledge on a per-hour basis (law firms, accounting firms, doctors). Other kinds of companies, those that provide other services or manufacture products, look for opportunities to add value to existing revenue-generating activity by adding I-stuff to their profitability equation.

For example, the DuPont Company, originally a manufacturer of gunpowder, was also an early champion of safety programs and safety education. Several years ago DuPont's CEO asked whether it would be possible to develop a revenue-producing activity using the Company's storehouse of safety knowledge. The result is what is now called DuPont Safety Resources, which provides safety consulting services and training courses and sells a range of safety products. This is but one example of how a company can convert I-stuff embedded in the company culture into a new revenue stream.

Jim O'Shaughnessy, retired Vice-President of Intellectual Property for Rockwell International, learned from his experience in licensing IP that there is more to creating value through licensing than merely cross-licensing your patents to avoid litigation:

> We believe that you can manufacture something better when you design it specifically with manufacturing in mind. Likewise, you can extract value from an asset better if you create it with extraction mechanisms in mind.
>
> We were not particularly wedded to patents. Of course, good stuff got patented. Some things we didn't patent. [For some] other things we may have had patent applications pending, but we would strive to extract value even before patents were issued. So it was the whole medley of intellectual property or I-stuff that we looked at as the fodder for both creation and extraction.
>
> In the early days of IP management, most companies became familiar with a simple patent license (sometimes called a "naked" patent license). In simple patent licensing, an outlicensing company unblocks the licensee's path to market. No I-stuff, such as knowledge or know-how, is transferred with the license, rather, the license lifts the exclusion granted to the patent owner in favor of the licensee. This grant is done in return for a payment. In this transaction, the value tends to be disparate. The party receiving money is typically getting more value than the party paying the money. All you've done is remove an impediment—unblock an existing path to market.
>
> On the other hand, when you shift away from a (naked) patent license and look at a license of I-stuff (technology, know-how, and show-how) the I-stuff is most valuable when it is aligned with the complementary assets of the receiving party, that

is, the licensee. The value proposition shifts rapidly and dramatically because now the license is enabling. You are embedding within the receiving organization's I-stuff a variety of intangible assets. Done properly, you are providing them with intellectual assets that align with their complementary assets. You are providing them with an enhanced capability for making continuous improvements in that technology, especially if it remains a collaborative relationship. As you begin to expand the scope of what is granted under the license to include technology (in addition to the legal rights of exclusion), you begin to enable the licensee's business proposition, and the arrangement becomes beneficial to both parties.

When we consider licensing-in a new technology, we look for a potential partner who has I-stuff that can be blended seamlessly with our own I-stuff to create new revenue streams or to reduce costs. Such arrangements may also speed the time to market or provide an enhanced level of technological prowess (the latter particularly when the I-stuff you in-license is the licensor's core competency that you're tapping into and a core deficiency, or weakness, in your own organization).

At Procter & Gamble there has been a radical shift in company practices relating to the commercialization of I-stuff. When interviewed in 2000 for *Edison in the Boardroom*, Jeff Weedman, Vice-President of External Business Development at P&G, talked about how the company had moved away from being a "product-revenue only" firm to one that obtains significant revenue through licensing its intellectual property. When interviewed for this book, Weedman was able to discuss P&G's further shift toward more I-stuff transactions, as well as the novel way his business development activities are measured:

The word "licensing" is no longer part of my department's name, nor does it appear in my title. That change is not just symbolic; it's really a more accurate reflection of what our role should be. What we're about for P&G is value creation, the increase of value for our shareholders. Accomplishing those two objectives involves two broad streams of activity. One is extracting value from things that we've already created, while the other is to accelerate current innovation. In addition, we find that in order to fulfill these objectives we can also create value by tapping into capabilities external to the firm. So it's no accident that we just call ourselves external business development at this point.

Part of my unit's I-stuff is found in the way we approach a business or licensing negotiation with an external organization. When we sit down to "negotiate," we don't spend a lot of up-front time talking about the royalty rates or what should be the value to you and the value to me. The most productive thing we talk about is how we can marry our capability and yours to build the most value. We consciously focus the conversation on how we can jointly make the pie bigger. Once both sides understand our negotiation intent, then we can begin to discuss how to make this new future happen. Later in the negotiation process, we say, all right, what is the legal structure that would best enable that value creation potential? Once we begin discussing the legal structure for the transaction, we're in the home stretch. We will continue to explore what the legal structures are that allow us to extract the most value. Sometimes it's a license. Sometimes it's a revenue share. Sometimes it's a swap. Sometimes it's a supply agreement. I honestly don't care, because if I can create value that is recognized by the internal businesses, they don't really care whether it's cash on the barrelhead or reduced operating costs or preferred access to technology. Nobody cares as long as we all agree on the increased value to P&G.

Steve Baggot, Director External Business Development at Procter & Gamble, says, "People don't come to work at P&G thinking about creating and leveraging I-stuff. On the contrary, our focus is on identifying new opportunities for new products in our marketplaces to meet the needs of our consumers. When an opportunity presents itself, we then drill down to the building strip to see what I-stuff we need to support the opportunity, and then we use it as necessary to get the most value from the opportunity."

According to Scott Frank, President of BellSouth's Intellectual Property Management and Marketing Corporation, "In the late 1990s, as we were seeing competition for the first time, BellSouth realized that intangibles needed to play a much bigger role in the business. Thus, we began to bundle our intellectual property with our I-stuff, such as relationships, know-how, and complementary business assets in order to compete more effectively in our markets. By identifying, developing, and leveraging our intellectual property and I-stuff, BellSouth has added hundreds of millions of dollars to its bottom line."

In the Commercial Airplanes division of The Boeing Company, there has been an evolution in developing profits from more than airplane sales. According to Jeanne Suchodolski, "The division now earns significant revenue by licensing certain parts drawings and knowledge to qualified entities. BCA has developed a significant knowledge base that may be included as know-how in out-licenses of this information. Similarly, the division also licenses other aircraft information (manuals, blueprints, software) to enhance and enable maintenance, repair, modifications, and overhaul of aircraft. Much of this information also comes from codifying I-stuff held by BCA. By capturing the necessary I-stuff and packaging it in a form that can be licensed, the division has not only developed a new sustainable revenue stream but has also provided its customers with value by expanding their choices and the availability of solutions in the marketplace."

Whether monetizing IP or I-stuff, companies are creating processes to lead managers through the complexities of intangibles licensing. (See Exhibit 4.4).

EXHIBIT 4.4   I-Stuff Case: HP's Probe Storage Problem

Since being featured in *Edison in the Boardroom* (2001), HP management decided in 2003 to create a new business function focused solely on licensing its intellectual property (IP) and I-stuff within the Office of Strategy & Technology. HP appointed Joe Beyers, Vice President of IP Licensing, to lead this new organization. In its first two years, the IP Licensing office quadrupled the IP value HP realized from licensing its technology.

Within the computer storage industry, HP is a leading innovator, with over 3,500 patents and hundreds of products in that industry segment alone. In the mid-90's, HP started investing in probe storage technology [within HP this technology was known as Atomic Resolution Storage (ARS)] at HP Labs Japan. This program focused on increasing the density of data storage by several orders of magnitude with nanometer scale mechanics. The goal was to radically improve the cost-performance ratio for all kinds of non-volatile memory products. Think of ten terabytes in a one-inch cube.

Over the course of several years, the ARS program successfully evolved with HP investing in the research with a team of over 60 technologists at HP Labs in Palo Alto, CA, Tokyo, Japan, Boise, ID and Corvallis, OR. More than 150 patents have been granted and many applications are in progress.

There were, however, several difficult business and technical challenges ahead of the ARS program when, in 2003, because of tight budgets and a change in product strategy, HP decided not to continue the ARS program. HP's IP Licensing (IPL) group immediately started a licensing program investigation to determine the feasibility of transferring the technology to leading players in the storage industry.

Typically, to develop and deploy a technology licensing program in HP, an IP Licensing Director leads a cross-functional team through a six-step process to secure IP management approval for out-licensing:

1. Evaluate technology readiness and competitive position (possible roadmaps) to determine "What can be licensed?"
2. Evaluate organizational, ownership, partners and technology transfer issues to determine "Who can help deliver the technology?"
3. Organize patents and other IP (find, rate, prioritize, manage)
4. Develop the licensee value proposition to determine "Who and Why?"
5. Evaluate carve-out with Corporate Development and selected VCs (earlier the better)
6. Determine the technology valuation and financials ("The Business Case")

In this case, the IP Licensing Director Joshua Rosenberg led a team consisting of the ARS Technologists from HP Labs and an IP Attorney from HP legal to develop a winning technology licensing package. This licensing package included the core set of patents, trade secrets and trademarks associated with the ARS R&D program. This team explored many possible uses of the broad set of technology developed over a ten-year period, including its use in fields ranging from probe storage to nanolithography processing to automotive lighting products.

The IP team also determined a valuation for the know-how and patents to be licensed and then began to actively look for partners with vision and expertise in the storage industry to help commercialize this exciting technology. Several companies immediately approached HP expressing interests to take a license, including consultation with HP technologists on possible applications of the technology. In discussions with potential licensees, the HP team confirmed not only the strength and value of the patents, but more importantly the value and importance of the know-how. Potential licensees were in fact interested only if the know-how was part of the deal because it would significantly speed-up their product development process.

In 2005, HP concluded its first ARS license agreement with a company that has an ongoing probe storage program of its own. HP will be providing technology transfer as well as access to relevant patents. Aside from the royalty revenue that HP receives, a technology license is a validation for the entire technology team, leading to increased job satisfaction by successfully transferring useful technology from "off-the-shelf" to revenue producing for HP and the licensee.

Michael Pierantozzi, Director, Strategy & Intellectual Property Licensing, Hewlett-Packard

John Tao, director of Corporate Technology Partnerships at Air Products, explains that his company has built an infrastructure not only to create but also to extract more value from its intellectual assets. "On the extraction side, we have found that potential customers are really interested in the know-how associated with the IP, and this significantly increases the value of the transaction. Thus, managing the way we capture the know-how in the value creation step is of critical importance, in addition to the intellectual property." Tao adds, "Air Products has changed the way it manages its intellectual assets in recent years by establishing a new process and organization. The Corporate group defines the intellectual asset management process and each business manages its associated IA. We also have added a licensing group to aid the businesses in licensing out technologies."

In addition to extracting value through external transactions, value may be extracted from I-stuff through purely internal activity. In most internal cases the value extracted is in the form of cost reduction. Vince Grassi, director of Global Learning and Knowledge Management at Air Products, discusses how the company's "best practice" system was able to generate significant cost reductions with internal I-stuff:

> The Air Products air separation best practice community has been in place for more than six years. As an example, the review committee received a best practice recommendation from an operator in one of our Canadian air separation plants. This plant had a flow meter on the plant's water inlet line but not on the outlet line. (We don't generate a lot of water in our air separation plants, and we also don't consume much either.) Nevertheless, there is a slight consumption of water inside the plant, so there is less water going out than what we have coming in. If you have two meters, one at each end of the plant's water lines, you could get credit for the difference. An operator in the Canadian plant noticed that if they put both meters in, there was a potential for a $50,000 annual savings. The operator said, "Well this is a great best practice; everybody should be doing this; it's not written up in our standards anywhere; why don't we submit this one?"
>
> The way the best practice system works is that anyone can submit a best practice; then it gets reviewed, and a determination is made whether to distribute it or not. In this particular case, the review committee believed that most of the plants were already doing this. However, they decided to release it. It went out to 75 of our air separation plants around the world. Four of our plants weren't already doing this. These plants implemented the idea in less than one month. So if you multiply five by $50,000, this simple idea was worth a quarter of a million dollars to the company. The operator that submitted this best practice was given a cash award to reinforce the sharing and reuse of knowledge behavior we encourage.
>
> This example illustrates an important lesson that we have learned from the transfer of best practices. That is, there is a lot of knowledge that one group takes for granted that others can leverage. Without a systematic approach to transferring knowledge we might not otherwise be able to capture, we would be missing tens of millions of dollars each year in benefits.

Best Practice 2: Be Prepared to Challenge Your Business Model

As noted earlier in this chapter, companies leveraging their I-stuff quickly learn that the firm's traditional business model may not apply to the extraction of value from its intangibles. A new or different business model may be more suitable. For example, a number of Cargill's business units focus their business model on relationship-building with customers. This focus has led to more and better business opportunities for both parties. Jerry Rose, President of Cargill's McDonald's business unit said, "We've attained such a deep level of understanding with McDonald's that we're often involved in solving problems and shaping McDonald's policy in ways that have nothing to do with the direct sale of our products or services." One example of this is the McDonald's breakfast burrito. Although popular with customers, the breakfast burrito proved challenging to make in the store. It required chopping onion, cooking eggs, mixing in sausage, and rolling it all into a tortilla. Sunny Fresh Foods, Cargill's Baldrige-award-winning egg products company, came up with a precooked product. McDonald's employees can simply ladle the premixed, precooked product onto a tortilla with cheese and then heat and serve the product. This new approach to preparing the breakfast burrito was accepted by McDonald's and incorporated into its breakfast product operations, with significant cost reductions for McDonald's and a new product offering for Cargill. "Such successes create even more new opportunities for Cargill," according to Rose. "The breakfast burrito is a good example of how Cargill business units that work with McDonald's have been innovative and high-performing. As a result, McDonald's has been willing to give us more new opportunities."

As some companies begin to understand I-stuff better, they also bump up against the question of the business model. Mark Radcliffe is a Senior Partner at DLA Piper Rudnick Gray Cary USA LLP, where he manages the Technology and Sourcing Group. He has been assisting companies in the "open source" industry. The open source business model represents a major shift in how software is developed and distributed: Most open source licenses require vendors to make the source code of their software available to licensees at no charge. They also require that licensees be permitted to modify and distribute the software to third parties at no charge. As Mark notes: "The open source business model represents a dramatic shift in the role of customers from users of the product or sources of information into active participants in product development. Open source companies receive information on bugs in their software much more rapidly than in a "closed source" business model. Also, since the source code is available, customers may themselves provide corrections to the bugs.

Successful open source companies spend significant effort in developing relationships with their "communities" of developers. These communities provide reactions and feedback on new functions the software company is proposing as well as on developing new functions the customer community wants. The development of software in the open source model is more rapid and often less costly to the developing company. SugarCRM, for example, had its open source CRM software completed and translated into 30 different languages by third party developers, within less than a year."

Celine Monette, former Director of Scientific Communications and Professional Education for a global pharmaceutical company, describes her experience in understanding the relationship between company business operations and the company business model:

> While working for a global pharmaceutical company, I managed the Continuing Health Education team, responsible for scientific activities and education. We worked to educate healthcare professionals about recent advances in diseases and disease treatments. It is important for the benefit of the patient that the drug knowledge is shared between the pharmaceutical industry and the medical community. In order to do so, we would prepare the scientific and clinical community for new scientific information and drugs my company planned to introduce several years before the drug was released. For example, we would prepare the diabetes-physicians community for the introduction of a new anti-diabetes drug by providing information on the disease, current treatments, and the clinical studies including the studies of our prospective drug, all well in advance of the release of our new drug. Our business model called for us to operate in series with the medical sector and the commercial sector. We would first provide scientific information and continuing health education to the medical community; once the product was commercialized, that was followed by the sales force.
>
> Wanting to know the degree to which our efforts contributed to company revenues, we launched an effort to determine the nature and degree of value that our activities brought to the revenue stream. When we examined our operations in support of the company's sales activities, we not only found ourselves touching on the internal business model, but we found ourselves questioning whether it was the best one for the company to use.
>
> So, when we focused on the professional education business model and how the new scientific and medical knowledge could be transferred more efficiently and in a shorter time with better scientific support to the commercial sector, we found how it could be significantly improved. We then changed our internal business model from one of simply delivering continuing health education directly to doctors to what I call the leverage model of working with the institutional players in the healthcare system, the medical organizations, and the medical faculties in universities across the country, to create a more integrated system of delivering high-quality and ethical continuing health education. This allowed my company to focus its resources on partnership management and thought leaders knowledge exchange in addition to continuing health education.
>
> You asked me about whether there were any lessons I learned from this analysis. I think the major lesson was that when you are dealing with intangibles, you've got to be willing to challenge the existing business model. Business models that companies may have relied on in the past may not work at all for converting intangibles (such as knowledge or know-how) into value for the firm.

A further example of a company creating a new, I-stuff focused business within a large existing value-chain company is the story of InnoCentive® and its creation within Eli Lilly and Company.

InnoCentive is a Web-based online process that matches top scientists around the world with interesting and relevant R&D challenges. It also enables companies to reward scientific innovation through financial incentives. Its origins are described by Alpheus Bingham, the Founder and current CEO of InnoCentive and former Vice President of Lilly's business innovation unit, e.Lilly:

"The initial idea for an external source of innovation was hatched in concert with our Director of Knowledge Management, Aaron Schacht. At that time, late 1999 and early 2000, our Chairman Sidney Taurel was launching a program called Leadership Five, which formed a group of executives to examine selected elements of the company's business and to make recommendations for change or improvement. The business element they examined had to do with some of the transformations that were occurring at the time in the middle of the dot.com era.

We were pushing a change in the business model while the Chairman, himself, was beginning to pull for information and thoughts on changing business models. As a result of the serendipitous timing, a separate unit of the company was established, which we named e.Lilly. This experimental group was created to look at current technology tools that enhanced the present performance of the business as well as to look for alternative ways in which the business could be done. InnoCentive was launched out of that unit, as one of its first outcomes. (Others have subsequently been incubated and launched from this same unit of the company.)

InnoCentive (www.innocentive.com) is a Web community of problem solvers made up of scientists and technical people around the world; it pairs them with companies looking to find solutions to certain R&D problems. It allows companies to harvest the I-stuff of thousands of minds around the world and pay a reward only if a solution is found. It also allows bright people in places like China or India to tackle interesting and challenging problems in their home country without emigrating and creating a brain drain.

Although this concept may appear radical, if not heretical, for a pharmaceutical company with a large internal R&D group, it really tackles the "Not Invented Here" syndrome by forcing companies and individuals to realize that the best and brightest minds are not all employed at their company. People with bright ideas are everywhere, and the more people you can have working on a solution, the higher the odds of success are.

The business model for how InnoCentive needed to operate was very different from the pharmaceutical business model used by Eli Lilly and Company. Nevertheless, the company recognized that this was a different kind of business; no thought was given to requiring InnoCentive to adopt the company business model.

On the contrary, it was encouraged to develop and implement a business model that would succeed."

Best Practice 3: Manage Your Brands

A brand is a business "asset" that is a pure intangible. It is more than a trademark or logo, more than a retail company's trade dress. It represents an identity and image created by the company to enable a product or service, a technology, or the corporation to form a relationship with a customer. Some companies consider a brand to be a promise made to its customers. Other companies use their brand to convey their core values or their business intent to their current and potential customers. Brands are found in retail environments and in industrial environments. Increasingly, government and institutions create brands to represent themselves to their clientele. A brand represents the organization's image and reputation, and it "promises" that the applicable product, service, company, or technology will meet a certain standard of quality and/or other attributes.

For some companies, who sell little in the way of physical products, the brand is often the company's major asset. Consider Coca-Cola. The company doesn't manufacture or sell soft drinks. It sells syrup to its network of Coca-Cola bottling companies. In Coke's case, the implied promise of quality and reliability is delivered to the customers consuming its soft drinks by the brand that appears on each container of Coke.

In the best-practice stories that follow, we explore several aspects of brand management. The first involves the speed and sophistication of the process of developing a brand management capability. The next delves into the issues involved in branding a technology as opposed to products and services, which we see frequently. Then we explore what goes into branding a corporation. Finally, we look at how several companies have been able to extract value directly from their brands, developing sustainable revenue streams for their organization.

DEVELOPING A BRAND MANAGEMENT CAPABILITY

Visa International is a company whose business requires that its brand be immediately accepted by customers and merchants alike, all over the world. Its brand on payment cards and their acceptance by merchants implies a security of transaction. Creating, maintaining, and managing a global brand such as Visa is a major task. Karen Gullett, Senior Vice-President of Global Brand Management, discusses how Visa manages its brand:

> Visa International exists as a common link between our member banks and the merchants around the world to facilitate commerce. We're an association structure comprising a core center of Visa Worldwide Services and six different regions.
>
> Visa is a brand that has always worked as an alliance brand with local members in their markets. For a payment card to have value, it needed to work beyond any one bank's individual geography so the common brand of Visa was created to serve the needs of many owners. Visa has always been a very decentralized company with most marketing efforts designed by regional executives to meet "local" objectives. To create a global brand in this environment, Global Brand Management is very precise in defining global strategies and requirements that are then implemented and refined by the local markets to address their specific business and cultural needs. The global brand positioning defines the Visa promise, "empowerment through ubiquity, reliability, security and ease of use," that we expect the brand to fulfill no matter where the stakeholder encounters Visa. The regions "translate" it to meet their specific business and cultural conditions. So, from the global brand positioning, we have six different advertising taglines that express our core promise and its underpinnings in ways that are market relevant, for example, "Visa: All You Need" in Canada and "Visa. Life Is Now" in Brazil. As with all brands, the strategies must be built from insights that are relevant, with the power to differentiate. For Visa to work on a global and local basis, the core strategy must have meaning at a global level, with the ability to be scaled up or down as need be depending on market development.
>
> We have a global brand management function at Visa International that resides in a core Worldwide Services office. We're responsible for identifying the core brand strategy and architecture, for providing the necessary tools and resources that are needed to implement the strategy, for assessing the continued relevance and impact of the strategy, and for ensuring compliance with brand standards.
>
> Visa World Services leads and chairs the Global Brand Management Council, which is comprised of the most senior brand and marketing executive in each region and at Visa International. We come together quarterly. We are in touch with council members weekly, if not daily. This constant flow of communication reflects their role in representing the local business demands and serving as global leaders regarding the issues related to brand management. Specific functions of the Global Brand Management Council are to:
>
> 1. Refine and recommend global brand strategy including positioning and architecture.
> 2. Recommend global market research requirements.
> 3. Approve and advance branding recommendations for product platforms.

4. Approve all tactical brand-related standards including related variances and waivers.
5. Approve global sponsorship/partnerships.
6. Determine borderless segment targets and approve initiatives.
7. Share business best practices.

A single brand that is used across the corporation and its product portfolio must be able to meet specific needs, while also extending across our lines of business. Visa is used to support payment businesses in the consumer, small business, commercial/government, and corporate channels, and in almost every case this is in an alliance relationship with the Member's brand and often with their particular product brand. Visa and our promise must provide a cohesive thread across these many avenues, adding value for each and maintaining its integrity in and of itself.

The Visa brand management story is an example of how an organization evolved a proactive and methodical approach to branding. Some organizations, however, do not have the luxury of time to create and implement a brand—a technology company whose I-stuff achieves instant market success, for example. Such was the case for Thomson and their mp3 technology. Thomson's main brand experience before mp3 was with RCA branded televisions. Thomson owned the RCA patent portfolio and had been achieving a large and profitable revenue stream from its patents for some years. Television set manufacture and sale at that time represented a fairly mature market, in which the business was in "harvest" mode. Thomson's television business had become one of product commoditization and stable manufacturing processes. For such a business, distribution was more important than branding. As a result, Thomson's experience with branding was quite limited. Henri Linde, Vice President New Business, discusses how Thomson created and managed the brand that technology created:

At the end of the 80's, Thomson began to work with the Fraunhofer Institute on compression technology. Based on this collaboration, the two firms made a proposal to the Moving Picture Experts Group (MPEG) organization on a compression format that went much further than other proposals (of which 2 had already been accepted). There is MPEG layer 1, MPEG layer 2, and MPEG layer 3. (MPEG layer 3 became shortened to mp3.) In 1991, mp3 became part of the international compression standard.

Several things happened to mp3 that created the environment within which our branding efforts took place. In 1993, Fraunhofer and Thomson put the mp3 code onto an internal Web page. That Web page was hacked and the code stolen. As a result, the code was illegally distributed across the Internet. During the course of 1993 to1995, the Internet became more known, and that's where mp3 actually took off.

Prior to 1995, we had been working to license the technology through business-to-business arrangements. However, while we were implementing our B-to-B strategy, there was an underground (and illegal) distribution of popular songs. Also, computer technology was changing; computers had become fast enough to allow creation of a real-time copy of a CD in a smaller footprint. (Smaller footprint was important because hard drives were in the megabytes then, so they couldn't hold a full CD-worth of data.) But the instant you could put a smaller copy of the CD on a hard drive, your computer was suddenly able to hold larger quantities of music. In what seemed a short space of time, you had lots of people with music that they had created, sharing it through their e-mail.

We were focusing on B-to-B applications; we weren't focusing on the branding or the format of the transmission. However, when consumers started utilizing the technology, when the consumers actually created this market, they also created the "mp3" brand. That's when I started thinking about it and said well, we can't protect "mp3," and we can't fight it either. This movement is too strong and I don't know of any other examples in marketing where both the technology adoption and the brand creation have been totally market driven. Suddenly we were into a very different brand situation. mp3 having technological cult status was cool, it was hip, it was different, and it was spread by word of mouth . . . it wasn't controllable by Thomson anymore.

We had to decide whether we wanted or needed to interfere with this spontaneous and market-driven brand creation process. Ultimately we decided to change our product distribution strategy and not hinder the viral nature of the brand evolution.

For Thomson, the question we faced was whether this new "brand" was one to be associated with a market fad, or would the market fade away once these customers left college? (We had noticed that the primary group of people using mp3 was those with computer skills, time, and access to broadband capability. That meant students in colleges. Had colleges not gone to broadband so quickly, and had computers not been a requirement for colleges, then the file-sharing services wouldn't have grown to nearly the extent that they did.) In other words, we are wondering whether these people, when they graduate, get a job, get married, and have children, will still spend their leisure time playing with mp3. At the moment it is unclear whether mp3 is a brand to invest in or one to ride on through its phase of popularity. At Thomson we must just wait and see.

DEVELOPING A CORPORATE BRAND

For many of us as consumers, our initial relationship with a company is based on the brand and the implied brand promise. As consumers, we know that Coca-Cola will guarantee that any Coke purchased anywhere in the world will taste the same. The U.S. postal service will deliver the mail regardless of the weather, and so on. However, in some industries, the brand promise has not materialized or has shifted. The pharmaceutical industry is such a case. As baby-boomers enter retirement, they are increasingly interested in all aspects of their health care. This has led to people wanting to know more about the company behind the drugs they are taking. On the pharmaceutical company end, they have spent years creating product brands. Corporate brand management is different from product brand management. At the pharmaceutical firm Eli Lilly and Company, Rob Smith, Director of Public Relations and Corporate Branding, explains how Lilly has worked to internalize its emerging corporate branding:

In the past, pharmaceutical companies like Lilly focused more attention on the reputation of their product brands and less on their corporate image. For example, when we marketed Prozac, nearly everyone was familiar with that brand, but far fewer people knew anything about the company selling it. However, the dynamics have really changed in the market. Patients, physicians, and payers (such as governments and HMOs) are increasingly interested in the reputation of the companies making and selling medicines. They want to know that the company they're dealing with can be trusted: Will their products do what they say they will do? Will this company be one that is transparent and shares all of its clinical data? Will this company be focused on truly innovative medicines and not just "me-too" drugs? Now, more than ever, it's important to think about our actions and how they will impact our corporate reputation. This is not just a nice thing to do, it is something that is very, very important in terms of generating incremental value for our customers and shareholders.

When you think about branding, it is easy to think only about marketing and big advertising campaigns. We view our corporate branding initiative more broadly at Lilly. Most importantly, it is an issue of organizational cultural change. We are striving to have every employee around the world think about the actions they take and how those actions will reflect on the reputation of the company. By having our employees aligned around our brand strategy, which places a special emphasis on breakthrough products and being reliable and trustworthy, we believe that we can meaningfully enhance Lilly's reputation in the eyes of our customers. To do this, we've conducted brand workshops around the world, highlighting real-life business problems that we face and then putting those through the lens of the corporate brand. Another good example is the Chairman's Ovation Awards that our CEO, Sidney Taurel, gives to employees around the world. Over forty thousand Lilly employees are eligible, and ten receive this award. Last year the focus was the corporate brand. He selected ten people that he felt were truly "living the brand." These individuals were lifted up in a very significant way as exemplary employees who were conducting their jobs in a way that will help us earn the kind of reputation we want with stakeholders."

As the Eli Lilly and Company story points out, most companies building a brand want to make sure the values and brand promise are internalized within the company and its employees. Some companies, however, are focused on defining the promise and the corporate brand and image. Cargill faced such a challenge. Ann Ness, Director of Advertising and Brand Management, explains their journey:

> Up until the late 1990s, Cargill did not have a well-articulated company brand. For years Cargill viewed itself as a commodities company and saw no reason to develop a high profile brand. As a commodity based business, Cargill focused on delivering what we said we were going to, when we said we would, and at the price that had been agreed upon. While there were several strategic business units (SBUs) with strong brands in their respective markets, there was little or no customer association of these brands with Cargill. When Cargill would acquire a business with a recognized brand, it would allow the business to continue to use and nurture the existing brands. People working in the acquired company would continue to identify with the legacy brand names, so Cargill grew to feel, act, and behave like a holding company.
>
> In 1999, senior management decided to implement a major transformational business change strategy. The transformation recognized the need to manage the company's image in the business world and the realization that managing the Cargill name, or brand, could bring benefits to the company. A visible Cargill name would send a strong message to the organization, to Cargill's customers, and to the market at large that Cargill was being reborn as a new company with a new strategy.
>
> With this new direction and a new, visionary strategic plan, we began looking at the Cargill name from a totally different perspective. We recognized that Cargill was a big, complicated diverse company wherein different SBUs could develop different ties to the Cargill brand depending on the strategy, their current market recognition, etc. In this way, it would be easier for people to make a new association with Cargill or to have their existing association reinforced. Interestingly, as soon as we started talking about Cargill as a brand, business units began speaking about the value of their brands and, at the same time, saying that the Cargill brand did bring some advantages but had the potential to bring a lot more. They were very persuasive and we collectively came to the conclusion that there would be a much greater value to Cargill to manage its brand name for success. So the plan came to be to organize Cargill under a strong central master brand with associated subbrands . . . much like GE.
>
> Cargill's vision is to be the recognized global leader in nourishing people. This suggests that all of the business units that support and nourish people (physically through food, intellectually through opportunities, etc.) would carry the Cargill name into the markets they serve with this positive nurturing people association.
>
> A key part of Cargill's new brand strategy involved a considerable amount of I-stuff, although we didn't recognize it as such at the time. At Cargill we knew there was a great deal of difference between how our competitors and we approached customers and conducted business. But it was very surprising to us to learn that people outside

Cargill did not necessarily recognize or appreciate these differences. Cargill has a culture that is not inclined to brag, and so Cargill hadn't managed, in any affirming way, large broad statements about either the company or its ambitions. Customers' perception of the Cargill brand tended to be based on their perception of the Cargill individuals they knew. Further, since Cargill is privately held, there is little opportunity for financial analysts to get to know Cargill, so the financial community route was not available to help others learn about Cargill and what we stand for. Obviously, there needed to be more work done around developing the image that we knew was inside Cargill.

There are also behavioral characteristics associated with the Cargill name that would be reinforced throughout the organization. Behavior, reputation, integrity, doing what you say you're going to do, a company culture of Our Word is Our Bond—are all aspects of I-stuff and are all a part of the interactions we have with our employees and our customers. With this new strategy, Cargill is moving in the direction of taking all of its I-stuff, its knowledge, its expertise, its skills and capabilities, its people, and bringing that to bear in a customer solutions environment. You have to have an entirely different way of getting people to perceive what you have and what you're bringing to the table.

For us to be successful in transforming the nature of the relationship with our customers from commodity based to solutions based and then realize the opportunities that are there, the traits of collaboration and innovation are critically important. A customer working with Cargill knows "win/win" means both the customer and Cargill win. This is a recipe for an enduring relationship and the sustainability of the organization. It is critical that our customers see us as being collaborative. And that, of course, becomes the foundation for moving ahead to a broader or expanded relationship. As to innovation, historically Cargill wasn't necessarily perceived as being innovative. But, if Cargill is to make the strategic move from a commodities business model to a customer solutions business model, then innovation is critical to achieving success. We are making progress, and the Cargill brand strategy is working. The Cargill name and brand has become widely recognized and appreciated for all the right reasons. In the food arena, the company is recognized as one of the top five companies to do business with . . . and this is directly attributable to the Cargill brand strategy efforts. Stan O'Neal, CEO of Merrill Lynch, in a meeting in Minneapolis a couple of months ago, said "Cargill is one of the most respected and sophisticated companies in the world." This remarkable statement attests to the results of Cargill's customer focus, innovation, and high performance . . . or, stated another way: Collaborate, create, and succeed. We are pleased that the awareness and reputation of our company is growing from day to day.

Extracting Value from the Brand

Finally, we have all seen how many companies involved in direct retail activities have long been using their brands to obtain direct revenue. Examples include the home team's caps and shirts sold at baseball games, Disney characters sold as stuffed animals, and companies extending their brand by licensing it to be used on noncompany products. However, industrial companies are learning that when others use their brand in an industrial setting (with permission), this use creates significant value for them. According to Scott Frank, President of BellSouth Intellectual Property Management and Marketing Corporations:

> In 1999, BellSouth Intellectual Property started out by licensing its patents and copyright protected software. This was during the telecom and economic boom, and we experienced immediate success. However, in the early 2000s when the bubble burst, many companies cut back substantially on their software and technology spending. Therefore, we began to focus more of our efforts on leveraging the BellSouth brand. One reason we did this is because we noticed that when we allowed companies to issue joint press releases with us, usually their stock would immediately increase. This helped us better understand the value of our BellSouth brand to other companies.
>
> We since have experienced great success by associating our brand with a variety of products and services offered by top tier companies. For example, we licensed the BellSouth brand to one of the top security systems companies in the country, Protection One, who did not have much of a southeastern presence and now calls itself BellSouth Security Systems from Protection One in our region. We have now done a significant number of brand leveraging deals with companies that want to be associated with a brand that stands for reliability, dependability, stability and much more. By more fully leveraging the brand, we've added value to BellSouth with new royalty streams, an expanded bundle of products and services for our customers, and highly profitable lines of businesses.

Conclusions: Beyond Leveraging

Leveraging a firm's I-stuff can generate major revenue growth, but it often requires a significant change in the corporate mindset and operating methods. As Einstein is reported to have said, "We shall require a substantially new manner of thinking if mankind is to survive." If this new way of thinking is done to the exclusion of the other activities on the Value Continuum, companies may be focusing on short-term results at the expense of the long term. I-stuff commercialization through leveraging activities must be integrated across all business units and business functions. To the degree that I-stuff commercialization through leveraging activities absorbs management attention, they are unable to move the company to integration of I-stuff activities across all business units and business functions. Equally, a focus on I-stuff leveraging to the exclusion of other perspectives could mean the company does not consider using its I-stuff as the basis for sustaining the firm in the long term.

5

INTEGRATING THE PORTFOLIO OF I-STUFF

C OMPANIES OPERATING ON the Integrating Path focus on two aspects of I-stuff management: using their I-stuff strategically to benefit the firm and managing I-stuff residing both within and outside the firm (see Exhibit 5.1). These firms are focused firmly on bottom-line performance. They recognize that I-stuff has strategic implications and that an I-stuff management strategy must be fully integrated with the corporation's business strategy. They also know that they must develop a system for measuring and managing their I-stuff. Finally, companies on this path must prioritize their use of I-stuff company-wide, and even outside their corporate boundaries. Much of what companies accomplish on the Integration Path involves being aware of and managing relationships, both those inside company boundaries and those that transcend company borders.

EXHIBIT 5.1   The Einstein Value Continuum Highlighting the Integrating Path

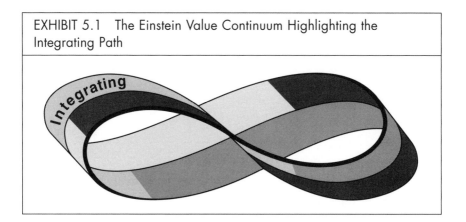

Thought Leader Comments

The Challenge of Building Value with I-Stuff

It is only in the last ten years that it has become axiomatic to believe that the intangible assets of an organization represent most of its value. This radical change in perspective however has not reflected itself in the way we manage our organizations today. For the most part, we still lead organizations the same way as when we saw most of the value creation coming from the exploitation of tangible assets. Yet we recognize that intangible assets need to be managed in a very different way. So, why have we yet to adapt the way organizations function to optimize the value we create with intangible assets?

The simple answer is that organizations have not figured out how to systematically leverage their intangible assets. We intuitively know that intangible assets are quite different in nature from tangible assets and that they need to be managed quite differently. The preponderance of intangible assets has fundamentally changed the rules of the game for business. The real difference is that tangible assets are by definition scarce, whereas intangible assets are by definition abundant. Intangible assets are in fact as much of a commodity as the air we breathe. But when incorporated into a business model and an organizational framework, their value can be leveraged. Branding, for instance, is available to everyone but it is only when it is incorporated into the framework of an organization and its relationship to customers that value can be generated.

We need a new perspective with which to lead and structure the organization as we define the new rules of the game. The challenge is that the old ways are firmly anchored in leadership habits, cultures, and structures that are now obsolete. A major portion of the value of most firms is in their intangible assets; this "balkanized" configuration also makes it much more difficult to strategically plan for the development of the capabilities and relationship that form these assets. This is why I believe that we will continue to see the emergence of new structures and roles to shape organizational configurations that will bring greater convergence between individual and organizational capabilities and the need to build customer relationships.

In this new context, we need to question things that are taken for granted, assumptions that the management team too often sees as proven facts as opposed to perceptions that were true at one point but no longer fit the reality of the business environment. We need to renew and develop capabilities much faster than in the past. Our focus has to be on the ultimate goal of building customer relationships, not on preserving the means that are more familiar to us. We achieve this only if we strive at every step to provide superior customer-perceived value in the marketplace. This is only possible if we look at the marketplace, from the perspective of the customer, not from the perspective of the manufacturer. We need to bring the customer perspective to every activity in order to demonstrate our brand promise and to respond effectively as new trends emerge.

Because intangible assets now represent the largest share of the value of most firms, we have no choice but to manage those assets actively in order to optimize the performance of organizations in their respective market place. The stocks that comprise these assets are made up of the individual capabilities of the members of the firm—we call that Human Capital; the organizational capabilities—we call that Structural Capital; and customer/supplier relationships which we call Customer Capital. These three stocks are connected and grow based on the exchange of knowledge between the individuals, the organization and the customers/suppliers. The knowledge strategy of an organization is geared to build the capabilities and the relationships that form the intangible assets of the firm. The growth of the intangible assets in turn determines the economic performance of the firm. As such, the intellectual capital framework is a representation of the "stocks" of intangible assets, while knowledge is the electrical current that runs between these assets to grow the human, structural and customer capital.

When it comes to the management of intangible assets, we will need to adopt an approach that is less controlling in nature, one that takes more of a systems view of the organization. We need to consider how to shift from a "make and sell" business logic to a "engage, sense, detect, collaborate and innovate" orientation with the organization functioning as a network which is open to its stakeholders. The organization that will have the best ability to create value from I-stuff continuously generates and renews capabilities to achieve breakthrough performance by enhancing the quality and flow of knowledge and by calibrating its strategy, culture, systems, and structures to the needs of the customer and marketplace. This is an organization with a high level of collaboration and interdependence and a superior ability to partner both internally and externally. In fact, this organization is the "partner of choice" that can readily complement its own capabilities with those of others, including its customers, to optimize value creation, innovation and agility. It is through "open networks" that the organization detects patterns in the marketplace as they emerge. It also responds to these new patterns in a proactive manner. As a result, there is no accumulated lag time between market place changes and the reactions of the enterprise. So "just-in time" evolution of the enterprise vis-à-vis the marketplace takes place as a result of the knowledge flows which generate the capabilities and relationships required to deal with new challenges as they emerge. This is an organization that:

1. Develops and leads itself in creating the relationships it wants with its customers
2. Takes an integrated, systemic view of the organization and takes action with many levers at once

3. Uses branding to actively shape the culture
4. Seeks to be a "first mover" and make market
5. Accelerates the development of capability and harnesses them strategically
6. Ensures that knowledge is flowing freely from the outside-in to collaborate, learn, and make strategy
7. Uses the development of the "strategy-making" capability to constantly renew itself and build new coherence with the emergent market place

It is with new DNA that our enterprises will be able to more fully leverage the intangible assets that will give them dynamic advantage in the market place. The context has changed already: There is no choice but to create this new order of organizations.

Hubert Saint-Onge

Companies on the Integrating Path of the Einstein Value Continuum share several characteristics. First, they know that I-stuff is the basic component of value creation for the organization and they want to find ways to use it strategically.

Second, they realize that I-stuff value may be measured on several dimensions. Most of us are familiar with the traditional accounting framework and how it registers value. It counts up the value exchanged in transactions and records them on the company's accounts. In other words, accounting looks backward and records the value of transactions that have already occurred. However, the value of intangibles such as I-stuff lies largely in the future. I-stuff is valuable because of what it can do for the organization next month or next year. For this reason, we cannot rely on traditional accounting to help determine the value of I-stuff. Companies on the Integrating Path are defining other ways of measuring and valuing their I-stuff.

Finally, because it is often impractical for a company to invent everything it needs, more and more companies are seeking outside knowledge and know-how and developing ways to create and extract the value for themselves. The successful (although discontinued) partnership between Disney and Pixar for making animated movies was a classic example of I-stuff symbiosis.

WHAT INTEGRATING PATH COMPANIES ARE TRYING TO ACCOMPLISH

For companies integrating their portfolio, the focus of I-stuff management has been on three separate and related areas:

- *Linking I-stuff strategies with the overall corporate strategy and objectives.* The value of I-stuff to an organization largely depends on the degree to which it supports or enables company business strategies and activities. Companies on the Integrating Path focus on identifying the kinds of value they want to obtain from their I-stuff and the role it will play. Once those are known, they can develop an I-stuff strategy for producing the desired value.
- *Measuring I-stuff.* Firms on the Integrating Path need to define and describe their I-stuff in terms that are meaningful to the company, its business strategy, and its business activities. Because the traditional accounting framework is not able to measure intangibles adequately, firms must create new ways to measure their I-stuff, ways that relate their intangibles to the company's business activities.
- *Leveraging and expanding the management of I-stuff outside the corporation.* A company's I-stuff often extends outside the corporation, in the form of "customer capital" the I-stuff is used to interact with suppliers, customers, and competitors. Likewise, a company may benefit from using another company's I-stuff. Companies on this path are seeking ways to leverage their own externally focused I-stuff as well as the I-stuff of others.

I-Stuff Strategies

Creating an I-stuff strategy is as new as the concept of I-stuff itself. Only a few firms have created strategies for managing their non-IP intangibles. What is an I-stuff strategy? It is, simply, a business strategy that incorporates I-stuff. If a traditional business strategy is the set of decisions and activities that firms implement to achieve their business objectives, then an I-stuff strategy is the set of decisions and activities firms implement to use their I-stuff in support of the business strategy.

Like a traditional business strategy, an I-stuff strategy should identify the kinds of value the firm seeks from its I-stuff, how the company's I-stuff can support the business strategy, the activities to be pursued in providing that support, timetables (when appropriate), and the assignment of responsibilities to make things happen.

We have written several times about the recommended methods of creating an IP strategy.[1] Companies tend to follow one of two approaches. The first

---

[1] P. Sullivan, *Profiting from Intellectual Capital* (New York: John Wiley & Sons, Inc., 1998), 108–111; P. Sullivan, *Value-Driven Intellectual Capital* (New York: John Wiley & Sons, Inc., 2000), 137–143, 251–260; and J. Davis and S. Harrison, *Edison in the Boardroom* (New York: John Wiley & Sons, Inc., 2001) 46–47, 97–103.

approach goes back to business basics and builds on the company's mission, values, and business strategy to identify the I-stuff the company needs and how it will be managed to support the business strategy. The second approach is to identify the current issues facing the organization, identify the kinds of value that I-stuff can provide, and then determine how it will be created and managed to support the business strategy.[2]

MANAGING ACROSS ORGANIZATIONAL BOUNDARIES

Until relatively recently, firms tended to keep all their I-stuff well within their corporate boundaries, and employees interacted with other companies only for very limited reasons and only after a careful delineation of the "rules of behavior." However, today many business opportunities lie outside the corporate boundaries. Outside I-stuff may involve technology, market- or customer-related knowledge, or licensing activities with another firm. Joint ventures, can be an example of outside I-stuff activities. The participating firms often jointly staff the effort, with each firm providing people and expertise in different areas.

Opportunities to manage I-stuff across organizational boundaries raise several questions. The first is whether the opportunity is sufficiently attractive for both firms to pursue it. If it is, the companies must then identify the I-stuff they need and determine which partner will provide what. Another question concerns where the I-stuff will come from: employees, suppliers, other stakeholders, or external parties. Finally, the parties must determine how the I-stuff is to be shared, the degree of sharing, and responsibilities of each party are confidentiality of the I-stuff that is managed across organizational boundaries.

MEASURING THE VALUE OF INTANGIBLES

Companies want to measure the value of their intangibles for numerous reasons. A few of these are: for use in financial reports to external parties (investors, regulators, and others); for merger and acquisition discussions; for decision making about value extraction; and for leveraging the firm's intangibles in day-to-day business operations.

---

[2]For a more complete discussion of the valuation of intangibles, see Appendix E.

There are three different *standards* against which intangibles value may be measured:

1. *Internal value to the organization.* This is the value an intangible provides for the organization and/or to the business in its day-to-day operations
2. *Value in trade.* This is the value of an intangible if the organization were to trade it for currency to another company.
3. *Value related to an external standard.* This is the value an intangible has when measured against a standard of value outside the organization, usually either Generally Accepted Accounting Principles or market capitalization.

No one measurement method has yet been devised that can credibly measure value for *all* reasons and across all three standards. At the very least, though, a value measurement must be (1) capable of measuring value across all three measurement standards, and (2) capable of measuring value in context.

Among the popular methods for measuring the value of intangibles to the organization, each is useful for measuring a unique set of factors.[3] Some of the more popular value measurement methods are:

- *Accounting method:* based on Generally Accepted Accounting Principles and largely restricted to measuring value at the time of a transaction. Accounting can only measure intangibles that are purchased.
  - Positives: well-accepted framework and method for measurement in financial terms, works well for tangible asset measurement; can measure individual intangibles, groups of intangibles, or all intangibles of the organization.
  - Negatives: unable to measure value in absence of a transaction; unable to accommodate multiple contexts.
- *Market capitalization method:* values intangibles based on their contribution to the firm's capitalization in the marketplace.
  - Positive: good for measuring large groups of intangibles, particularly when their contribution to market capitalization is necessary.
  - Negative: not good for individual intangibles or for value-in-trade circumstances.
- *The "capitals" method:* divides the firm's intangibles into a series of "capitals" (e.g., human, customer, structural); relates these to performance

---

[3]For a more complete discussion of the valuation of intangibles, see Appendix E.

ratings and measures the change in the performance of the selected capitals over time.

- ○ Positives: most useful when alignment of intangibles with business strategy is required; measures all organizational intangibles.
- ○ Negative: not capable of measuring individual intangibles or groups of intangibles.
- *Indicators method:* does not measure intangibles directly; identifies indicators of performance for the corporation and measures changes in these indicators over time. Some of the performance indicators may relate to intangibles.
  - ○ Positive: well-accepted business method.
  - ○ Negative: cannot measure value in currency terms.
- *Value streams method:* recognizes that intangibles may create multiple simultaneous value streams in multiple contexts; identifies and quantifies actual and potential value streams to estimate the current and potential value of an intangible to the owner (in the owner's context) or to a potential buyer (in the buyer's context).

None of these popular methods meets both of the desired criteria: (1) an ability to measure value across all three measurement standards, and (2) an ability to measure value in context.

Best Practices for the Integrating Path

Companies on the Integrating Path utilize the following three best practices: 1) creating and implementing an I-stuff strategy, 2) managing relationships across organizational boundaries, and 3) measuring your I-stuff.

Best Practice 1: Create and Implement an I-Stuff Strategy

There are many ways to create and implement an I-stuff strategy. Two contrasting approaches demonstrate this point. Although both approaches evolved over time, one emerged from a focus on core values and the other evolved from a need to bring core capabilities to new business opportunities.

S.A Armstrong Limited is a privately held Canadian family company that has been in business for more than 70 years providing fluid handling equipment. Charles Armstrong, President and CEO of this innovatively managed company, describes the process he and the company went through to evolve an I-stuff strategy that matched the company's business strategy:

Our business strategy has been to evolve from a generic product company (manufacturing and selling pumps and related equipment) to a customer solution-provider. One of the significant challenges of managing such a transition is the nature of the dialogue between a salesperson (who may or may not be a company employee—it could be a distributor or representative or agent) and the customer. To be consistent with our strategy, we didn't want our salespeople to just sell products but to collaborate with the customer in order to understand the customer's issues and help solve them.

The challenge we faced was how to develop an I-stuff supporting strategy that called forth the wider capabilities of the organization and encouraged people to work side by side with each other and the customer to configure customer solutions.

The first piece we tackled was making the values of the company explicit, so that people had a common terminology for discussing and internalizing the company's mission, vision, and brand promise to the customer. We achieved this through a company-wide initiative that involved conducting values surveys and values workshops.

We then focused on creating a culture where employees are prepared to share knowledge. We also put in place the technology infrastructure to support this activity. Since 1991, we wanted to have a single global platform where our businesses could transact with one another and our customers on a global basis. At that time, this was an enormous undertaking. Over the next 15 years, in no small part owing to evolving technology, we achieved that goal.

The second piece we tackled was leadership restructuring. Instead of having hierarchical general managers and geographies as the focal drivers of our business plans, we created a Leadership Board comprised of nine people from different disciplines and geographies but equal in terms of their expected contribution. Board members are responsible for delivering the strategy and business plans of the business on a collective and shared accountability basis.

This means that the leadership of the organization actually has to practice working in a collaborative way, in order to achieve the business results. It's not without struggle that mutual success and shared accountability are driven to other levels in the organization. However, without the leadership of the organization demonstrating and working collaboratively, it is simply unreasonable to expect disparate parts of the organization to work together and demonstrate a collaborative intent with the customer.

Our work with values and leadership gave us the means to ensure that our strategy and culture were woven into our brand and that they were derived from the values of the organization. We believed our brand had to be fully embraced inside the company in order for it to be a significant experience for our customer.

Our best day is when our customers take us alongside to their customers, so that we have an opportunity to collaborate on a solution for the ultimate customer. By the nature of our business, we are only a part of an overall end product or end solution, and so the more capable we are at working externally with others, the more successful we can be. In other words, the more capable we are in delivering value to that overall end product or service, the more valuable we'll be to our customers. That is how we measure the success of our I-stuff strategy at S.A. Armstrong Limited.

The Dow Chemical Company's evolution of thinking about why and how to develop I-stuff strategies followed a different path. Because Dow frequently establishes new businesses around new technologies or new market opportunities, its focus became how to bring the power of the company's intellectual capital (IC) to each new business to improve its odds of ongoing success. Here Bruce Story (Intellectual Capital Director, Plastics), Nancy Schrock (Senior Intellectual Capital Leader, Dow Ventures), Tony Frencham (Business Director, Plastics), and Theresa Kotanchek (R&D Director, Dow Ventures) discuss Dow's IC strategy:

At Dow there is a big difference between IP strategy and IC strategy. IP is intellectual property (in our case largely patents, trademarks, trade secrets). IC encompasses much more. It includes not only IP but also the knowledge and other intangible assets that must be brought together to successfully execute the business strategy and to build a valuable and sustainable business.

Although all businesses are expected to have an IC strategy, such a strategy is particularly relevant to newly developing businesses and established businesses pursuing new growth opportunities. As these emerging opportunities are pursued, an integrated and visionary IC strategy better positions the business to extract long-term, sustainable value from its intangible assets—an essential ingredient to "creating your future."

Indeed, for the majority of new businesses, we must evaluate the opportunity through an IC lens, because IP would likely not yet exist. Although we do develop a strategy for getting the most valuable IP that we can, we spend the bulk of our time on creating the IC strategy that can include how we build and align both the internal and external resources, knowledge, capabilities, customer relationships, and all the IC that goes into building a successful business. IP is only one small component, although it depends on the industry and the market as to how important the IP is itself.

In Dow's early days of intellectual asset management we were focused on IP. That experience taught us several things. First of all, we learned that until you implemented an IP strategy, you couldn't fully understand the inadequacy of an IP strategy alone. The reality is that most of the companies in the world have IP, and most have some sort of IP strategy. But an IP strategy that focuses on supporting the business is just one step in creating competitive advantage. And, when you implement one of these, you soon realize just how little you knew about what other intangibles were available to support the business beyond just IP. Those intangibles may be internally or externally obtained. Our Hygiene and Medical business may be a good example of how this works. This team within Dow Plastics was assembled to focus on building a more profitable business aimed at selling plastics to the global hygiene and medical market. It was a business that we were not managing to best effect because we did not fully understand the industry complexity and our organization was not aligned well with that industry at the time. Aside from looking at the organization of the industry, we also quickly identified that it was an industry with an extremely high level of IC complexity.

When the Hygiene and Medical business team first started, we initially created an IP position within the business. The team didn't yet have a good understanding of the full range of intangible resources the business could command or whether the IP position we had was adequate.

When Dow first viewed the Hygiene and Medical business through a market lens, we were nothing more than a supplier of raw materials. Once the business team began looking at how to grow the business, we realized that one of our biggest resources was Dow's IC, along with some supporting IP. Ultimately the IC which the team identified fed into the creation of a new business strategy. On the heels of the new business strategy, the team was able to put together a preliminary IC strategy for the business. (As you can see, this is an iterative process.)

With the Hygiene and Medical team's focus on IC and the changes it made in its business strategy, the perception of the industry changed: from Dow being viewed as a company supplying raw materials into Dow being seen as a company that understood branding, marketing, and positioning within the industry. This change in the perception of Dow in this target market resulted in several key brand owners and fabricators involving us at the front end of projects, rather than at the back end. Involvement in the early stages of product development can give us a better position within the competitive business landscape and enable us to capture enhanced value.

Before Dow's Hygiene and Medical Team recrafted our approach to the industry, there had been only two competing raw materials suppliers who were seen as successfully capturing the value they delivered. Both had consumer product business lines and understood how to manage and value their IC in a consumer markets environment. When we entered the market, we soon raised ourselves to this level. At that point one of the brand owners (i.e., downstream customers) approached us and offered to share their product and business plans and to meet with us to conduct a sharing of how each company managed their IC.

That experience, and others like it, has led us to a clear understanding of the Dow process for creating and implementing IC strategies. When Dow starts up a new business (or wants to rejuvenate an existing one), we examine the proposed business strategy, identify all of the internal and external IC necessary to support or even revise that strategy, and from there develop an IC strategy. The IP strategy follows and arises out of a determination of the IP that is needed in order to create a valuable and sustainable business.

Dow's IC strategies include knowledge, know-how, relationships, and all other intangibles, in addition to IP. We spend a lot of time on IC, deciding how we will build the resources, the knowledge, the capabilities, the customer relationships, and all of that I-stuff that goes into building a successful business.

Best Practice 2: Managing Relationships across Organizational Boundaries

Companies managing across organizational boundaries sometimes take on another organization's employees and integrate them into their own operation, or send their own employees to be integrated into the operations of others. Although this is not yet a widespread practice, companies that manage across organizational boundaries have already learned several lessons.

The first lesson is that in the cross-organizational enterprise you must take on your partner organization's goals as your own. Only in that way can you ensure a consistency of focus on the part of your employees as well as theirs. The second lesson is that your employees are now part of a larger process than when they were simply working for their own organization. Third, you and your employees must learn to tailor knowledge and know-how in ways that enable your partner organization while still providing value to your firm as well.

Hubert Saint-Onge believes that managing an organization "in silos" will no longer be adequate for most organizations. He stresses that companies will increasingly find themselves managing across organizational boundaries:

> Increasingly, the marketplace imposes a need for collaboration both internally and externally to organizations. Knowledge is actually created as people collaborate to apply what they know to resolve specific issues. This will even be the case when the collaboration includes people from different backgrounds and functions.
>
> Customers are asking for integrated solutions. Those integrated solutions very often do not correspond with the way organizational silos work. What's more, no organizational structure seems to be able to meet the shifting needs and preferences of customers and their requirements for integrated solutions.
>
> More and more customers want the supplier to give them solutions that are ready for them to use in their own context. More and more, they refuse to have to assemble for themselves what the organizational silos provide in segmented ways. They refuse to do the work of the supplier. As a result, it is becoming more and more difficult to meet the needs of customers through a hierarchical organizational structure.

This is why more and more organizations now have to function on the horizontal (i.e., cross-organizational boundaries) axis as well as on the vertical (i.e., within an organizational silo) axis. In the end, this new blend produces a matrix geared to providing integrated solutions.

Another example of cross-organizational management of I-stuff that illustrates Saint-Onge's points involves the Canadian manufacturer S. A. Armstrong Limited. Charles Armstrong discusses how a move to partnering and collaboration led his company into a cross-organizational set of arrangements:

London's Heathrow Airport is constructing a new Terminal 5 (T5). It is currently the largest construction project in Europe. It will cost 4.2 billion pounds (about $7 billion) to build and will handle 30 million passengers a year. At any peak time there will be 5,000 people on the construction site. It's an enormous project.

The mechanical contractor, AMEC, wanted to bring forward the completion date of the mechanical work by using offsite-packaged modules. It was determined that this would help reduce the critical path of construction by many months, simplify congested site logistics, and improve the quality of site commissioning.

Armstrong worked with AMEC on a number of different things: plant efficiency, offsite packaging, and equipment controls. As a result of our "collaborating" and "problem-solving" values, we've been working with AMEC and others to reduce the overall operating costs, to simplify installation, and to reduce the number of interactions on site.

We're working in a world where owners, contractors, manufacturers, and consulting engineers have struggled working tightly together, where the behaviors are often not closely aligned, and where collaboration is not the norm. We have a notion of what collaboration in a business context requires. It's about building trust and sharing knowledge. The T5 project is a structured, real-time process-in-practice, building capabilities for both individuals and organizations throughout the value chain.

One of the questions that we are often asked is: How do we manage these integrated customer/organization teams? Today, the answer is that it's very specific to a particular project. Fundamentally, we understand collaboration to be a function of our organization's values (service, collaborating, learning, innovation, and "making it happen"). In the business context, the prerequisites are shared values, organizational structures, and capabilities, supported by an enabling IT architecture. The capacity to learn from practice, and to calibrate to our customer needs, is the activity.

Procter & Gamble is another company that operates across organizational boundaries. Similar to Armstrong, P&G found itself involved in an opportunity in which a nontraditional joint venture offered the prospect of significantly enhanced value to both companies involved. Jeff Weedman and Steve Baggot of P&G tell the story:

> The I-stuff we want to talk about is associated with Glad Press'n Seal. This product is actually a film with millions of microscopically sized dimples. At the bottom of each of those dimples is a small bit of adhesive that will stick to surfaces other than just the film itself. The real breakthrough innovation was figuring out how to make random-shaped dimples so that when the film rolls up on itself, it has mountaintops touching on mountaintops or bottoms, never nesting in the valley, so it doesn't stick together.
>
> It was clear that the market for this product roughly divided into quarters: A quarter of it was held by Glad, a quarter by SC Johnson, a quarter by Reynolds, and a quarter of the market was private label, which was the fastest growing segment.
>
> When we ran the numbers, it was clear that the cost to establish a brand equity in a huge market with well established competitors, all with very good trademarks, would be relatively large for one product in what was, by P&G's standards, a fairly small category. (We also didn't own a brand name.) We decided to seek out a partner from within the community of potential entrants and to do that via an "auction."
>
> We had a number of companies come in and look at this wrap technology, along with a trash bag technology and some others. The technology portfolio we put on the table and the proposition that accompanied it was: "Do you want to license any one of these technologies or the bundle of technologies; and what would you be willing to pay for it?"
>
> The deal that ultimately emerged was with Clorox. It was one that I think is a terrific example of balancing each company's capabilities and each company's strengths. For example, what Clorox got in this deal was not just technologies that were eventually marketed as Glad Press'n Seal™ and Glad ForceFlex;™ but they also got the right to additional improvements invented at P&G on any of our businesses that had application in the food wrap, plastic container, and plastic bag market.
>
> The Glad business was unlike any of Clorox's other businesses. It didn't have a lot in common with their bleach business, and it didn't have a lot in common with their charcoal (Kingsford) business. It had a lot more in common with P&G's businesses that dealt with high-speed processing of paper and plastic films than it did with any of the Clorox businesses.
>
> One outcome of this approach is that Clorox was able to tap into P&G's robust innovation pipeline. We agreed to allow Clorox to utilize P&G's R&D capabilities to support the Glad joint venture. So there are actually quite a few P&G employees working on the Glad business and bringing their embedded I-stuff directly into the joint venture. They stayed P&G employees, but they're paid for by the joint venture.
>
> As we negotiated the deal structure with Clorox, it was important to us to align our economic interests as well as facilitate a productive working relationship going

forward. We wanted to focus on building share, sales, and profits and not spend a lot of time continuing to negotiate between Clorox and P&G. If P&G only got paid for the I-stuff that we brought them at closing, we'd be incentivized to continue to try sell to them new I-stuff all the time as opposed to focusing on building the total business.

When we raised this concern with Clorox, they agreed that it could drive our relationship in an unintended direction. Both parties decided to better align the interests of both companies so that if the Glad business grew, it would grow for both Clorox and for P&G.

As a consequence, the deal was structured so that P&G would receive 10 percent of the total Glad business with an option to purchase an additional 10 percent (an option that we have since exercised). In exchange, P&G contributed to the joint venture the portfolio of technologies that included what was eventually marketed as Glad Press'n Seal and Glad ForceFlex. Another outcome was that we included further P&G inventions that were in the plastic wrap, trash bag, and container field of use as part of the deal so that there was little reason to negotiate IP going forward.

In laying out the governance for the joint venture, we realized that Clorox should be in control; they had the category knowledge, they had a terrific trademark in the Glad brand, they had the consumer expertise, and they had the manufacturing capability. They brought a known, highly valued brand equity, a knowledgeable selling organization, and a category expertise. We were bringing technology and technological I-stuff and current technologies as well as a pipeline of superior technology and I-stuff, a consumer understanding, and a lot of technical know-how. The marriage of Clorox and P&G capabilities has made for a very interesting and profitable joint venture. The fact that we acquired the additional 10 percent of the Glad business is evidence that we see this joint venture as a good economic opportunity for us.

Finally, Cargill is a company that made a significant commitment in the mid-1990s to change its business model in order to bring the power of the company's I-stuff to bear on customers and their problems more effectively. In pursuing this goal, Cargill has learned several lessons about what it takes to manage its I-stuff across organizational boundaries. John Raley, Intellectual Asset Manager at Cargill, relates some of these:

> Managing and leveraging I-stuff across organizational boundaries can be a challenging endeavor because it requires a new point of view, a different assessment methodology, and a different plan of action. Historically, companies embarking on a growth path looked inside themselves to see what new opportunities could be developed from their core competencies and/or what acquisitions would complement their core competencies and open up new opportunities.

To manage and leverage I-stuff across the boundaries between organizations, it is necessary to take stock of the knowledge the organization has, ideate on potential extrapolations of that knowledge to new opportunities, identify the required, yet missing, pieces of knowledge, and then work with other organizations that can fill in the gaps. To do this successfully there must be an introspective fluency in the core competencies of the organization and an extrospective fluency to extrapolate those competencies into business opportunities that lie outside the organization's comfort zone. Success requires unusual people and unusual senior management support, made even more rare by the past mantras of "stick to your knitting, focus on your core competencies, etc."

Cargill is a large, global enterprise in the agricultural and food chain businesses. Its Emerging Businesses unit was challenged to grow new, significantly sized opportunities based on Cargill's wealth of knowledge of the components that go into foods. The Emerging Businesses unit comprises just a handful of people yet it funds the efforts of 40 to 50 other people, most of them outside the Cargill organization, in pursuit of this challenge. The business model the unit follows calls for tapping into the collective knowledge of the company, ideating about possibilities, and then leveraging I-stuff across organizational boundaries to make those possibilities become reality. For example, fundamental chemical research can be done at universities, market research can be done by professionals in that field, product application development work can be done in partnership with other companies, etc. If an idea develops into a successful business, the decision can then be made to acquire the operation, sell it, establish a joint venture, etc. By not developing infrastructure before the need is proved, considerable costs can be avoided. And if the effort is not successful, minimal damage is done since each of the parties involved has not developed similar infrastructures and can continue on based on their core competencies.

One of the ideas being worked on in Cargill's Emerging Businesses unit is to use Cargill's knowledge of agricultural oils (soybean oil, canola oil, corn oil, etc.) and adapt that knowledge to develop products based on renewable agricultural oils that would replace oils derived from petroleum, a non-renewable resource.

Starting with knowledge of the chemistry that affects odor, color, and other properties of agricultural oils, as well as the requirements for a consistent quality raw material supply chain, Cargill has partnered with universities and companies strong in fundamental chemistry to develop the knowledge of how to modify the molecular structures of agricultural oils so as to mimic petroleum-based oils. Cargill has also partnered with companies that use petroleum-based oils to make other products. The list of possibilities is quite extensive, and many opportunities are being explored. Just recently, a producer of bottled water started packing their product in a "plastic" bottle made from corn. Also, patent applications have been filed describing the production of polyurethane foams from vegetable oils instead of traditional petroleum oil. The breadth of opportunities for oils derived from agricultural sources is seemingly endless. The results are products made from a renewable oil source that can substitute for products made from a non-renewable oil source, which makes good business, environmental, and social sense.

Managing and leveraging I-stuff across multiple organizations to make this success happen has been and will continue to be challenging. It requires thinking "inside the box" as well as "outside the box" at all times. But the effectiveness of discovering new opportunities and the efficiency of leveraging the I-stuff of other organizations versus creating/recreating that knowledge within an organization can save millions of dollars and many years of effort.

Best Practice 3: Measuring I-Stuff

Recognizing the difficulty in measuring the value of intangibles, companies have developed a variety of approaches over the past decade or so.[4] Each approach attempts to resolve a specific management issue or assist with a particular aspect of intangibles management. Exhibit 5.2 shows a few examples of these management concerns and the intangibles measurement approach(es) that attempt to deal with them.

No one method for measuring I-stuff value is particularly useful for measuring the "operational" value of I-stuff or for supporting decision making around resource allocation to I-stuff activities. The following account describes how one I-stuff manager found a way to measure the operational value of her organization's I-stuff. According to Celine Monette, former head of Scientific Communications and Professional Education for a global pharmaceutical company:

> My experience in measuring I-stuff started in 2000, when I headed the Professional Education Department for the Canadian division of a global pharmaceutical company. Our approach was to prepare the healthcare professionals and the Canadian pharmaceutical market, for innovations such as new scientific information and drugs the company would be introducing in the future. This was done by activities of sharing our scientific and medical knowledge and by continuing health education. It was accomplished by developing long-term partnerships with medical organizations, building relationships with influential medical professionals, exchanging knowledge, and by doing high-quality and ethical continuing health education and research in education. I felt it was important to be able to measure the value this created in order to properly reflect the return on past and present investment in the department's activities and its impact on the product life cycle. Because my department operated as a cost center, the amount of value it

---

[4]For a more complete discussion of value measurement relating to I-stuff and to intangibles, see Appendix E.

created was not directly measurable through the company's finance and accounting system.

Virtually all of my department's intangibles were I-stuff. We comprised staff from several different pharmaceutical companies, universities, healthcare systems, and several different iterations of the company itself. All of our processes and methods were devised and immediately implemented by the staff directly. We had no written processes or methods. We were a classic I-stuff organization.

One of the important questions we needed to answer was what amount of investment (budget) was optimum each year in order for my department to function. Under the then current circumstances, the amount of budget to be allocated to us was based on a collective guess. In addition, I had determined that in order to respond to the company's business strategy my department would require more human resources. This meant that we needed a way to assess the human resources needs in financial terms. Finally, I wanted to know whether we should invest more in one therapeutic area versus another one.

I turned to The Canadian Institute for Chartered Accountants (CICA) and ICMG for some advice. I learned through them that because of the way my organization was financially structured, it did not have a top and a bottom line. For organizations that do have a top and bottom line, it is possible to conduct analyses to determine what happens if certain things are done. For such organizations, one can determine whether a project or an activity increases or decreases the amount of investment necessary, or how it affects the return on investment. But in the case of a cost center, it is not possible to know whether the "right" amount of investment in the activity is being made or whether the organization is spending the company's investment on the "right" things. In addition, understanding that accounting works by tallying transactions, we knew that the transactions that would be influenced by the work of my group would be transactions that would occur many years into the future. So I couldn't assess the impact that my current year's budgeted activities would have on the firm's bottom line until several years in the future, if then.

Following my discussions with the CICA and ICMG, I determined to define the kind of analysis that I would like to commission in order to be able to routinely identify the value my organization was bringing to its company. After several iterations, I settled on the following as the nature, scope, and objectives of an engagement I wished to commission:

- To develop the capability to *measure* the contribution of activities and initiatives in *creating value* for the company, both quantitatively and qualitatively, addressing both tangible and intangible sources of value
- To be able to *track* the department's value creation *performance over time*
- To be able to *predict* the effect of new strategic initiatives on the value created by the department
- To value the impact of the department's efforts on product life cycle, both historically and in the future

In discussions with ICMG and the CICA, the first big challenge they identified was how to measure the contribution to value creation for the company when there isn't a top or a bottom line. Further, even if there were, an accounting approach would involve using financial data from the past to help make decisions about operations in the future. In the dynamic work of pharmaceuticals, that didn't seem to be particularly helpful. It seemed to me that would be like looking in a rear-view mirror to find the answer. I needed to look ahead.

We determined that the only way to respond to my engagement objectives would be to use a modeling approach where we would try to figure out the links between the amount the company invested in the forthcoming year, the way in which that investment was allocated to specific continuing health education activities, and the linkages all of that had to future revenues. Such a model could allow us to estimate the incremental impact of any investment in the continuing health education as well as how well alternative allocations of that investment within the department produced bottom-line results for the corporation.

The challenge of course is that because it's incremental and you're looking ahead, you can't prove it after the fact. It's like driving a car; you're steering as you go, making constant course adjustments as opposed to looking backward and trying to figure out where you came from.

We decided to structure the questions we wanted to find answers to. The first question we sought to answer was: What was the impact of the value created by the department for the company? As part of this activity, we were able to look at the life cycle of each product and show how that life cycle would be affected, which is really a revenue curve, through continuing health education. This allowed people to see the impact on different projects of having continuing health education or not having it. It also allowed me, as the department decision-maker, to make tradeoffs between where people should be focusing their time in order to meet the educational needs of the healthcare providers and to get the best payoff for the corporation.

Building on the answer to the first question, our second question was how to develop and codify the informal decision-making process that was already happening within the team but hadn't been committed to paper. This would involve unpacking the decisions that each person made in the course of building that strategy. Such an unpacking and codification process could spread each individual's knowledge more broadly within the medical education department. It would have the additional benefit of allowing us to involve others outside the department in our allocation decision-making processes. I believed that codifying the heretofore informal decision-making processes was important to getting a better understanding of what the interactions were here, both within and external to the department.

When I began to share the ROI model within the company, I got two kinds of reactions. One group of people got it instantaneously and viewed it as a decision model. They recognized that, while it is difficult to evaluate to a certainty, and even if it were not precise, it would certainly help in predicting the best action to take to optimize resource allocation in terms of future profitability for the firm. The second group had trouble with the model because they viewed it as a measurement model. They were already comfortable with the rearward-looking transaction model that the company was using. So it was hard to change that—that way of thinking.

All of the foregoing notwithstanding, overall it was well received. People were really curious about it, and some people were even looking at what we were doing and thinking about developing similar processes for themselves.

Let us turn from the measurement of I-stuff value in an operating organization to the general problem of measuring value at all. Bill Swirsky, Vice-President of The Canadian Institute of Chartered Accountants, discusses how the accounting organizations of several countries have come together to determine whether and how the development of a new value measurement method might be encouraged. This new value measurement approach should not be burdened with the rules of accounting yet should be capable of measuring the value of intangibles and should not be constrained by the accounting framework but also complement that framework:

In the early 1990s, the CICA began tracking the emerging measurement and reporting issues of the "intellectual capital" movement. Without understanding its full implications for business performance, we recognized that the emerging IC community could be talking about something of strategic importance for the accounting profession and our stakeholders. Encouraged by the movement, we sponsored our own contribution in 1993, a project called *Performance Measures for the New Economy.*

Our early efforts were focused on "shoehorning" IC into traditional financial statements. In 1997, however, we came to the conclusion that trying to put IC into financial statements was bound to be unsuccessful for a variety of reasons. Further, we realized that financial measurement for intangibles produced an inaccurate answer to the *wrong* question: What is the financial value of the firm's IC? We concluded instead that the right question was: How can we measure the value that organizations create? We came to realize that traditional accounting is based largely on recording transactions, and in so doing (quite well) what it actually measures is the *realization* of value that was previously created through R&D and other forms of innovation.

At this point, we learned about the existence of the ICM Gathering and saw it as a group of like-minded people from whom we could learn more about intangibles and value measurement. We joined the Gathering and began a fruitful journey with a group of colleagues with similar interests.

Having come this far, CICA sponsored a project to invent ways to measure organizational value creation from the perspective of both shareholders and stakeholders. We called it Total Value Creation®, or TVC®. The project was successful;

we produced a model and an approach to the measurement of the value created by an organization. With TVC® we had a good solution for measuring total value at a company level but found that it could not be assimilated by accounting firms and institutes. We then sought to put together a consortium that would focus the Big Five accounting firms on developing TVC® further. Our colleagues in the profession were not ready to invest in such a solution. With hindsight, there are probably two reasons why we couldn't get traction. First, our professional colleagues had not yet agreed with our definition of the problem, and second, for the accounting firms, each had a branded initiative that overlapped with our proposal in many aspects; all saw committing to TVC® as a financial and IC drain on resources they would wish to see used for their own commercial ends.

Still believing that the issue was "how to measure the amount of value created by an organization," we decided to take a different tack. We sensed that a number of accounting institutes around the world could agree that measuring and reporting on value was an important and worthwhile challenge. We then focused on collaborating with them to resolve the problem. Thus the Value Measurement and Reporting Collaborative (VMRC) came to be, comprising the accounting institutes of Canada, the United States, Australia, South Africa, and Germany.

VMRC went through the usual period of finding its focus. It settled on what we now call the New Paradigm Initiative (NPI). The purpose of NPI is twofold: in the short term, to identify and categorize all of the current approaches for measuring value; and to provide measurement professionals with a comprehensive listing of methods, including an assessment of what each does well (i.e., the issues each is best at facilitating and the level in the company where these issues are most frequently observed). In examining these current approaches, we also intend to evolve a listing of criteria specifying what a new, not-yet-invented approach for measuring value would ideally contain.

VMRC has begun to produce results. We've already published a discussion paper on the NPI Web site called "Re-discovering Measurement." We've catalogued more than 80 value and performance measurement approaches that have emerged in the past 15 years, and we have developed an online system that enables NPI participants to see for themselves how these approaches compare with each other and with VMRC's initial set of measurement concepts and criteria. We are assembling a total list of criteria and expect to be able to make it publicly available in the near future.

We think all of this will contribute to our collective ability, as measurement professionals, to develop a new, internally consistent, systemic model for measurement that both parallels and complements traditional accounting and financial reporting; it needs to be synergistic with other initiatives calling for enhanced disclosures, it must rest on a solid conceptual foundation, and ultimately it must meet the needs of stakeholders for new insights into an organization's value and performance.

Conclusions: Beyond Integrating

Integrating the organization's I-stuff involves a step upward in management thinking. For many older or more traditional firms, taking such a step may prove challenging, whereas for newer or less traditional firms it may simply be a part of doing business. Integration of the firm's I-stuff and deciding whether to align it with the business strategy, whether to manage it across organizational borders, or whether to measure its value will require new and different attitudes and perspectives for any firm. We challenge firms to accept Einstein's statement; "The important thing is not to stop questioning." However, firms that are successful with integration will find themselves identifying more challenges and opportunities for building, leveraging, and sustaining through their I-stuff than ever before.

6

SUSTAINING THE CORPORATION THROUGH I-STUFF

COMPANIES ON THE Sustaining Path have a long-term perspective on the firm, its activities, and its place in industry and society. Firms on this path have achieved a fundamental shift in their view of value, away from short-term business goals and objectives and toward the long-term fundamental value the firm creates. For firms at the Sustaining Path, shareholders are no longer the ultimate group for which the firm creates value; shareholders become an important stakeholder in the firm, albeit one with a special financial interest. However, firms on the Sustaining Path recognize that shareholders are only one of a number of stakeholders in the firm.

Because of their long-term view, firms on this path become interested in organization-wide renewal, focusing their I-stuff management on the renewal and re-use of I-stuff and on developing sustainable value streams through their I-stuff. Firms with the sustainability perspective find that finance-based reporting, by itself, is no longer sufficient for the now expanded set of stakeholding individuals and groups wanting to know about all the firm's activities and intentions. (see exhibit 6.1)

Thought Leader Comments

I-Stuff and Corporate Sustainability

Sustainability has become a term too easily used and too often misunderstood. In the corporate world it can attract headlines, such as reports about how corporations are at fault for permafrost melting in Siberia or the polar ice caps shrinking because of carbon dioxide emissions from factories; or it can be a hidden unresolved item in the corporate boardrooms about the long-term viability of a business. In the latter context, it is interesting to note that an analysis of the top 3000 listed companies in the U.S. shows that less than 30% were on that list 20 years previously.

The financial reporting realm has been dominated by a focus on the firm's tangibles such that shareholders came to be focused on a single metric—the earnings per share number.

The narrow and incomplete focus on short-term performance and on financial metrics such as earnings-per-share is only of interest to short-term stock traders who focus on the regulatory disclosure requirements for shareholders.

But there is a new and more wholesome view, wherein stakeholders in an organization seek information on the measurement and reporting of intellectual assets, intellectual property and the value streams of innovation portfolios, the challenge of reporting on continuous organizational renewal and sustainable development, the methodologies of presenting information for the long-term institutional investor as well as the community of stakeholders. There is an unmistakable movement to disclose information that escapes the grasp of the accounting lens.

In 2003, the CICA released a Research Report on measuring "Stakeholder Relationships, Social Capital and Business Value Creation." This research posited that companies could be categorized into three "levels" of stakeholder sensitivity. The first level companies are labeled as "Compliant": Their primary focus is avoiding harm to stakeholders: for instance, by attempting to minimize environmental damage and protecting the health and safety of employees.

Companies at the second level are "Responsive": doing their best to meet reasonable stakeholder expectations regarding economic performance, environmental impacts, and role in the community.

At the third level, companies are "Engaged": Here the objective is maximizing economic, social, and environmental value for all stakeholders—not solely the shareholding class.

I-stuff provides the energy needed to drive the transition from simply avoiding harm in relations with stakeholders, to maximizing value for everyone. At this level, sustainability is not just about the environment, or continuous renewal and innovation inside the organization. It is about inter-relationships viewed as systemic and dynamic—part of the economic eco-systems within which the organization can prosper and remain relevant.

I-stuff can be seen as a connection between what is important to people, in their various stakeholder roles, how the organization defines success over the long-run, and how it behaves day-to-day in its various relationships with stakeholders. In other words, I-stuff provides connectivity between values, and value creation.

The organization uses its I-stuff as the major means for reaching its business objectives. It can then measure its long-term success, as well as progress along the way as a check on the degree to which it is successful in managing and focusing its I-stuff on important business goals. Information on organizational I-stuff and its uses is one of the most powerful pieces of information a company can send to its stakeholders.

An organization claiming to be concerned about long-term sustainability, but only measuring accounting performance, runs the risk of undermining its very credibility. Measuring and reporting the broader and more sustainable aspects of performance, such as I-stuff and its associated value creation activities, is still a work-in-process; the journey is not without uncertainty. But the rewards to our corporations and all of their stakeholders will be its own reward.

Bill Swirsky, Vice President, The Canadian Institute of Chartered Accountants

What Is Sustainability?

"Corporate sustainability" became popularized during the Rio Earth Summit in the early 1990s when the challenge was to find sustainable solutions to address environmental, social, and economic issues. *Forbes* magazine, in its 2002 Worldwide edition, used this definition: "Corporate sustainability is the umbrella for an expanding set of largely stakeholder-oriented challenges touching key aspects of business performance, competitiveness, and even survival."

The Gathering perceives corporate sustainability in two ways. Sustainability with a capital "S" describes how the firm acts or interacts with its community and with society on a long-term basis. For many companies, particularly those involved with basic commodities or environmentally challenging materials or products, long-term corporate sustainability has become intertwined with environmental responsibility in addition to the economic and social responsibilities. Some large international companies became leaders in making corporate sustainability a centerpiece of their internal cultures as well as in their external reporting. Typically, these companies have long-term visions extending out for decades, and environmental issues may be central to their very survival. Examples in the United States include Dow, DuPont, Georgia Pacific, IBM, and Intel. In Europe a list of such companies would include Royal Dutch Shell, IKEA, British Petroleum, DSM, and DaimlerChrysler. In Japan, one finds Toyota, Honda, Canon, Ricoh, Mitsubishi Electric, and Tokyo Electric, to mention but a few.[1]

But Sustainability with a capital "S" is not our primary interest here. Sustainability as it concerns the Einstein Value Continuum is thought of with a small

---

[1]"The Evolving Business Case for Corporate Sustainability," *Forbes* Worldwide Edition, September 2, 2002.

"s." For I-stuff management, sustainability is concerned with how the firm's current decisions affect the future in its day-to-day decision making around making its profits.

The Characteristics of Sustainable Corporations

Sustainability for business organizations does not mean preservation or permanence; rather, sustainability for businesses must be thought of in terms of adaptability, flexibility, and persistence; some even describe sustainability as organizational Darwinism. Sustainable corporations have a number of characteristics in common. For example, sustainable corporations:

- *Manage themselves for continuous economic growth.* This dimension of management activity has two very strong elements. First, the sustainable corporation manages itself internally so as to improve and enhance its innovation and productivity continually. On the external front, sustainable corporations constantly review and seek to enhance their market relevance as well as their relevance and importance to the firm's external stakeholders.
- *Control and influence their destiny.* Sustainable firms recognize that they have the ability to control their own futures and exhibit a willingness to do so. These firms are quick to adapt to changes in their external environment. They have a culture of organizational change and a willingness to depart from the familiar. Their organizations lack complacency and exhibit a drive for continual renewal. They demonstrate a corporate capability for foresight and an ability to adapt as required to create their own future.
- *Demonstrate a sense of longevity.* Sustainable firms focus on dynamism and movement, not on preservation. Their view of the future extends beyond the life cycle of their key products or important technologies.
- *Have strong core values that are aligned.* Sustainable firms imbue themselves with values that are focused on the long term, values that are reflected in how the firm acts and reacts with its customers, its suppliers, its employees, and its shareholders. Business values concerned with sustainability may include such items as honesty, integrity, ethics, and fair play. Sustainability Path company values are in alignment with their internal and external environments. Internally, they are consistent with and supportive of the activities and attitudes necessary for the business strategy to succeed. Externally, they are equally consistent with and supportive of the needs and values of the firm's key stakeholders and stakeholding groups.

WHY ARE STAKEHOLDERS IMPORTANT?

Corporations exist in a complex network of interdependent stakeholder relationships. The term "stakeholder" has been defined as any individual or group that can affect, or is affected by, the achievement of a corporation's objectives.[2] For most corporations, key stakeholders include employees, customers, investors, government regulators, suppliers, community residents, and, in some cases, environmental and other advocacy-based organizations.[3] Increasingly the business community is becoming aware that a corporation's long-term value may be created by the contributions of multiple stakeholders, with multiple perspectives on what is "valuable" for them in their own relationship with the corporation.

How a company engages its relevant stakeholders to address its unique sustainability issues can have a direct bearing on its access to markets and capital, its ability to attract and retain quality employees, the efficiency of its operations, and its reputation and brand value. In short, how well a company manages its I-stuff for sustainability and how it keeps its stakeholder community informed and positively disposed to its business and social responsibilities is a measure of how successful it is and will be in sustaining itself in the long term.

It is interesting to consider investors as one of the corporation's stakeholding groups. It is known that only a small portion of investors focus on short-term goals. While relatively few in number, these investors often drive near-term stock prices and have an impact on markets far in excess of their relatively small numbers. Also, because the stock market cannot measure the contribution of a company's intangibles, the long-term potential value is overlooked for the short term results that can be measured and which respond to the short-term investor's interests. But short-term investors are unlikely to care about the corporation as a sustainable entity and, therefore, are not the kind of investor that sustainable corporations desire.

Shareholders who are long-term investors are more desirable; long-term investors may be viewed as stakeholders in the corporation and, as such, may fulfill a broader range of roles for the corporation than purely financial ones.

The result of the above discussion is to suggest that sustainable corporations may find it to their advantage to find ways to actively seek out investors

---

[2] T. Donaldson and L.E. Preston, "The Stakeholder Theory of the Corporation: Concepts, Evidence, and Implications," *Academy of Management Review*, 20, (January 1995): 65–91; R.E. Freeman, *Strategic Management: A Stakeholder Approach* (Boston: Pitman, 1984).

[3] Canadian Institute of Chartered Accountants, *Stakeholder Relationships, Social Capital and Business Value Creation*, Research Report, 2003, 3.

whose interests in the corporation are long-term and who would be happy to find themselves cast as stakeholders as well. For the firm, it is easier and perhaps even more powerful to keep its stakeholder community informed and participative when more of them are investors as well.

SUSTAINABILITY AND I-STUFF REPORTING

There is a history of discussion and initiatives around whether and how companies should report their intangibles to interested parties outside the firm. One school of thought leans toward the financial and posits that firms should report their intangible assets on their balance sheet just as they do their tangible ones. A significant difficulty with this approach concerns the inability of the financial and valuation communities to devise methods that ensure the unambiguous valuation of intangibles. Another school of thought decrees that it is important for outsiders to know about the *use* of intangibles. This leads to the belief that the firm should identify its more important intangibles and, for each, describe how it is expected to be used (narrowly) in the creation of profits. Still another perspective on reporting takes the view that firms should identify all their intangibles, as well as the groupings of intangibles with the greatest potential business interest for the firm, and discuss (broadly) how the firm intends to manage these for improved business performance (profitability, social responsibility, and other factors).

The major initiatives on the reporting of intangibles have been centered in North America and Europe. The European view of intangibles is an asset-based one. As a result, European approaches to intangibles reporting tend to focus on schemes that require a standardized format for defining the "capitals" of the firm (e.g., human, organizational, relationship) and for the firm to identify "how much" of each reside within the firm, along with some information about how the firm intends to manage its key intangibles in the near future. For some years firms in Sweden have been reporting on their intangibles (intellectual capital). The Ministry of Technology and Economics in Denmark published a set of guidelines for the reporting of intellectual capital in (2002). Currently, there is a movement in Germany to create a "knowledge balance sheet" (*Wissenbilanz*), with governmental and institutional groups meeting to devise a format for companies to use.

In North America the focus on intangibles is quite different. Whereas the Europeans view intangibles as something to be managed, the North American view is that they are available for exploitation in the pursuit of profits. With the latter in mind, and with a clear focus on financial reports, the effort has been to create standard approaches for companies to use in reporting on their intangibles through the Management's Discussion and Analysis (MD&A). The purpose of the MD&A has been to provide a narrative explanation, through the eyes of management, of how a company has performed in the past and its future prospects. The MD&A is intended to integrate historical and prospective information as well as financial statements and business analyses; together with the financial statements, this information is meant to impart useful knowledge to investors and other readers. Although originally intended as a regulatory document to supplement the financial statement, the MD&A now complements the financial statement and has become the locus wherein North American companies can report on any aspect of their intangibles that they wish. The companies that publish so-called triple-bottom-line reports reflecting economic, environmental, and social impacts often contain relevant intangible indicators.

North American firms have resisted the creation of separate intellectual capital reports, such as those found in Europe. In North America, companies fear they may open themselves up to litigation by unhappy investors, who, not understanding the tenuous nature of intangibles and their use in business, may feel they have been misled by statements about the potential use of intangibles in the business.

Despite all the discussion and activity surrounding intangibles reporting, in most countries such reporting remains voluntary. For this reason, companies must decide on their own whether and what to include in an intangibles report. The temptation for many companies is to include information that is supportive of short-term business goals or activities. Experience has shown, however, that once an intangibles report has been published, third parties look for follow-on reports that contain follow-on information on items mentioned previously. Giving in to the temptation to produce self-serving information in a report may prove to be problematic later on, or even an impediment to change.

One school of thought (and one with which the authors agree) is that much of the value of reporting on the firm's intangibles comes with the increased knowledge and visibility the firm obtains by the simple process of developing the information for its own sake. Often publishing such a report internally can be very effective.

The Importance of Values to Sustainability

Values may be thought of as the ideals that shape and give significance to our everyday lives. They are reflected in the choices we make, the priorities we set, the decisions we make, and the actions we take. In an individual's role as employee, the person's individual values drive his or her day-to-day decision making. The values of a firm represent the consensus beliefs of its individual members. The sum of the values contained within the firm's boundaries—its collective values—influence the worldview held by its employees. In cases, where there are differences between the "official" values of the firm, as espoused by top management, and the values of employees, significant dysfunction is likely to occur. For example, in such a circumstance it would be unlikely that employees would implement top management's strategies and plans effectively.

For sustainable corporations, the values of the firm and the values of employees must be closely aligned. Without such alignment it would not be possible for the collection of individuals comprising the firm to deal with the range of internal issues that arise as the firm grows toward a sustainable state. It would be fair to say that without alignment between the values of top management and the values of employees, firms are unlikely to mature to a sustainable position.

What Sustaining Path Companies Are Trying to Accomplish

The aims of Sustaining Path companies are to:

- Define sustainability for the organization, and the roles therein for I-stuff
- Understand how employee and corporate values enable sustainability
- Report on corporate progress toward sustainability.

For companies using their I-stuff as a major element in their sustainability activities, the focus of I-stuff management has been in several important areas.

Best Practices for the Sustaining Path

Best practices for the sustaining path include:

1. using I-stuff as a catalyst for corporate sustainability,
2. using values to enable employee and
3. corporate sustainability, and I-stuff reporting.

Best Practice 1: Using I-Stuff as a Catalyst for Corporate Sustainability

The use of I-stuff as a catalyst for corporate sustainability is accomplished by different organizations through different means. Some organizations seek to renew their I-stuff continually as the path toward corporate sustainability.

EXHIBIT 6.1   The Einstein Value Continuum: Highlighting the Sustaining Path

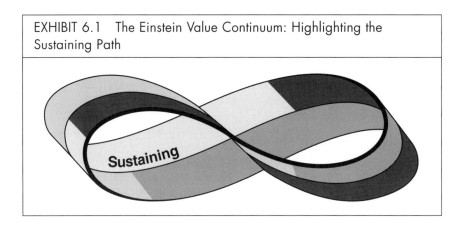

Sustaining

Others look for new and different ways to exploit the I-stuff they already have. Still others seek to use their I-stuff as a way to influence their stakeholders. Eli Lilly and Company shares an example of a strategic dilemma that touched on the company's sustainability efforts. Rob Smith, Eli Lilly and Company Director of Public Relations and Corporate Branding, outlines how the organization used its values as well as nonstrategic I-stuff in a method for resolution:

Pharmaceutical companies seek sustainability just like any other business. In our external environment are stakeholder patients involved with a number of diseases with declining patient populations for whom we have provided medicines that alleviate or cure. We are eager to maintain our good relationships with these patients, yet we are mindful of our investors and the need to make a return on investment. Occasionally the choice between what is economic and what is desirable gives rise to a devil's choice: We can't bring ourselves to abandon a patient population in need, but we still must focus on profitable opportunities. In 2001 we faced this very dilemma and found a way to use our I-stuff creatively to develop new ways to service such a population while still maintaining our focus on profitable patient populations. In short, we used our I-stuff to solve a difficult sustainability problem for the corporation.

At that time our business strategy focused on discovering and developing new medicines in four therapeutic areas: neuroscience, endocrinology, oncology, and cardiovascular diseases. At the same time a new form of tuberculosis, multidrug-resistant tuberculosis (MDR-TB), was emerging as a global health crisis. TB is often thought to be a "disease of the past," but it is re-emerging. (One-third of the world's population is latently infected.) There is a rapid increase due to HIV/TB co-infection. (In some geographies 75 percent of HIV-infected patients are also TB infected.) Each year, over 300,000 new cases of MDR-TB are diagnosed in more than 100 countries.

Lilly had been manufacturing two drugs, older antibiotics that are part of the treatment protocol for MDR-TB. They are two fairly complex drugs to manufacture, and Lilly has been the single supplier of them around the world. But these two drugs were patented back in the 1950s and 1960's. Continuing with their manufacture and sale would be inconsistent with our new business strategy.

Normally, once a drug is off-patent, generic drug manufacturers begin to make and sell generic versions of drugs. In the case of MDR-TB, very few generic makers have come forward to manufacture and sell these drugs, largely due to the increased treatment complexity of this disease. Treatment for MDR-TB requires the use of second-line drugs and a treatment duration that is longer (up to 24 months versus 6 months for first-line drugs); that is more expensive (up to 100 times); that results in more side effects; and that requires complex diagnosis.

We decided to explore whether we could take our manufacturing technology— our know-how and other I-stuff—and actually transfer it to manufacturers in geographical locations where the disease is most pronounced.

To accomplish that, we created the Lilly MDR-TB Partnership (which has become a model for public-private partnerships) involving the cooperative efforts of the pharmaceutical industry, government bodies, international organizations, and academic institutions. This program is multidimensional, dealing with all aspects of the MDR-TB problem, from drug supply to treatment and from surveillance to evaluation. In addition to being the only MDR-TB program, it is also one of a few transfers of technology programs in the pharmaceutical industry. Its primary goal is to train healthcare personnel and increase the supply of the critical drugs needed to treat MDR-TB to meet the treatment goal of the World Health Organization (WHO). A secondary goal is to improve the production capacity for these two products closer to where the disease is more prevalent: Latin America, Africa, Asia, and some segments of the prison population in Russia. By transferring manufacturing technology, not only do we increase the supply of the products in the countries that need it most, but we also play a role in helping regions become independent in their care of MDR-TB.

So what does Lilly get out of all of this? We get to re-use knowledge that we created 40 to 50 years ago in a new way and to tackle a global health issue more effectively. This is consistent with our philosophy of supporting the company's external stakeholders, in this case several countries, patients, and components of the healthcare industry combating this disease. Internally, it allows us to concentrate on areas of core competence, specifically the four main therapeutic areas defined in our business strategy. We could not have come to such a positive resolution of our dilemma if we had not been able to manage and transfer the company's outdated but still effective I-stuff associated with these MDR-TB drugs.

Best Practice 2: Using Values to Enable Sustainability

Sustainability Path companies, well aware of the fundamental power and importance of values to the management and longevity of the firm, use this knowledge in interesting and different ways. Some companies use values as a way to align members of organizations or project teams in order to improve innovation and productivity. Other companies use their knowledge of values to create alignment around the corporate brand and its promise to customers. Still others use values to help resolve dilemmas involving thorny strategic issues.

Jim O'Shaughnessy, former Vice President of IP at Rockwell relates how values were used to reduce conflict and increase innovation and productivity:

When I joined Rockwell, the company in general had a very good culture. The group in which I was working did not. When you think about culture from either an anthropological or sociological point of view, what you understand is that cultures are deeply ingrained and don't readily change, or don't change very much very fast. I was facing a situation in which things had to change—it couldn't just be that this was our culture and we were stuck with it.

When I undertook a preliminary investigation, I was led to a group active in the analysis of organizational values. From my study of the topic, I came to appreciate that what glues an organizational team together is its shared values. By the way, values aren't just another term for culture. It is the disaggregation of that term culture into its moving parts; when you pull it apart, you can understand it and when you understand it, you can manage it. So I engaged that group to do a values assessment and to work with us in order to understand the shared values of our part of the overall organization.

This is not to say that everybody within a team has to have the same values. However, unless everybody on the team has a core set of shared values, the team is not working to its highest potential. Indeed, if one or more members do not share these values, they can be positively destructive of team work. So, there's a lot to be learned by a study of values, and as I say, the atomization of culture and the ability to respond truly to the needs of people to be led in a way that is completely congruent with what they value. The absence of this objective is sure folly. Regarding our team, a number of constructive things happened. One, we smoked out people who paid only lip service to what we called culture. We also unearthed some dysfunctional behavior, and truly destructive behavior. Once we understood those sources of team dysfunction, we could properly address it at its source. Those individuals who compromised team integrity were provided with out-placement services, moving them out of our organization, and giving them the opportunity to get on with life elsewhere.

We found almost immediately a change in the energy of the team. We weren't spending a lot of time in stupid fights catalyzed by people who didn't share these values and who were disruptive. There was much more positive energy in the team.

Also, our communications became crisper. We understood what was important. That productively impacted daily teamwork and also contributed to insights when it came time for recruiting. We said: Why bring in somebody who lacks this intersection with our value set? And we took the position that we would rather have someone who shared our core values than someone who was truly brilliant and an outstanding player but who lacked those values. Team cohesion meant that everybody could contribute better.

Organizational teams are glued together by values, and if you're expecting a high-functioning team, you benefit greatly from the coalescing factor of those shared values.

Clarica, the Canadian insurance company, wanted to create a company-wide environment in which every person in contact with customers or with the public would present the same company face and information. To accomplish this, it was decided to learn the degree to which employees shared the espoused corporate values and, if there were differences, to reduce any gaps that might exist:

> To identify the values espoused by different groups as well as the overarching principles guiding the culture, Clarica conducted a survey of 8,000 people that included all employees as well as 3,000 financial advisors in the field. The results of this survey allowed us to identify the different strands of values in the organization as well as the values that were shared across the board. It gave us the DNA of the organization. The survey results identified the key values held by people in the organization. We then looked at our strategic direction and at our brand to identify where we needed to insert new values into the existing fabric in order to align the culture. Within the fabric of the existing values, we then added the values that we felt were missing in order to reinforce on the brand, primarily, and, secondarily, the strategic direction of the firm. This was done based on the premise that whereas you can't fundamentally change a culture, you can stretch the culture in a desired direction by pulling certain lower priority values into a higher priority position in order for the fabric to fit the strategic direction and the intent of the brand better.
>
> The core values were then translated into the behaviors that operationalized the values for our organization; in other words, we defined the values in behavioral terms, checked to see whether these behaviors were being practiced, and identified gaps in our behavior that reflected gaps between our desired set of values and the actual values that our employees were practicing. Finally, using this information, we were able to embark on a program to better inculcate and practice the values that were more consistent with our strategy and our brand image.

Best Practice 3: I-Stuff Reporting

As already discussed, companies on the Sustainability Path must decide whether to report out on their intangibles and, if so, what to report. Whereas companies in Europe, particularly those in Scandinavia, have a history of intangibles reporting, and a generally agreed perspective on what to report, such is not the case in North America. In North America, because the focus of intangibles is on creating and extracting value, reports of intangibles and their use tend to be focused on the company's annual financial report. In particular, there is a movement around including this information in the company's Management Disclosure and Advisory (MD&A).

Rob Smith of Eli Lilly and Company discusses the evolving thinking process of the corporation as it decides on the recipient of information on the company's intangibles and what kind of information it will be:

At Lilly we have a complex network of stakeholders: individuals or groups that receive value from their relationship with us (and we receive value from them), although not financially or through ownership of our stock. At one end of the stakeholder spectrum we have the local governments and communities where we work and live. For example, we are one of the largest employers in our hometown of Indianapolis, Indiana. We consider the Indianapolis local government as a stakeholder. We want to make sure that we have a good relationship with the city government where we work, with businesses (suppliers and others) that can have a positive impact on the operations of our company, and with governments and businesses in the communities in which we live.

We also have a wide range of international stakeholders, be they the governments of countries in which we operate, or nongovernmental organizations that are a part of a country infrastructure. We also have a diverse set of stakeholders within the health care industry, including patients, medical personnel, hospitals and clinics, medical researchers, and insurance companies.

Although Lilly exists, in part, to make money and to provide our investors with a return, at the same time we believe we must also be a good corporate world citizen. As we have illustrated in one of the other stories you've put into this book, there's a lot of tension between the pursuit of financial returns and being a good world citizen. At least in our case, it has on occasion meant that we have found ourselves sacrificing a bit of shareholder value in the short term in order to be socially responsible in the longer term. We think that's just good business.

For example, if we learned that there was some bad news about one of our products, some companies in that position might be tempted to withhold such information to generate a short-term financial benefit. At Lilly that would be unthinkable. It not only goes against our pursuit of long-term profitability, it also is in violent conflict with our core values.

Our core values contain a strong emphasis on corporate responsibility. For example, in 2004, our total philanthropy was over $400 million in cash and product contributions around the world. We have a history of protecting the environment in everything that we do. And just within the healthcare community, we have very generous patient assistance programs. So, the question we continually ask ourselves is:

What is the best way that we can pull all those things together into a credible report to our stakeholders? Not just to blow our own horn or talk about how great we are, but we seek an objective format that is informative and consistent with what other companies use to share Lilly's activities on corporate citizenship and the record of which we are proud with our external audiences. You don't act socially or corporately responsible just so you can report it. You do it because of who you are and in response to your corporate values. Nevertheless, there is an outside audience that likes to learn about these things, and we continually seek the most appropriate way to keep them informed. That has been Lilly's motivation for putting together its social responsibility report.

We have always known that handing out an annual report containing one or two paragraphs on corporate responsibility would not be particularly helpful. If you look at annual reports, you see that a number of companies are really paring those things back and just focusing on the financials and some key company highlights. (This applies to their financial reporting in general, not only the annual reports.) If you take a look at our annual reports, the last one is fairly bare bones. It really cuts to the chase. There's not a lot of gloss. There's not a lot of color.

We want to focus on the major results we've achieved and some key activities within Lilly. We want to communicate with stakeholders who care about these issues. These people are not so much interested in what our sales were last year as in what kind of company we are: how we're treating the environment, how we're treating our customers, our suppliers and our employees.

Looked at from another perspective, these thoughts reflect the fact that Lilly (as well as other companies) has recognized that stakeholders are different from shareholders. Whereas shareholders benefit directly from the financial aspects of the company, stakeholders are interested in other kinds of value. The social report that we create is intended for the stakeholders, many of whom may not be shareholders of the company.

CONCLUSIONS: BEYOND SUSTAINABILITY

A fundamental concept underlying the idea of business sustainability is that of continual renewal. Any company traveling down the sustainability portion of the I-stuff management path may anticipate some feeling of relief when the end of that path is on the horizon. However, because of the magic of the Einstein Value Continuum, companies that master the management of I-stuff for sustainability (and come to the end of the sustainability portion of the path) find themselves back at the beginning, with Building, Leveraging, and Integrating enticing them to yet more I-stuff management experiences.

As a book of best practices in the management of I-stuff, this book is incomplete. To explain what that means, let us make a comparison to *Edison in the Boardroom.* The companies contributing best practices to *Edison* had been involved with managing IP for quite some time, and all could say definitively that their contribution represented a best practice. But, for the companies contributing to *Einstein*, this is not necessarily the case. Many of the companies profiled in this book are in the process of exploring I-stuff and its relationship to firm value. These companies see their efforts as a work-in-progress. This journey is just beginning.

As the authors look back on the concepts and ideas in this book as well as on the company experiences in implementing them, we ask ourselves: Have we learned any core *truths* or have we experienced any new insights from putting this book together? Any intense intellectual effort, such as writing a book, is a learning experience. In the case of *Einstein* this is particularly true. Whereas *Edison* was written from the business perspective surrounding IP, it focused on one "silo" of value and information. But I-stuff crosses many silos and perspectives. This has been an intense intellectual experience for the authors as we have tried to "simplify" intangibles to one perspective while maintaining the integrity of all views. Suffice it to say, we have learned more from this enterprise than we thought possible. While we could make lists of things we have learned as well as things we have come to see in a new light, there are two particularly core ideas that stand out:

1. **I-stuff is the fundamental source of value for organizations**—There is nothing more basic than the realization that companies make money from the ideas of their founders, employees, customers and other stakeholders. I-stuff is at the center of every organization. Some companies never understand or acknowledge it, yet they survive. Others embrace it and seek to actively manage it and to use it for their long-term sustainability. Organizations in the former group tend to be relatively short-lived, while those in the latter are most likely to persevere and sustain themselves well into the future.

2. **Stakeholders are as important to organization success as is I-stuff**— Shareholder value required the firm to place the needs of one stakeholder group above all others. This has led to highly dysfunctional corporate behavior over time. Today we realize that a company has a network of stakeholders (employees, customers, suppliers, communities, governmental agencies, etc.) that can help it steer itself through the minefields of business, law, regulation, technology and politics, in order to increase the firm's odds of sustaining itself over the course of time. This view of stakeholders requires companies to identify who are their main stakeholders and better understand how to respond to their needs

and concerns and also how to utilize these relationships to feed into their own I-stuff renewal.

The intangibles management community continues its journey to understand and to capitalize on the full range of the firm's intangibles. For firms who began their intangibles journey with intellectual property, the shift to I-stuff is the obvious next step. For firms who are beginning their journey directly with I-stuff, we hope this book contains information that is helpful. But for all I-stuff managers: The value you find will be in the journey and not in the destination.

As Einstein is reported to have said, "Truth is what stands the test of experience." Whether this view of intangibles "stands the test of time" remains to be seen; however, the future will bring the truth soon enough.

7

PROCTER & GAMBLE: PROGRESSING BEYOND INTELLECTUAL PROPERTY

FROM ITS BEGINNING in 1837, Procter & Gamble (P&G) has been at the forefront of technology. Commitment to invention has fueled revolutionary advances for consumers such as Ivory, Crisco, Tide, Crest, Pampers, and the osteoporosis drug Actonel. Today, P&G is number 1 or number 2 in all the global categories in which it competes and now, with the acquisition of Gillette, has 22 brands with annual sales of at least $1 billion dollars each. P&G continues to be a global leader because more than 165 years after the company was founded, innovation is still a cornerstone of its success. P&G invests $2 billion in research and development annually (more than $5 million every day) and has a research force of more than 7,500 employees worldwide. This significant R&D investment delivers results: P&G holds more than 28,000 patents globally. However, just as creating leading products to improve the lives of consumers is a key priority of the company, P&G has come to realize that managing the intellectual property (IP) and I-stuff that lead to these innovations is equally vital.

CHANGING A CORPORATE CULTURE

Historically, as the company became bigger, reaching annual sales growth targets became more challenging. New sources of innovation, as well as deriving greater return on investment, became paramount. P&G Chief Technology Officer Gil Cloyd recognized the great potential for technology transfer early on. He explains, "With such a strong R&D commitment, there are naturally many promising technologies that will never see their way into an actual P&G product. These intangibles—whether they are patented technologies, ideas, or know-how—represent a huge potential for P&G in terms of both income and future product development."

Changing a corporate culture is a lofty challenge, particularly for older companies with deeper roots. For more than a century, P&G closely managed its intellectual assets to ensure its stronghold in various consumer product sectors. Patented new technologies increased the company's portfolio, and many contributed to new and better products, but most were not commercialized because they were not aligned with P&G's core strategy. "These patents—as well as the accompanying know-how—languished indefinitely. They not only didn't make money for the company, they were a financial liability," said Cloyd.

Under A.G. Lafley, P&G's president and CEO, the need to lead change and focus relentlessly on winning with the consumer by delivering superior value became standard at P&G. As A.G. Lafley said in 2001 in an address to R&D new hires, "We're making the choices required to accelerate top and bottom line growth over the long term: making choices about what to do and what not to do. We're choosing where to play and how to win."

"The inevitability of change and the need to lead it, not react to it, is one of the things I believe in most strongly. One of the distinguishing characteristics of great institutions is that they have an enduring capacity for renewal. P&G is a great institution and we are continuing to change for a simple purpose—to be a more innovative company, more focused than ever on global brand leadership, and even better positioned to win in the global marketplace."

The Promise of Intellectual Assets

Over time it became more and more evident that intellectual assets held greater promise than just the products they were destined to deliver. Technology, know-how, and even the people who conceived them constituted a promising but virtually untapped revenue stream for P&G. As a consequence, several leaders from P&G's R&D organization put forward the proposal that additional value could be derived beyond the simple commercialization of intellectual assets in P&G products. In fact, other companies would gladly pay to use P&G's innovations. Out of this realization, P&G's External Business Development (EBD) organization was born.

Opening P&G's vault has been an evolutionary process. Jeff Weedman, P&G Vice-President of EBD, has seen this transformation first hand. "For decades, P&G was on the defense, carefully guarding secrets through patents and firewalls to the outside. We would occasionally look to the outside for resources to create or improve our products, but only in a limited circle—usually suppliers or universities that we had a research relationship with. And we certainly would never dream of sharing our own innovations with external companies," he said.

"Today our culture is different. External focus is integrated across the company. Everyone from business managers to scientists to external relations [people] continually looks for ways to create value by finding external capabilities that can drive our businesses and [by] extending our intellectual property to others. It is not just a strategy, it is a mindset."

How They Did It

In the 1990s, P&G accelerated its intellectual asset management program by creating an internal Global Licensing group of five managers, led by Weedman, whose sole purpose was to mine and optimize P&G's vast patent portfolio. In doing so, the company realized the significant cost savings of trimming its patent maintenance fees. It soon became clear that strategic management of its IP had profit as well as cost-saving potential. Initial successes, such as the licensing of a proprietary calcium technology to Tropicana, allowed the group to cover their costs in less than two years. The P&G Global Licensing initiative had effectively underscored the importance of further exploring what value was hidden within company walls.

In 1999 P&G went a step further by declaring itself "open for business." It announced a "three- to five-year rule" stating that any technology would eventually be available for sale or license—even to a competitor. Still in effect, the internal rule states that all P&G technologies default to licensing consideration three years after first in-market introduction, or five years after the patent has been issued. It allows P&G a period of exclusivity but ensures that promising innovations won't be nursed indefinitely. It also allows P&G to realize a financial benefit from its research investment, even if a technology does not make it to store shelves as a P&G product. The three- to five-year rule was a turning point for P&G culture. It signified that not all innovations had to be put into P&G products for their value to be realized; there are other legitimate ways to extract value from technology.

At the same time that P&G was establishing its licensing program, the landscape for Intellectual Property management was changing externally, as well. Books like *Edison in the Boardroom*[1] had brought greater awareness and legitimacy to this type of endeavor. More and more companies were awakening to the benefits of IP portfolio value extraction.

---

[1] J. Davis and S. Harrison, *Edison in the Boardroom* (New York: John Wiley & Sons, Inc., 2001).

Because of the recognized upside potential, P&G continued to refine its organization and practice. Senior management announced that profits from external arrangements, such as licensing, would flow back to the global business unit that had created the technology or facilitated the licensing deal, rather than to Global Licensing, as had been the case previously. In addition, P&G Global Licensing changed its name to External Business Development to reflect its expanding mission and brought in additional staff to service internal customer needs.

"The culture changed almost overnight," explains Weedman. "There just hadn't been enough incentive to identify technologies that would be better commercialized or licensed elsewhere. In fact, it wasn't even top-of-mind to more than a select few. Opening our company doors required a completely different way of thinking, and it began at the top. Permitting business units to optimize underutilized technology to improve their bottom line was critical. Now we use a concerted IAM strategy integrated across all businesses not only to make the most of our intellectual assets, but also to help shape corporate strategy."

EBD became a company moniker synonymous with value extraction. Some business units positioned their own staff within EBD to help identify profitable opportunities and to further the business unit's skill-set. EBD was no longer solely about reactive or even proactive patent management; indeed, it was no longer just about patents. Today, EBD works closely with internal customers to determine their needs and to facilitate the use of external assets to meet them.

In addition, A.G. Lafley wanted every aspect of P&G to be more externally focused: "I want us to be the absolute best at spotting, developing, and leveraging relationships with best-in-class partners in every part of our business. In fact, I want P&G to be a magnet for the best-in-class—the company they most want to work with because they know a partnership with P&G will be more rewarding than any other option."

Moving the Technology Forward

"Creating a revenue stream from P&G's technologies is no longer our sole consideration. We also help to move technologies forward by working with external sources. There has been a palpable shift in how our business units see this external sourcing. Before, there was a pervasive 'not invented here' syndrome; this has shifted to a recognition that technologies and solutions can be 'proudly found elsewhere,'" said Steve Baggott, Director, EBD. "If P&G is seeking a technology that does not fall within our core competencies or can be found elsewhere more quickly and more economically, it only makes sense to source it externally. The result is a better product that has been created faster and cheaper than if we had produced it in-house from beginning to end."

Such coordination led to a landmark joint venture to launch new products in plastic bags, wraps, and containers—revolutionary in that the partnership married two long-time competitors.

As one of the world's leading experts in the high-speed manipulation of film in diaper and feminine hygiene products, P&G was developing promising plastic film technologies. After years of development, P&G test-marketed a revolutionary new plastic food wrap under the name Impress. The wrap utilized millions of food-safe adhesive-coated microscopic dimples to adhere to surfaces, such as cookware, rather than needing to stick to itself, as do less effective conventional plastic wraps. Test market results for the wrap were very promising: The wrap rose to number one, even though there was a significant price premium and competitors had defended aggressively. At the same time P&G was continuing to hone its proprietary ForceFlex™ technology. ForceFlex is a new type of flexible elastic film that gets stronger as it is stretched. An outgrowth of research on diapers, ForceFlex was a natural for use in garbage bags.

Both technologies showed great potential. However, P&G realized that the marketplace was already dominated by companies well established in the plastic film business and knew that it would be costly to establish P&G's brand equity in this category. Furthermore, P&G did not intend to establish an extensive category presence.

Rather than allowing the technologies to die on the vine, P&G packaged all the patents, equipment, related know-how, and test marketing results and shopped the technologies around.

"We had a strong package, since one of the technologies had already been successfully test marketed," said Weedman, who marketed the film technologies to other companies. "We took the portfolio to all of the current category leaders, some international interests, and even some players who were not in the plastic wrap business. We even had an internal bid—a P&G business unit that was interested in finishing the development and commercializing the technologies. It was a close call, but ultimately it came down to economics: How can we get the best return on our investment? And since we ultimately retained a stake in the business, we also had to consider: who can get the products to market faster?"

Ultimately, it was The Clorox Company, maker of Glad® products, which showed the most interest. Rather than license the technology, P&G and Clorox entered into a joint venture that launched two groundbreaking new products in less than two years.

Although Clorox had a great established brand and excellent go-to-market ability, P&G was able to bring more than just plastic wrap technologies to the joint venture. The exclusive use of a range of current and future patents, trademarks, and proprietary technologies that have application in the plastic bags, wraps, and containers business was also included.

"P&G channels all of our related innovations to the joint venture, which not only allows P&G to retain a stake in the technology but also saves resources, as we no longer have to run an auction for technologies in this sector," said Weedman.

P&G also made available approximately 20 full-time employees dedicated to the Glad business. Clorox supplies all additional personnel and manufacturing equipment and contributes its Glad bag, container, and wrap business.

"This joint venture combines the power of the Glad brand and organization with Procter & Gamble's strong R&D capabilities," said Benno Dorer, Vice-President-General Manager, Glad Products Division. "By collaborating on the many innovative technologies that P&G brings to the joint venture, we've already launched two great new products that have quickly become huge in-market successes. Together, we have taken the Glad business further than we could have without the partnership—we have brought products to market more quickly, and consumers, retailers, and our shareholders benefit from it greatly."

Although P&G did not compete with Clorox in the plastic film business, it is a staunch competitor in other sectors including water purification, surface cleaners, and the cleaning mop business. This presented challenges in forming the joint venture, but neither side saw these as insurmountable.

One primary hurdle was simply how to maintain an appropriate firewall for both sides, so that neither company would inadvertently communicate proprietary information. P&G sent two senior employees to help lead the Glad business from the Clorox headquarters in Oakland—employees who had the knowledge and experience to ensure that only appropriate information was exchanged. In addition, P&G asked a member of its senior management to be on the Glad joint venture Board of Directors.

"Having a senior executive involved sent a clear message that this initiative was an important priority for the company. P&G employees think and act like owners, so it was important that they saw our commitment to making this work," Weedman said.

Following on the heels of Glad Press 'n Seal® wrap, the Glad joint venture launched Glad ForceFlex trash bags just one year later, using another technology that P&G has brought to the relationship.

Today the Glad brand has increased its market share in both the trash bag and food wrap categories. Because of its profitability, P&G increased its interest in the Glad joint venture from 10 to 20 percent of the global Glad business, the maximum allowed under the agreement.

"This is a terrific example of balancing each company's capabilities and strengths. By combining forces we were able to move the product to market faster and begin seeing a return on our joint venture sooner. This partnership was significant for another reason. It told the world not only that P&G is open for business but that P&G realizes there are different ways of doing business," said Weedman.

Ready for a Joint Venture?

1. **The upside economic potential is huge.** Don't enter into joint venture on simple, run-of-the mill ideas. Think "groundbreaking."
2. **The cultures of both organizations are compatible.** This can be tricky if potential partners are competitors. However, P&G and Clorox share core values, a similar vision on going to market, an emphasis on the consumer, and a focus on building brands that provide superior performance and value.
3. **The venture will be supported internally.** Early on, P&G had the strong support of both the CEO and CFO. In addition, positioning P&G employees within the joint venture brought it "home"—rather than having it seen as an isolated deal in California. It sent the message to employee-owners that the joint venture was a part of P&G.

"CONNECT + DEVELOP"

Following on the success of initiatives such as the Glad joint venture, P&G has made an even greater commitment to seeking external sources to develop products better, cheaper, and faster than if they were solely developed internally. As part of its "Connect + Develop" strategy, P&G announced its goal of accessing 50 percent of new ideas, technologies, and products from external sources. A.G. Lafley issued a challenge to the company. He said, "Historically, over 90 percent of our innovations have come from inside our own organization. I want to see 50 percent or more coming from external partnerships. I honestly believe we can increase our innovative capacity fivefold by collaborating more effectively with external partners. I want to create an environment in which there is an open market for ideas, for capital, and for talent. More specifically, an environment in which big ideas can attract the capital and talent they need on the strength of the idea itself no matter where it comes from." As of this writing, P&G has achieved approximately 35 percent of its in-market innovations from external sources, up from about 10 percent in 2000.

"Connect + Develop" is about extending P&G's capability to develop and commercialize innovations whether they originate within our walls or not. Through Web-based consulting resources we have extended P&G's R&D force from 7,500 scientists to hundreds of thousands," explains Larry Huston, Vice-President, R&D, Innovation and Knowledge in charge of "Connect + Develop." "This accelerates the work of our own scientists and helps P&G bring more innovations to the market that truly meet the needs of the world's consumers."

A key element in the "Connect + Develop" strategy is effectively utilizing the Internet to match technical needs with the right innovators around the world who have technology solutions and "ready-to-go" products that P&G can utilize.

In 1999 P&G joined a select group of other Fortune 100 companies as an initial investor in *yet2.com*. Based in Cambridge, Massachusetts, *yet2.com* provides intellectual property consultancy and licensing services to world-class international clients. *yet2.com* and its online marketplace promote technology licensing and transfer. Its clientele consists of over one-fourth of the Fortune 1000. *yet2.com* draws on its global network of technology leaders in thousands of companies across all industries, to establish productive dialogs quickly. In addition to being an investor, P&G has utilized *yet2.com* services for both bringing in and taking out technologies. This has resulted in profitable connections that otherwise might not have been made.

P&G also utilizes the resources of NineSigma, Inc., a leading company in the field of innovation sourcing. NineSigma provides the methodology and infrastructure for linking companies with outside technology in a wide range of scientific fields. NineSigma has Ph.D.-level program managers that both search and proactively solicit technological solutions for its clients.

"Web-based resources such as *yet2.com*, NineSigma, and InnoCentive link research and development worldwide across technologies, across companies, across geographies. It is important in such an interconnected world to map yourself to the right people who complement your capabilities. As a result, a new dynamic has emerged: Know *who* is as important as know *how*," said Baggott.

Accelovation

P&G has collaborated with outside partners for generations—but the importance of these alliances has never been greater. Searching the World Wide Web to identify and connect with the talents and technologies of today's most prepared minds can be a daunting task. However, with the help of a company called Accelovation, they've found an effective way to scour the Internet for everything from consumer insights to radical new technologies in P&G categories.

Accelovation is a high-tech startup that is leading the creation of a new generation of tools to understand markets. Accelovation was started in 2003 when the founders recognized that current approaches to monetizing IP are highly inefficient, manual, and costly. Often businesses today face challenges in identifying market opportunities, knowing how best to exploit portfolios of existing inventions, and knowing how to reach beyond their company boundaries to understand broad innovation landscapes. Accelovation's solution is a search-based approach that extracts key market insights from online data and transforms the Internet into an organized, actionable decision-making tool for IP and business professionals.

"Accelovation has condensed the billions of pages of text contained in the Internet into portfolios of technologies and market assessments that have allowed P&G project teams to quickly focus on relevant Web pages rather than wading through the millions of 'hits' one usually gets when searching the Web. It's an amazing search tool," remarked Baggott.

Mining Know-How

P&G continues to move up the evolutionary spectrum of intellectual asset management. They have realized the value of patent and trademark management, from both cost savings and profit perspectives. They've reveled in the value created through joint partnerships, as well as the products and product improvements made available by bringing in external resources. They have seen the profits from licensing technologies and brand names. The millennium marked another milestone: mining the value of P&G's greatest asset, its know-how.

"At P&G, we've always prided ourselves on the superior products we provide to improve consumers' lives. These are tangible items, as are the technologies that go into them," Weedman explained. "But we've always been equally proud of our organization—not just what we do, but how we do it. We have great minds with great ideas. These assets—the intangible ones—are equally responsible for making P&G what it is today. So why not try to extract value from them as well?"

Reliability Engineering

Another cultural advance was in store for the consumer products giant. In order to realize value from its nontangible intellectual assets, P&G would have to codify and systematize ideas—making tangibles out of intangibles. One of its first great successes was codifying and marketing a proprietary process known as Reliability Engineering.

In the 1990s, in an effort to improve manufacturing quality and drive down cost, P&G product supply built up a suite of tools and methodologies. Developed in conjunction with scientists at Los Alamos National Laboratory and the early work of W. Edwards Deming, Reliability Engineering involves the analysis and prediction of failures—when and how they occur—to increase manufacturing productivity. By 2002, Reliability Engineering had saved P&G more than $1 billion worldwide. For example, it helped P&G transform manufacturing efficiencies in a range of assembly lines that make consumer products ranging from diapers to fruit juice. In P&G's Atlanta fruit drink bottling plant, productivity rose by 44 percent. Given its wide range of application across industries, Reliability Engineering held great potential for other corporations as well.

P&G's first Reliability Engineering pilot project with an external company showed that it indeed held great promise. The pilot project proved that the tools were applicable outside P&G and that they could result in significant savings for other companies as well. However, P&G had provided the pilot company with strong internal support to help implement Reliability Engineering, support that P&G could not replicate on a large scale.

P&G entered into an exclusive agreement with BearingPoint Inc. (formerly KPMG Consulting) to market the Reliability Engineering supply chain solution under the name PowerFactor, marrying P&G's manufacturing expertise with BearingPoint's consulting ability to take solutions into the marketplace. "PowerFactor helps manufacturers across a wide range of businesses increase productivity, make prudent capital investments, and increase production without sacrificing quality. It dramatically improves a company's ability to fix what's worth fixing and take the resulting savings directly to the bottom line," said Mary Anne Gale, Vice-President, Global Supply Chain Operations for P&G.

Each PowerFactor customer is treated individually, receiving only the methodologies from the toolkit that apply to them. The client company is given an estimate for how much they can save and also how much it will cost to license its customized toolkit from P&G. BearingPoint provides marketing, implementation, and customer support—and it shares licensing revenue with P&G. Since its launch in 2002, PowerFactor has been commercialized in a broad spectrum of industries, including transportation, utilities, retail grocery, and commercial products. These industries have saved a cumulative $150 million, with over $25 million of that coming from capital avoidance. P&G realized an unexpected benefit: As PowerFactor improved over time through its use in other companies and industries, P&G actually found more internal applications for the toolkit they had originally created.

"PowerFactor is a significant move for P&G for many reasons. Obviously, it paid off for our own manufacturing business, saving more than a billion dollars. But this process intended to *save* money now *makes* money, too. Most important, we now see the value of codifying and marketing our know-how. People will pay for our ideas," said Mike Hock, founder of P&G's Know-How commercialization practice.

Indeed, P&G continues to find value in know-how across many areas of the company. P&G has always been known for its keen awareness of the consumer, the result of decades of best-in-class market research. In 2004, P&G announced that it had granted an exclusive license of its proprietary "Gen-3" consumer behavior model and "Virtual Launch" new-product testing method to BASES, the leading global provider of simulated test marketing services. BASES is incorporating the model and methodology into its forecasting model and is leveraging its experience in new-product forecasting to improve the "Virtual Launch," ultimately supplying it back to P&G for its marketing needs. In the end, both sides are ahead: BASES improves its own ability to evaluate and optimize new product initiatives, and P&G's promising methodology ("Virtual Launch") is being further developed by an entity for which development is a core competency, making the methodology ready for P&G's use faster than if it had finished development internally.

"In time, the market research technologies accelerated through our partnership with BASES will be available to the general marketplace as well as P&G. By combining P&G innovations with external expertise, our ideas not only help ourselves—they help raise the bar for the industry," said Kim Dedeker, Vice-President, Global Consumer & Market Knowledge.

In their effort to mine for company gold, P&G has uncovered yet another underutilized asset: its retirees. P&G is well known for the quality of its employees, the best and brightest. They are given the formal and on-the-job training that shapes their professional careers. Also, because P&G is predominantly a promote-from-within company, employees think and act as owners, finding solutions, improving processes, and instituting positive changes in their respective functions. The challenge is how to tap into this valuable human capital after retirement.

In 2003 P&G was a founding member of YourEncore, a retiree services company that recruits highly experienced retirees from R&D disciplines and makes them available to member companies to solve technical problems on a time-bound, short-term basis. The arrangement allows retirees to work on their own terms, but taps into the great minds that were developed through years of training and experience within P&G walls. YourEncore is open to technical and engineering retirees from other companies, as well.

"YourEncore gives P&G the opportunity to draw on the skills of our own experienced retired scientists and allows access to talented technical retirees from other companies who are often able to share new insights and experiences," said P&G Chief Technology Officer Gil Cloyd.

THE VALUE OF EMPLOYEES

P&G also realizes the value of its current employees, in terms of their contribution to the business and also the need to allow continued professional growth. For example, one benchmark arrangement transferred all IT infrastructure work and many P&G IT experts to Hewlett-Packard (HP). This highly structured partnership ensures that P&G employees get the opportunity to work and grow in a company for which their expertise is a core competency, whereas P&G gets the benefit of the employees' knowledge and experience, enabling HP to deliver better service for lower cost.

This partnership also strongly positions P&G to execute its goal of tapping external innovation. By transferring non-core work to a partner company, P&G can maintain its focus on its core business, while still ensuring that, through its partners, it will continue to grow and innovate in areas that remain key in keeping the operational aspects of the business on the cutting edge, ensuring efficiency, delivering maximum results, and providing the lowest possible costs.

P&G's ten-year partnership with HP is the largest of four such key P&G relationships. Also included are IBM, for employee services support, Jones Lang LaSalle, for facilities management, and an additional contract with HP for Transaction Accounts Payable.

"These partnerships deliver three main strategic wins for P&G," said Linda Clement-Holmes, General Manager of Information and Decision Solutions and Global Business Services Governance.

"They let us focus on making premium products for our consumers, without sacrificing innovation in IT and other business support areas. They also allow us to save on costs, while increasing service. And, they ensure that our employees' expertise continues to grow, while still benefiting the company."

P&G also realizes the value of its current employees by providing their expertise to help improve the services of external contractors for "backroom" functions that are not core competencies for the company. For example, an arrangement that created an exclusive IT contract with HP included transferring P&G IT experts to the HP payroll. The employees get the opportunity to work in a company for which their expertise is a core competency, P&G gets the benefit of the employees' knowledge and experience, and HP is able to deliver better service for lower cost.

P&G employees have long been encouraged to "think outside the box." Now the corporation itself is thinking and looking outside its *walls*—searching for atypical arrangements, for new types of partnerships, and for new ways of extracting value from its assets.

Today, intellectual asset management drives P&G corporate strategy across all business units. The pendulum has made a full swing from the early years of defending secrets to an integrated model of sharing resources both internally and externally. Through thoughtful and open-minded management of its diverse assets—from trademarks to patents to know-how to its people—P&G is setting a course for its future and for the consumer products industry that it leads.

APPENDIX A

HOW COUNTRIES AND REGIONS ARE HELPING THEIR COMPANIES CREATE VALUE FROM INTELLECTUAL CAPITAL

By Gordon McConnachie

Gordon McConnachie is Chairman of the Board of Scottish Intellectual Asset Management Centre. His credentials may be reviewed at: *www.gmcconachie.com.*

INTRODUCTION

Across the globe there is a growing realization among many business leaders, CEOs, and owners of small and medium-sized enterprises that there is latent value within the intellectual capital (IC) of most companies.[1] Much of this intrinsic value is not fully exploited, yet this does not have to be the case, as major companies such as Dow Chemical (in the United States), IBM (in the United States), Neste (in Finland), NXT (in the United Kingdom), and Skandia (in Sweden) have shown us.

The ground rules and best practices for creating and extracting value from an IC base have been developed, refined, and reported over the past two decades, mostly in Europe and North America.[2] The early pioneers in the field

In putting together this paper I acknowledge the assistance and advice of the following people, who kindly took the time to discuss aspects of this subject: Greg Allan, Daan Andriessen, Chiew Yu Sarn, Brendan Coady, Calum Davidson, Tim Hoad, Melvyn Ingleson, Khor Aik Lam, Alan Lung, Ian McCoull, Rob McLean, Geoffrey Oldham, Waltraut Ritter, Iain Russell, Caroline Sincock, Marien van den Boom, Audrey Yap, and others too numerous to mention and to whom I offer my sincere apologies for omitting them from this list. All provided excellent assistance and advice, and any errors or misinterpretations are solely my responsibility. I particularly wish to acknowledge the roles in relation to the IA Centre in Scotland played by Caroline Sincock in coming up with the concept; by Janet Brown, Ian McCoull, Greg Allan, and Calum Davidson for their commitment in bringing the concept to life; and by Wendy Alexander, who as Minister for Enterprise, Transport and Lifelong Learning in the Scottish Executive at the time had the vision to fund the initiative.

[1]Intellectual capital is the knowledge within an organization that has the potential to create value.

[2]Patrick H. Sullivan, *Profiting from Intellectual Capital* (New York: John Wiley & Sons, Inc., 1998).

are well known and essentially fall into two categories: far-sighted individuals and far-sighted large companies that saw and seized on the opportunities presented by those far-sighted individuals. At first, only a patchwork of larger companies benefited from their application of sharp IC management tools. There was little penetration into the core industrial base of society, and most of the innovations in this field took place in industry, not in academic circles.

Today, in our changing world, this first paradigm in the application of intellectual capital management is altering before our eyes. These two events, our changing world and the proliferation of sharp IC management techniques, are related; in this appendix it is my intent to shed some light on why the paradigm is changing to include companies of all sizes that apply and benefit from these techniques, why governments and academia are becoming increasingly interested and involved, why this is becoming an increasingly global phenomenon, and why the end result of this activity is a powerful business tool that complements the business process. It is, in fact, part of the business process, as companies seek to compete and grow in the developing global knowledge-based economy.

Consequences of the Knowledge-Based Economy

The developing global knowledge-based economy and its consequences for how businesses create value are the principal catalysts of a new awareness of the potential benefits that sharp IC management can deliver. The global knowledge-based economy has been described by Houghton as "emerging from two defining forces: the rise in *knowledge intensity* of economic activities and the increasing *globalisation* of economic affairs.[3] The rise in knowledge intensity is being driven by the combined forces of the IT revolution and the increasing pace of technological change. Globalization is being driven by national and international deregulation, and by the IT-related communications revolution. However, it is important to note that the term 'global knowledge-based economy' refers to the overall economic structure that is emerging, not to any one phenomenon, or to any combination of phenomena."

This knowledge intensity combined with greater ease in trading over the surface of the globe quite simply changes the rules of doing business. Competition

[3]John W. Houghton, "The Global Knowledge Economy," Support Paper #1, Centre for Strategic Economic Studies, Victoria University, Melbourne, Australia. This outline draws on J. W. Houghton and P. J. Sheehan, *A Primer on the Knowledge Economy* (Melbourne: Centre for Strategic Economic studies, 2000); and P. J. Sheehan and G. Tegart, eds., *Working for the Future: Technology and Employment in the Global Knowledge Economy* (Melbourne, Australia: Victoria University Press, 1998).

can now be more intense and immediate, and the knowledge component required to provide a business solution will often be more important. There are underlying basic requirements for a society to perform well in a knowledge-based economy, the most significant of which are access to appropriate education and lifelong learning, access to high-speed Internet, and a culture that encourages entrepreneurial skills, agility in conducting business, and a mindset that encompasses both traditional business values based on assets and the developing business values based on value streams. There are also underlying enablers that encourage the growth of a knowledge-based society: A significant enabler is an awareness and understanding of how to work the intangible assets in a company, especially the non-intellectual property (IP) intangible assets, in order to create and extract value—in other words, an awareness of sharp IC management techniques.

In any given society, important factors that affect economic growth in the context of the developing knowledge-based economy are the existing basic requirements and key enablers just described and the development of these into the future. It is therefore self-evident that many countries have considered what is required to be done and have addressed the issue of obtaining a critical mass in these skills as one of the means of ensuring the well-being of society. For these reasons, several countries are now pursuing the benefits of effective IC management along business lines and on a national scale, and they are doing so in very different ways.

THE ROLE FOR REGIONS AND COUNTRIES

Regions and countries can play an important role in informing and counseling their companies, especially small and medium-sized companies, about how to identify, develop, and use their intangible (knowledge) assets to create more profit or value. The span of possible activity stretches all the way from simply providing information, to active counseling and diagnosis, signposting, approving reputable providers of skilled consultation, and finally to providing financial support to develop the business both at home and abroad.

Several countries and regions are today the first movers in helping their local companies understand and take advantage of the opportunities to increase the value of knowledge in conducting business. The text that follows briefly describes what specific countries have achieved and is not intended to be a complete and comprehensive review.

National and cultural factors clearly play a role. In countries in which R&D activity is heavily funded by public money, through universities, institutes, and national laboratories, it is important to commercialize new technologies in order to obtain a return on their investment. In many countries, unlike in the United States, the bulk of the companies receiving public funds are small and medium-sized enterprises whose knowledge assets represent an often untapped lever for enhancing job creation and the quality of jobs within the country. In countries that do not possess a labor cost advantage, the so-called high-cost economies, it is imperative to find a way to differentiate their offerings in order to compete globally: squeezing value out of intangible knowledge assets is one way to achieve this. However, this route is also available to the low-cost economies, as low cost does not necessarily imply low skill.

In fact, the combination of low cost and a high skill base in certain industries can result in a significant competitive advantage. Therefore it can be argued that for developing large economies like China and India, or for companies with a significant knowledge base in any low-cost country, investing in IC management and rigorously applying the results can be a significant best practice and competitive advantage on a global scale.

SNAPSHOTS OF SOME COUNTRIES THAT HAVE INVESTED IN ICM

In these snapshots I look first at countries that have put together a coherent program to encourage their companies to incorporate intellectual capital management (ICM), the management of the intangible knowledge base, into their business activity. Among those countries, which I have chosen to call The Performers, are Scotland and Singapore.

Second, I mention a few countries or regions in which elements are in place to support companies in working their knowledge base but in which a coherent national policy is not yet apparent, or may not need to be if the underlying economic culture and support structure is vibrant enough. These regions and countries include North America, the Arab nations, the European Union, China, Denmark, India, Japan, Germany, South Korea, Sweden, Taiwan, the Netherlands, and the United Kingdom. I call these The Developers.

The Performers: Scotland and Singapore

Scotland has taken a deliberate look at what is required to remain competitive in the current global economy and has taken several steps which show not only a clear thought process but also a commitment to convert the roadmap resulting from this process into action.

Scotland is a small country located on the northwestern fringes of Europe with a population of about 5 million[4] and a GDP per capita of U.S. $27,700.[5] As part of the United Kingdom, Scotland occupies the 11th position in the World Economic Forum Global Competitivity Index for 2004.[6]

Scotland is somewhat equipped for the global knowledge-based economy in that educational standards and broadband accessibility are high; however, the entrepreneurial spirit is not as strong a component of society as it needs to be. Having formed a clear and realistic assessment of the present situation, the government and the development agencies in Scotland have developed a suite of measures that address the current opportunities.

In relation to the opportunities that flow from a sharper management of the knowledge base, the groundwork is contained in a blueprint for a society designed to be smarter, with the aim of remaining successful in a changing world. Out of this roadmap flowed the creation of ITI Scotland, institutes designed to harness the fundamental research skills, which are recognized as a national asset, and convert some of them into new high-technology companies on the ground. This roadmap also confirmed the initiative already under way under the banner "Proof of Concept Fund" to stimulate inventors and innovators separately to bring their ideas to market. Market failures were also recognized, including an honest admission that, just as in most countries, most business people had insufficient knowledge of the role intellectual assets could play in the future of their business: As a result, the Intellectual Asset Centre was set up. Future issues of concern include how the value contained in discoveries of all sorts in technical and nontechnical fields can better be factored into the decision process that funding agencies operate; how a value in context can best be placed on developing technologies, including a consideration of the probability of success; and how the nation as a whole can be mobilized to make the most of the time window opportunity provided by the developing world economy.

In April 1999, the Scottish Office produced a report addressing the fact that Scotland could no longer compete in the modern marketplace on the basis of a low-cost, low-skills workforce. The report set the direction for the subsequent initiatives directed toward making Scotland fit to compete more effectively in the world economy.[7] The intent brought to the surface in this report was translated into action through the concept of a "Smart, Successful Scotland," which

---

[4]National Statistics UK, www.statistics.gov.uk/cci/nugget.asp?id=6.

[5]*World Facts and Figures*, www.worldfactsandfigures.com/gdp_country_desc.php.

[6]"Global Competitivity Ranking for 2004," World Economic Forum, www.weforum.org/pdf/Gcr/Growth_Competitiveness_Index_2003_Comparisons.

grew within the country over the next few years and was encapsulated by a *Scottish Executive* report in November 2004.[8] The thrust of creating such a Scotland concentrates on the promotion of enterprise: on business growth and on the skills of individuals underpinning such growth. Subsequent initiatives have been driven by these premises.

Some of the steps taken in the last few years to boost innovation and the leveraging of knowledge assets have been the launching of ITI Scotland, the creation of the Proof of Concept Fund, and the decision to create an Intellectual Assets Centre for Scotland. The key intermediaries in conceiving and delivering these programs are the two Scottish development agencies Scottish Enterprise and The Highlands and Island Enterprise Network.[9]

ITI Scotland was created in 2003 to fund breakthrough technology developments in specific niches of the energy, life sciences, and tech-media sectors with a view toward exposing high-growth companies to new research and helping them to grow and expand on technical platforms.[10] Many of the components the institutes seek to foster are already in place: Scotland's innovation and academic reputations are world class. The institutes are designed to provide a strong link between fundamental research and company formation by funding and developing specific new technologies, which will then be positioned in the Scottish economy through startup companies, license, sale, or some other form of transaction. The funding level for this project is £450 million (U.S. $800 million) over a 10-year period.

The Proof of Concept Fund was established in 2000 to help researchers take their ideas and inventions out of the lab and develop them commercially into groundbreaking Scottish businesses: The fund is backed up by a suite of support activities provided through the Enterprise Network.[11] There have been six funding rounds to date, with the following categories available for funding: life sciences, microelectronics, food and drink, optoelectronics, digital media and creative industries, communications technologies, forest industries, tourism,

---

[7]*Scotland: Towards the Knowledge Economy. The Report of the Knowledge Economy Task Force*, Scottish Office, April 12, 1999.

[8]"A Smart, Successful Scotland: Strategic Direction to the Enterprise Networks and an Enterprise Strategy for Scotland," *The Scottish Executive* (November 2004); The Scottish Executive, *The Devolved Government for Scotland*, www.scotland.gov.uk/Home.

[9]Scottish Enterprise, www.scottish-enterprise.com; The Highlands and Islands Enterprise Network, www.hie.co.uk.

[10]ITI Scotland, www.itiscotland.com.

[11]Proof of Concept Fund, www.scottish-enterprise.com/sedotcom_home/sig/academics/proofofconcept.htm.

and energy. The program currently supports 172 groundbreaking projects worth over £28 million (U.S. $50 million) and in its first five years created more than 400 new jobs.

As the work described above was undertaken, it became clear that Scotland's companies needed to address a further issue. Companies knew very little about the threats and opportunities available through the use of IP, and they knew even less about their non-IP IC. A baseline study confirmed that there was a perceived need for a service to inform and coach Scottish companies about how to understand and use their intangible knowledge base in order to compete in the knowledge-based economy. Companies also needed to be directed toward reputable bodies capable of providing sound consultancy on issues that required attention. It must be said that most countries, if not all, would find a similar result if a baseline study were carried out: The difference is that Scotland actually did the work and acted on the results.

In 2003 Scotland created the Scottish National Intellectual Assets Centre (the IA Centre) to respond to these defined needs.[12] The Centre brings together in one place a range of expertise to help organizations realize their potential through managing their intellectual assets. Its charter is to deal mostly with the recorded assets of an organization that have a potential to create value; however, this cannot be done without considering the non-IA forms of IC as well, in other words the ephemeral and nonrecorded assets that are often vital to value creation.

As the organization's official publications describe, "The IA Centre is a first, in Scotland and indeed in Europe—a unique center to assist businesses in deriving value from their IA. Supported by the Scottish Executive, the Centre was developed in response to the demand from businesses to learn more about their IA. Initial studies showed that, despite the number of businesses asking for advice, there were still many more that were not aware (that they needed it or that it was available). Moreover, the value of unexploited IA lying in Scottish companies was judged to be several billion pounds sterling!"

Although the IA Centre has been in operation and fully staffed for only a short time, it represents Scotland's commitment to becoming and remaining a smart and successful country. Its focus is on Scotland, but it is also cooperating with similar developing centers in Europe and around the world. With annual spending of less than £1.5 million (U.S. $2.6 million) the Center represents a prudent yet far-sighted investment in the future. The initiatives Scotland has

---

[12]The IA Centre, www.ia-centre.org.uk.

taken are clearly driven by a desire for economic development, enhanced competitiveness, and improved living standards.

Singapore is a small country situated in the heart of Southeast Asia: It has a population of about 4 million and a GDP per capita of U.S. $23,700, figures very similar to those of Scotland.[13] Singapore, however, occupies the seventh position in the World Economic Forum Global Competitivity Index for 2004. Its small, open economy, although modern and internationally competitive, is nevertheless vulnerable to external shocks because the value of its exports is much larger than its GDP, and about two-thirds of its industrial output is exported. The government of Singapore has taken some well-thought-out and deliberate steps to safeguard living standards, built up by this country over the past 50 years, and in fact runs its economy in a manner similar to that of a large corporation.

Singapore is well equipped for the global knowledge-based economy in that educational standards and broadband accessibility are high and the entrepreneurial spirit is a strong component of society. Raising an awareness of the role played by IP and non-IP assets in the growth of profitability and value for companies is also part of the strategy that has been adopted. Singapore has chosen to start with IP and develop its support strategy from this base.

The task of promoting awareness of IP is being undertaken by the Intellectual Property Office of Singapore (IPOS).[14] Going beyond the traditional role of IP regulator, IPOS has actively tied the basic lessons in this field to business practice and driving IP tactics to fulfil the business strategy. In recent years, a stronger emphasis has been put on incorporating the knowledge assets into this argument, and the concept of IA management is a developing theme today in Singapore.

The Infrastructure Development Division of IPOS makes the link between IP and the development of businesses and is charged with supporting local business through both the creation and protection of IP and the noninfringement of IP belonging to others. This long-term engagement of IPOS has produced a suite of support activities and tools. The IP Consult program permits local businesses to attend monthly open consultation events at which issues related to IP can be discussed with a qualified IP attorney and consultants. The SurfIP Web portal has been developed to allow direct access to information and search facilities for all aspects of IP and is the first in a set of measures IPOS is putting in place to help businesses move up the value ladder; it is also the first step toward extending the support provided for IP to the entire intangible

---

[13]*Statistics Singapore,* http://www.singstat.gov.sg/keystats/mqstats/indicators.html#population.

[14]Intellectual Property Office of Singapore, www.ipos.gov.sg.

knowledge base.[15] The SurfIP portal lists a Singapore network of IP providers in various fields: This is an indication of the stage of development of IP and IC management in the Singapore marketplace.

Moving beyond awareness, in January 2003 Singapore launched the Singapore IP Academy, which was intended to be the focal point of education and research in the field of IP. The IP Academy aims to broaden and deepen knowledge and capabilities in IP creation, protection, exploitation, and management. As knowledge and innovation become key factors in boosting a nation's economic progress, the value of IP will become critical. The IP Academy will play a key role in Singapore's development into an IP hub.[16]

Once awareness is created, the next step is for businesses to integrate IC management practices. IPOS and the IP Academy are developing value-added tools and programs to help companies use their intellectual assets more effectively. Education, training, and counseling on IP and IA management are now increasing roles for these organizations in Singapore and for their local and international partners. These programs include events and coaching targeted toward the personal development of senior business people at the CEO, CIO, and CTO levels.

These measures are backed up by programs designed to support companies' internal and outward investment. Singapore's Economic Development Board (EDB) "exists in order to create sustainable GDP growth for Singapore with good jobs and business opportunities for its people," and is the government agency for internal investment in Singapore.[17] In recent years it has positioned Singapore well to attract IP-based foreign investments and projects. The EDB has at its disposal a Patent Assist fund, which provides qualifying Singapore companies with matching fund grants to assist in patent filing.

Likewise, International Enterprise Singapore (IE Singapore) exists "to help Singapore-based companies grow and internationalise successfully."[18] Its vision is to be an expert agency in firm-level growth, market intelligence, and internationalization strategies. As such, IE Singapore is the government agency for outward investment and expansion of local Singapore companies. Under this charter, IE Singapore operates an "IP for Internationalization" program that provides matching funds to support qualifying projects on IP and IP-related issues.

---

[15]SurfIp, www.surfip.gov.sg.

[16]Singapore IP Academy, www.ipacademy.edu.sg.

[17]EDB Singapore, www.sedb.org.

[18]IE Singapore, www.iesingapore.gov.sg.

Singapore as a nation has seized the challenges that are presented by its particular type of economy and its geographic location and has taken steps to support local industry and maintain living standards. These steps include building awareness and providing counseling services for IP as well as non-IP intellectual assets. Singapore has seen the changes taking place in the global economy today and is acting to stay ahead of the game. The driving forces again are a desire for economic development, enhanced competitiveness, and stable or improved living standards.

The Developers: Regions and Countries Developing an Approach

The path taken by a country or region depends on many factors, one of them certainly being size. Just as it is easier for small companies to be more agile than large ones, it can be argued that it is easier for small countries to be more perceptive and act more quickly than their larger neighbors. In this respect, small countries may have a distinct advantage in the early years of the knowledge-based economy, in that if they are faster to provide leading-edge support to their companies, the individual companies will have a greater chance of becoming or remaining successful.

There is one region and one country, however, that for quite different reasons may prove an exception to this inherent advantage for small nations. These are North America and China.

It can be argued that, irrespective of size, it is imperative that a country or region consider its existing competitiveness in the knowledge-based economy (including the awareness and competencies of its companies to work their intangible knowledge assets) and create and execute the appropriate plan to provide the required support.

Many of the regions and countries mentioned next are conducting such studies right now, as indeed are others not mentioned. I will concentrate on issues concerning the working of knowledge-based assets for value and touch on other interrelated issues.

In the large, free-market economy of *North America*, comprising Canada and the United States, competitive forces have created an environment in which knowledge can be freely traded as a commodity. In addition, the knowledge and information content of the economy becomes more significant each year. The concept of trading IP, with or without associated technology, is well established. The power of IC as a source of new products and services is beginning to be realized, as is the ability to extract value systematically from assets, tangible and intangible, through single or multiple simultaneous value streams.

In short, the North American region, by the very nature of its economy and culture, has taught itself many of the lessons that need to be learned in order to manage all the assets for value, including the intangible knowledge assets. In addition, it has abundant sources of information and expertise, which can be called on when the need arises. It is therefore not surprising to find that the United States occupies the 2nd position (closely behind Finland) in the World Economic Forum Global Competitivity Index for 2004, whereas Canada occupies the 15th place.

In Canada, there is a national network of 21 Centres of Excellence designed to "foster powerful partnerships between university, government and industry," whereas in the United States there is a network of National Laboratories.[19] These centers and many universities in both countries are highly active in licensing or commercializing know-how and technologies: The degree of sophistication they bring to technology development and transfer is a recognized best practice.

For these reasons, there are no formal programs for IC management in place to support local industry, and such programs may quite simply not be required.

The Arab nations of Bahrain, Egypt, Jordan, Lebanon, Saudi Arabia, and United Arab Emirates formed the Arabian Knowledge Economy Association in May 2005 at a meeting in Dubai.[20] Its primary purpose is to "achieve sustainable economic development and growth by preparing and enabling our people, enterprises, institutions, and societies to meet the challenges presented by, and to realize the benefits of, the emerging knowledge, technology and global business environment." This not-for-profit association places IC at the forefront of its thinking as "the only sustainable raw material for true growth." The key focus areas for the association will be knowledge leadership, innovation and entrepreneurship, research and technology, and economic sustainability and growth.

The clearly stated purpose of this association, which it is hoped will grow to encompass all Arab nations, is to achieve sustainable economic development and growth by preparing Arab country enterprises, institutions, universities, people, and societies to meet challenges and benefits from opportunities extended by the emerging knowledge, technology, and global business environment.

The European Union is a free trading block of 25 democratic European countries and is a work in progress.[21] Nominally the largest free-trade area in

---

[19]Centres of Excellence Canada, www.nce.gc.ca; USA National Laboratories, http://wotug.ukc.ac.uk/parallel/internet/www/sites/america/usa/national-labs.html.

[20]Arabian Knowledge Economy Association, www.akea-me.com/akea.asp.

the world, the union has embraced the knowledge-based economy as a major opportunity for prosperity.[22]

The European Council held a special meeting in Lisbon in March of 2000 to agree on a new strategic goal for the Union in order to strengthen employment, economic reform, and social cohesion as part of a knowledge-based economy. The European Commission has launched a medium-term program to ascertain the key initiatives required but has not issued any clear opinion about the need to provide companies with additional support to develop opportunities and profit from their intangible knowledge base.

A recent study showed that the efficiency of using knowledge within the 25 countries of the expanded European Union shows a remarkable spread, as indeed it does between individual companies.[23] These trends are valuable in helping individual countries and companies set direction.

The Innovation Relay Centres are the world's largest network for technology transfer: "This network, established in 1995 by the European Commission, comprises today 71 Innovation Relay Centres (IRCs) throughout Europe and encompasses all EU countries, and in addition Bulgaria, Iceland, Israel, Norway, Romania, Switzerland and Turkey, and one South American country, Chile. These centers have been created in order to facilitate the transfer of innovative technologies to and from European companies or research departments. As a mover and shaker in innovation, the IRC network has become a leading European network for the promotion of technology partnerships and transfer mainly between small and medium-sized companies (SMEs). The IRCs are innovation support service providers mainly hosted by public organisations such as university technology centers, chambers of commerce, regional development agencies or national innovation agencies. Most IRCs are set up as consortia. Each center is staffed by personnel who have extensive knowledge of the technological and economic profile of the companies and regions they serve."[24] The IRCs constitute a powerful tool in supporting European companies and a potential future route for ICM coaching, should this be considered appropriate.

At present, the European Commission is considering which initiatives should be created, but for the moment, countries are proceeding individually, with their own agendas. In the provision of assistance to companies in leverag-

---

[21]The European Union, http://europa.eu.int.

[22]Lisbon Agenda, www.europarl.eu.int/summits/lis1_en.htm.

[23]Ante Pulic, "Value Creation Efficiency at National and Regional Level," Knowledge for Development Conference, World Bank Offices, Paris, June 20, 2005.

[24]Innovation Relay Centres, http://irc.cordis.lu/.

ing their IC, the European Union is currently a patchwork of individual countries without a common policy.

China is a major economic power with a population of about 1.3 billion and a GDP per capita of U.S. $5,000, with an underlying annual growth rate close to 10 percent.[25]

In recent testimony before the U.S.-China Economic and Security Review Commission, the opinion was given that "China has transformed itself from the world's greatest opponent of globalization, and greatest disrupter of the global institutions we created, into a committed member of those institutions and advocate of globalization. It is now a far more open economy . . . and it is globalizing its institutions to a degree not seen in a big country since Meiji Japan. Adoption of the rule of law, of commitment to competition, of widespread use of English, of foreign education, and of many foreign laws and institutions are not just updating Chinese institutions but transforming Chinese civilization."[26]

There is no question that China is investing in building its future: A key turning point was its 1984 decision to invest heavily in innovation, and China is continuing to learn how intangible knowledge assets can be used more effectively by looking at ways to capitalize on its world-class fundamental research. Although the country does not yet have a coherent program, there is evidence of significant interest and data collection. Hong Kong, with its history of Western-style law, including IP law, and its ability to work in both the Western and the Chinese cultures, is clearly seen as "the intellectual capital center for the region."[27] It is probable that the development of a skill base in sharp ICM in China will result from a combined effort centered in Hong Kong and major centers within China such as Beijing, Guangdong Province, and Shanghai. The synergy of Hong Kong as a portal between China and the developed Western economies will be of immense value in this process.

China has the capability to move fast once it is convinced that it has identified the correct elements, and for this reason it should be classed as a large country that can move with the agility of a small one. The driving force will be economic improvement and the associated benefits for society. This is likely to have a fundamental effect on China's attitude toward IP, as China amasses more and more IP rights, which it will be required to enforce overseas.

---

[25]China Population, www.cpirc.org.cn/en/eindex.htm.

[26]William H. Overholt, Statement before the U.S.-China Economic and Security Review Commission, May 19, 2005.

[27]Bernard Kellerman, "Value, Not Cost, Is the Issue," *CFO*, September 1, 2004.

Denmark is a small country with a population of about 5.4 million and a GDP per capita of U.S. $31,200. It has taken the lead in Europe in investigating the role IC plays in the health and profitability of companies and has produced several groundbreaking initiatives, the most notable of which are the use of IC statements and the tool IPScore. The driving force behind Denmark's initiatives is clearly to maintain or enhance competitiveness. "An intellectual capital statement is an integrated part of company knowledge management. It identifies the company's knowledge management strategy, which includes the identification of its objectives, initiatives and results in the composition, application and development of the company's knowledge resources. It also communicates this strategy to the company and the world at large."[28] Such an IC statement comprises a knowledge narrative, a management challenge, a set of initiatives, and a set of indicators.

The Danish Ministry of Science, Technology, and Innovation published a guide to Intellectual Capital Statements in November 2000, and by April 2002 more than 100 companies had tested the system.[29] The practice of writing an IC statement is now common in Denmark. In March 2003 new guidelines were introduced, as well as a paper describing tentative methods for analyzing IC statements.[30] The Danish experience with IC statements shows that companies that create and use such statements, in general, achieve much better management of their knowledge base and possess one more powerful tool in managing their affairs and in communicating with their surroundings. The Danish government considers the program to have moved beyond its pilot phase and has handed over responsibility for its administration countrywide to the Danish Commerce and Companies Agency.

The Web portal IPScore is a further groundbreaking approach developed on the initiative of the Danish Patent Office. It helps Danish industry become better informed about the IP they possess and manage their IP portfolios better.[31] The portal includes features related to portfolio management, risk/reward balance, and portfolio value and covers both patents and trademarks. Originally offered free of charge, a revised version is now offered for sale. Although the revised version is built extensively on the experience and requirements of

---

[28]"Intellectual Capital Statements: The New Guidelines," www.videnskabsministeriet.dk/cgi-bin/doc-show.cgi?doc_id=138091&leftmenu=PUBLIKATIONER.

[29]Danish Ministry of Information, Technology and Research, www.videnskabsministeriet.dk/fsk/publ/2002/intellectualcapstatements/index.html.

[30]"Analysing Intellectual Capital Statements," www.videnskabsministeriet.dk/cgi-bin/doc-show.cgi?doc_id=138090&leftmenu=PUBLIKATIONER.

[31]IPScore, www.ipscore.dk.

Danish companies, consultants, investors, analysts, and patent agencies and is a fully professional tool, it must be cautioned that the field of ICM, of which IP management is a part, is a new and experimental field. As ICM issues are always highly dependent on context and time frame, business decisions derived from results achieved using such systems as IPScore are best confirmed independently by internal or external experts.

India is a large country with a population of about 846 million and a GDP per capita of U.S. $2,900.

India's current annual growth rate of GDP of 7.5 percent and its large population place this country on any future map of leading world nations. Technological and business development is centered on the major cities, and this hub-based approach can be expected to continue until India's participation in global trade reaches a critical mass. The economic development of India has significant potential, and ICM is already playing a meaningful role. The rapid growth of call center services to the world and India's leadership in computer programming are two simple examples of how the knowledge-based economy is benefiting India.

India has committed to a program of building expertise in IC and using it in business in cooperation with the ASEAN nations and the Asian Institute of Management.[32]

Japan is a large country with a population of about 128 million and a GDP per capita of U.S. $28,000.

For the past 50 years, Japan has been in the forefront of economic growth, and it is no surprise that Japan is embracing ICM to enhance its competitiveness. The first groundbreaking work in the IC movement was in Japan, with the original work of Hiroyuki Itarni, who studied the effect of invisible assets on the management of Japanese corporations.[33] The Japanese Ministry of Economy, Trade, and Industry has emphasized the role that IA management will play in securing the competitiveness of Japan in the future knowledge-based economy.[34]

Many working groups in Japan are studying the value of ICM, and although no formal support to industry is visible today, we can expect to see some significant and powerful initiatives in the future.

---

[32]Federation of Indian Chambers of Commerce and Industry, speech by Prof. G. S. Ugot, Centre for Executive Education and Lifelong Learning, ASEAN Indian Summit 2003.

[33]Patrick H. Sullivan, *Value-Driven Intellectual Capital* (New York: John Wiley & Sons, Inc., 2000), 238–44.

[34]METI, "White Paper on International Economy and Trade 2004," www.meti.go.jp/english/report/downloadfiles/gWP2004ke.pdf.

Germany is a large country in central Europe with a population of about 82 million and a GDP per capita of U.S. $27,600.

German technology is known and respected the world over, and the country boasts two of the most renowned research organizations in the world, the Fraunhofer Gesellschaft and the Max-Planck Gesellschaft. The Fraunhofer Patent Center for German Research, in Munich, not only handles patenting activities for the entire network but is also an institute in its own right. The center also runs the patenting, acquisition, and marketing activities of inventions from contracted universities, technical colleges, and companies, including technology consultation and deal-making. As such, the center is an example of global best practice.

No formal program is visible in Germany to help companies understand the new challenges of the knowledge economy and to extract value from these opportunities. However, the knowledge intensity in the German IT and technology industries alone suggests that such intervention may well be necessary, especially bearing in mind the large number of technology companies in the SME category, which make up the backbone of German industry.

The initiatives taken so far by Germany have concentrated on the creation of IC statements under the banner of a project entitled "Wissensbilanz" supported by the German Ministry for Economics and Labor.[35] It is proposed that this tool be used to harness the know-how in companies better and to allow it to be used more effectively. The project is based in part on earlier work carried out in Denmark, Sweden, and the Netherlands.

It is to be expected that some future project will be mounted in Germany to take advantage of the large amounts of IC in German industry, at least some of which is currently significantly underdeveloped.

South Korea is a medium-sized country in Asia with a population of about 48 million residents and a GDP per capita of U.S. $17,700. South Korea has built a sturdy economy based in large part on technology development.

To support its industrial base, South Korea regularly holds international conferences on issues related to knowledge assets. The 2004 Seoul International Intellectual Property Conference concentrated on global commercialization of technology developed in the Pacific Rim.[36]

To up the game in Korea, the Korea Intellectual Property Office, in cooperation with the World Intellectual Property Organization (WIPO) Worldwide Academy, is now offering e-learning courses on international patent regulations and IP basics. The course was first made available to students of Pusan Nation-

---

[35] Wissensbilanz, www.bmwa.bund.de/Navigation/root,did=61652.html.

[36] The 2004 Seoul International Intellectual Property Conference, www.korea.net/News/News/NewsView.asp?serial_no=20041031011.

al University and became available to 16 additional Korean universities in autumn of 2005.

The Electronics and Telecommunications Research Institute of Korea (ETRI) produced an IC report for the year 2004,[37] a groundbreaking event for South Korea and an indicator of the value placed on knowledge assets in this country. Chu-Hwan Yin, President of ETRI, has said that "The intention of publishing ETRI's IC Report is, internally, to acknowledge the true sources for long term competitiveness. Externally, we would like to let more people understand that the real value of research institutes lies in the sum of intangible intellectual capital rather than on tangible assets. We sincerely hope our efforts can initiate a new perspective for our government to locate where the core of national competitiveness and social welfare lies. Hopefully the new perspectives from our efforts will lead to concrete policies with emphasis on intellectual capital."

South Korea is clearly a country that is considering how to leverage its intangible knowledge assets in the best fashion; its progress will be well worth watching.

Sweden is a small country in northern Europe with a population of about 9 million and a GDP per capita of U.S. $26,800. Sweden has had a profound effect on our understanding of intangible knowledge assets.

According to Sveiby,[38] efforts to manage knowledge organization and to measure knowledge have been apparent in Sweden since the mid-1980s, in what has come to be known as the Swedish Community of Practice. The so-called Konrad Group began to track nonfinancial indicators with the purpose of encouraging knowledge-based companies to improve their public reporting; by 1994, 43 Swedish knowledge companies were using this approach. In 1991, Skandia AFS appointed Leif Edvinsson as the first IC director in the world.

This far-sighted approach has been continued in Sweden, in which the intangible assets of organizations are regularly considered in formulating business strategy. In line with this approach, Sweden has suggested that public funding be used to support an insurance system to help companies defend their IP rights, a concept of particular value to SMEs.[39] The concept of leveraging the intangible knowledge base for value is ingrained in the working culture of many Swedish companies. With the active private sector offering consulting, there may be no requirement for significant public sector support.

---

[37]ETRI, *Intellectual Capital Report 2004*, South Korea; courtesy of www.sveiby.com.

[38]Karl-Erik Sveiby, paper presented at the Personal Economic Institute Conference, Stockholm, October 1996.

[39]David J. Skyrme and Debra M. Amidon, "Innovation Action for Europe: Is It Innovative Enough?" www.entovation.com/gkp/eurovation.htm.

Taiwan is a mid-sized economic power with a population of about 23 million and a GDP per capita of U.S. $23,400. The economy of Taiwan is influenced both by its Chinese heritage and by the economy of the United States.

As part of its drive to remain competitive, Taiwan created the Taiwan Intellectual Capital Research Center (TICRC) in 2003 in the firm belief that future success is possible only if all the knowledge-based assets are used effectively and in context. The center is funded with public money, under the umbrella of the Department of Industrial Technology. TICRC claims that it is "the first local research center related to academic researches and managerial practices of intellectual capital. TICRC would like to be a bridge to connect between industry and academia, and to build up a practice and knowledge sharing community in Taiwan. Through participating in TICRC communities, the progress of theory and practice of IC in Taiwan can become a pioneer in the world for academic purposes, and our national competitive advantage can be triggered by our IC knowledge creation and diffusion in industry."[40]

The Netherlands is a small country located in northwestern Europe with a population of about 16 million and a GDP per capita of U.S. $28,600. The Netherlands is making its own mark on the European landscape in investigating IC and its potential. The Netherlands government has for some time studied this topic through its Ministry of Economics.

The first groundbreaking move was the creation of Technology Rating International (TRI),[41] which has developed a rating method that provides investors and entrepreneurs with sound insights into the commercial potential of an innovation project, as well as the value created by the project and the technology it uses, both on its own and in relation to the technology used by competitors. The purpose of TRI is to bridge the gap between innovators and investors by providing an independent, qualified technology rating that includes the intangible knowledge asset components.

A second groundbreaking move was the creation of the Center for Research in Intellectual Capital at the InHolland University, which is the first faculty of its kind in the Netherlands and, along with TICRC in Taiwan, one of possibly only two in the world. The purpose of the faculty,[42] led by Professor Daniel Andriessen, is to investigate the phenomenon of IC and to help organizations measure, manage, and report better on their IC. The Center concentrates primarily on finding practical solutions to problems experienced by knowledge-

---

[40]Taiwan IC Research Centre, www.ticrc.nccu.edu.tw/TICRCenglish/epaper/epaper200502Eng.htm.

[41]Technology Rating International, www.technologyrating.com.

[42]www.inholland.nl/index.html?folder=1532&SID=267BFC65-C5F9-4960-9CE9-142E3BAFB4A9.

intensive companies. The knowledge gained by the research of the Center will be shared with the students of InHolland University so that, armed with the most up-to-date insights, they will be prepared to play their own knowledge-intensive role in modern business.

The Netherlands is positioning itself to capitalize on the opportunities presented by the knowledge-based economy. Its unique mix of pubic sector research and vibrant private sector consultancy services makes it a country well worth watching.

The United Kingdom is a medium-sized country located in northwestern Europe with a population of about 60 million and a GDP per capita of US $27,700. The United Kingdom is taking significant steps to embrace the opportunities presented by the knowledge-based economy.

In 2000, Prime Minister Tony Blair stated, "I strongly believe that the knowledge economy is our best route for success and prosperity. But we must be careful not to make a fundamental mistake. We mustn't think that because the knowledge economy is the future, it will happen only in the future. The new knowledge economy is here, and it is now."[43] Many of the U.K. government policy initiatives designed to help U.K. industry meet the present challenges have been driven by this belief.

The principal initiatives visible to date that relate to intangible knowledge assets are the provision of almost complete geographic high-speed broadband Internet coverage, an emphasis on lifelong learning, the provision of a powerful information service by the U.K. Patent Office, and a portfolio of measures by the Department of Trade and Industry to inform U.K. citizens, particularly those in business, of the opportunities presented by these assets and their conversion into value streams. These initiatives are accessible to the entire United Kingdom and are additional to those measures taken specifically in Scotland, which is an integral part of the United Kingdom but with its own devolved government responsible for national Scottish affairs.

The official Web site of The UK Patent Office contains a wealth of information on all aspects of IP, including copyrights, design rights, trademarks, and patents. It is also the portal leading to online search facilities for national, European, and worldwide IP records.[44]

The Department of Trade and Industry (DTI) has overall responsibility for advising businesses. It has produced a headline informative brochure on

---

[43]Tony Blair, Keynote Speech, "Knowledge 2000: Conference on the Knowledge Driven Economy," The Knowledge Economy—Access for all 7 March 2000 http://www.dti.gov.uk/knowledge2000/blair.htm.

[44]The UK Patent Office, www.patent.gov.uk.

creating value from intangible assets[45] and a self-assessment tool to determine critical success factors for creating value from intangibles.[46] The DTI also operates an innovation portal, which provides information and coaching on various aspects of the innovation process, including the role of intangible knowledge assets.[47]

The developments described earlier in Scotland are being observed by the rest of the United Kingdom, in the same way that developments in the rest of the United Kingdom are being observed in Scotland; as appropriate, best practices will be refined and shared.

The economy of the United Kingdom is in the forefront of the developing knowledge-based economy, and it can be expected to be one of the leaders that will implant sharp IC thinking into the European Union.

FUTURE ROLES FOR GOVERNMENTS

As this short illustrative review has shown, there is a great deal that governments can do to help their companies take full advantage of the opportunities presented by the developing knowledge-based economy. The new paradigms introduced by this economic shift require new approaches and provide significant opportunities for intelligent first movers, be they companies, countries, or regions.

The benefits of intelligently working its IC base are now available to any company, and companies are well advised to consider which steps will bring the most benefit and to act on them. This applies to companies of all sizes, as well as to universities, nonprofit organizations, and organizations in the public sector. It is all about effectiveness, efficiency, getting the most out of what has already been created, and charting an even more business-intelligent future path.

Governments all over the world are considering what needs to be done, and some have already acted. In addition, the entire subject of IC is being studied in academic circles, and departments dedicated to IC are being set up. In the earlier years, big business led the way; today businesses of all sizes, government, and academia are beginning to walk hand in hand.

Perhaps the most important point about the new awareness of the power to be gained from intelligently working the IC base of organizations is that this

---

[45]"Creating Value from Your Intangible Assets: Unlocking Your True Potential," DTI, May 2001; provided courtesy of the programme manager Tim Hoad, www.intangability.com.

[46]"Critical Success Factors. Creating Value from Your Intangibles," DTI, 2004.

[47]DTI Innovation Portal, www.innovation.gov.uk.

awareness is global. Therefore, countries that choose to ignore this new wave do so at their peril.

The end result of all this activity is a powerful tool that complements business and societal processes and in fact is part of these processes. This tool provides a better understanding of what knowledge an organization possesses and how it can best be used, managed, traded, shared, and applied in order to create value.

There is an opportunity here for each country to pause, as some have done, conduct a baseline study of where they are today, assess where they can realistically progress in a given time frame, conduct a simple gap analysis, and draw a roadmap of how to get there. This is an opportunity that is simply too important to miss.

Appendix B

The I-Stuff Value Matrix

THE VALUE MATRIX evolved out of a Gathering meeting at which companies were asked to identify the value they extracted from their intangibles. Each company mentioned the kind of value it actually extracted from its particular mix of intangibles, as well as the kind of value it wished to extract. The kinds of value were captured on flip charts for subsequent analysis.

Several days after the meeting, Pat Sullivan plastered the company conference room walls with the flip chart papers and began to review them to see what patterns of value or groupings of like kinds of value might emerge. His initial ideas were shared with Gathering companies and, after several iterations and some discussion, agreement was reached on the structure of the value matrix as well as its contents.

The value matrix shown in Chapter 4 is reproduced here (see Exhibit B.1). The matrix has two dimensions. The x-axis contains a listing of the major groupings of company intellectual property (IP) and I-stuff, and the y-axis contains the groupings identified during the first analysis and refined over time.

Whereas a full value matrix would contain all categories of IP and I-stuff, the version reproduced here focuses primarily on I-stuff. One IP column has been retained to act as an example of the kinds of value companies seek from their IP. The remaining columns in Exhibit B.1 contain only I-stuff information.

The very brevity required for terms to appear in the table means that misunderstandings could arise about the meaning of each term. Thus the remainder of this appendix will be devoted to explaining the meaning associated with each of the terms in the table.

EXHIBIT B.1 Value Matrix

	Patents	Knowledge	Know-how	Relationships	Codified Information
Defensive Value	Protection (exclude others) Design freedom Litigation avoidance	Protection (trade secret), negotiation bargaining chip	Protection (trade secret), negotiation bargaining chip	Protection (trade secret), negotiation bargaining chip	
Offensive Value Revenue	Product and service revenue Patent revenue: sale, license, JV, SA, license	Sale, license, JV, SA	Sell, license, JV, SA	JV	Sell, license, JV, SA
Cost	Litigation avoidance, access to the technology of others	Litigation avoidance	Litigation avoidance	Litigation avoidance	Litigation avoidance
Positioning	Reputation/image, competitive blocking, barrier to competition	Reputation/image, barrier to entry	Reputation/image, barrier to entry	Reputation/image, barrier to entry	Reputation/image, barrier to entry

JV, joint venture; SA, strategic alliance.

Defensive Value

When organizations anticipate that others may try to use or practice a company innovation, they seek to create a series of defensive positions that will strengthen their ability to ward off any attack. By their very nature, defensive positions are passive. They can be thought of as a modern-day equivalent of the medieval castle. Castle builders created a series of different defensive structures, each intended to protect from some different form of attack. Walls were built to protect from arrows, stones, and artillery shells. Moats were built to keep attackers away from the castle walls, and so forth.

Modern companies seek defensive value created through several means:

- *Protection (excluding others).* Innovations protected by patents allow the patent holder to preclude others from using or practicing the innovation. Mere ownership of patents implies defensive activity.
- *Protection (trade secret).* Trade secret protection for an innovation typically requires that the company hold secret all information about the innovation. Companies seeking to use trade secrets as a defensive form of legal protection must ensure that they take steps to demonstrate that they can and do maintain the secret.
- *Design freedom.* The freedom to continue with ongoing research to explore in greater depth an area of innovation that is already protected by patent is considered design freedom. This means that companies that have already staked out an innovation position through a patent may not be denied the ability to continue to explore the position through further work and patents despite the existence of patents from others that may have been issued later.
- *Litigation avoidance.* Companies with large portfolios of IP and I-Stuff are not good targets for lawsuits by other, less well endowed, companies. Large and high-quality portfolios of IP and I-Stuff may often intimidate potential litigants and convince them not to pursue legal action.
- *Negotiation Bargaining Chip.* Patents and I-stuff may both be used as bargaining chips in business negotiations.

Offensive Value

The term *offensive value* may be interpreted to mean active (rather than passive) value. Whereas the several different kinds of defensive value just cited are all passive in nature, offensive values are active in nature. There are three major groupings of offensive value from intangibles: revenue-generating value, cost avoidance value, and strategic positioning value.

REVENUE-GENERATING VALUE

Value from Products and Services

Sale. Revenue may come from the sale of products and services that were developed, manufactured, distributed, and sold using the company's I-stuff.

License. Revenue may come from licensing others to manufacture and sell the company's products and services.

Joint venture. Revenue may come through joint ventures created for the purpose of generating some new kind of value based on the company's products and services that are developed, manufactured, or sold using the company's I-stuff.[1]

Strategic alliance. Revenue may flow from strategic alliances created for the purpose of obtaining access to markets the company would otherwise be denied.[2]

Value Directly from Intangibles

Sale. Revenue flows from the sale of the innovation's legal protection (its patent, copyright, or trademark) or from the sale of I-stuff associated with the company's products and services.

License. Revenue flows from licensing the intangible itself.

Joint venture. Revenue flows from a joint venture in which the company's contribution is its I-stuff.

Strategic alliance. Revenue flows from a strategic alliance in which the alliance is around the company's I-stuff.

Integration. The integration of I-stuff into company operations may create value that is indirect. Employees with very specific skills—how to oper-

---

[1]Joint ventures are created for companies to gain access to complementary business assets they otherwise could not have access to.

[2]Strategic alliances are entered into in order to obtain access to markets a company might otherwise be denied.

ate complicated machinery or how to install and set up a factory, for example—possess I-stuff whose integration into company operations is valuable.

Cost-Avoidance Value

Minimizing litigation costs. High-quality patents may be a key factor in minimizing a company's litigation costs. A patent that is well written and valid may dramatically reduce the possibility that its owner will be sued for patent infringement.

Accessing the technology of others. Patents are often more valuable than cash when a competitor needs access to a patent owned by another firm. Technology competitors may be able to establish licensing agreements when other forms of negotiation fail.

Strategic Positioning Value

Reputation/image. Some companies use patents as well as legally protected innovations as measures of reputation or image in the marketplace. For example, IBM, 3M, and Texas Instruments are examples of companies whose reputations rest on their ability to provide customers with products based on the latest technology. These companies all have substantial portfolios of high-quality patents. Their portfolios bolster their image of technology leadership, which helps them compete in their respective marketplaces.

Competitive blocking. Patents may be used to block competitors from entering certain technology businesses. When one company has a commanding patent position, others may feel themselves precluded from participation and may not enter the field.

Barrier to competition. Companies already in business and having a commanding position in either relevant patents or I-stuff, or both, may successfully create a barrier to new entrant companies by virtue of the existence of their patent and I-stuff portfolios.

Being a player. In some industries, in order to be considered a "player," a company needs chips to bring to the table—in other words, evidence that it belongs in the game. A portfolio of patents or known high-quality I-stuff is such evidence.

Appendix C

Updating the Concept of Complementary Business Assets

By Patrick H. Sullivan and James P. O'Shaughnessy

James P. O'Shaughnessy is a frequent speaker and the author of several articles on IC management. He recently retired as VP Intellectual Property from Rockwell International. He can be contacted at *jim@jposhaughnessy.com.*

In a groundbreaking 1986 paper, economist David Teece introduced the concept of *complementary business assets* (Cbas).[1] In business operations, CBAs "complement" the ideas and innovations of the firm's employees. Together they make it possible for the firm to evolve an idea, either in form (from a raw idea to a finished product) or location (from the manufacturing plant to a retail location), into a product or service that a customer will buy.

Originally conceived to help explain why first-time innovators don't necessarily realize the full potential of an innovation, CBAs have since been discussed in the context of what has become known as the "resource-based theory of the firm." Teece theorized that "In order for such know-how to generate profits, it must be sold or utilized in some fashion in the market. In almost all cases, the successful commercialization of an innovation requires that the know-how in question be utilized in conjunction with other capabilities or assets. Services such as marketing, competitive manufacturing, and after-sales support are almost always needed. These services are often obtained from complementary assets."[2]

Developed before the emergence of the "knowledge economy" using a simple manufacturing firm as the model, the resource-based theory has been acknowledged by firms large and small as useful in understanding how to extract the most value from company innovations where tangibles are concerned. However, because the management and commercialization of *in*tangibles is still in its infancy, there is not yet sufficient experience to make a definitive assertion about whether CBAs also leverage the value of intangibles.

---

[1] D. Teece, "Profiting from Technological Innovation: Implications for Integration, Collaboration, Licensing and Public Policy," *Research Policy* 15 (1986): 285–305.

[2] Ibid., 283.

Nevertheless, for most firms that are both commercializing intangibles and knowledgeable about CBAs, the early consensus is that the same concepts apply to intangibles.

Teece and his colleagues later suggested that the fundamental question in the field of strategic management is how firms can achieve and sustain competitive advantage. He contrasted two perspectives on creating and maintaining competitive advantage for the firm. The dominant paradigm in the field during the last two decades of the 20th century, the competitive forces theory, is concerned with firm positioning in the marketplace. It encourages companies to find "unmet demands" in their markets and to provide products and services to meet these demands. Having established a competitive position in the market, the theory then emphasizes the actions a firm can take to create defensible positions against competitors. The alternative to the competitive forces theory is concerned with firm-level efficiency. In the "resource-based" perspective, competitive advantage can be developed, deployed, and protected through the use of internal combinations of tangible and intangible assets. Key among the tangible assets are the firm's complementary business assets, which complement the firm's innovations.[3] These ideas expanded on the concept of dynamic capabilities but added nothing further to the definition or understanding of CBAs.

Although academics have continued to write about the role of CBAs in commercializing new technologies, few new insights have emerged about what comprises them, how firms actually use them, or how firms create profits through them.[4]

Subsequently, the member companies of the Intellectual Capital Management (ICM) Gathering, an international group of large technology companies actively concerned with managing their intangibles, further defined and provided examples of CBAs based on the experiences of their companies. Pat Sullivan, a co-founder of the Gathering, would later apply these supplemental thoughts about the CBA concept to his consulting and economic work. For example, as an economist who routinely valued intangibles, he recognized that CBAs could have a significant effect on the value of an intangible such as intellectual prop-

---

[3]D. J. Teece, G. Pisano, and A. Shuen, "Dynamic Capabilities and Strategic Management," *Strategic Management Journal* 18, no. 7 (1997): 509–510.

[4]See, e.g., M. Tripsas, "Commercializing Emerging Technologies through Complementary Business Assets," in *Wharton on Managing Emerging Technologies*, G. S. Day, P. J. H. Shoemaker, and R. E. Gunther, eds. (New York: John Wiley & Sons, Inc., 2000), 175–176; and P. Christman, "Effects of 'Best Practices' of Environmental Management on Cost Advantage: The Role of Complementary Business Assets, *Academy of Management Journal*, August 2000.

erty (IP) or I-stuff. His insights into applications of the CBA concept to valuation caused him to observe:

> It is much too simplistic to assume that a potential licensee would pay a royalty unassociated with the status of the licensee's complementary business assets related to the intellectual assets. Thus we must be cautious not to trivialize the valuation analysis by failing to take into account all of the factors of leverage, and the characteristics of complementary business assets that constitute one of the most profound factors in the equation.[5]

Sullivan further described how CBAs are being used in the extraction of value from intangibles, identifying their role in the process of making commercialization decisions. He also discussed the role of CBAs in mergers and acquisitions and as a source of profit for the enterprise.[6]

A DECADE OF WORKING WITH CBAS

In its earliest meetings, during 1995 and 1996, the companies of the ICM Gathering embraced the then existing view of CBAs. They had observed empirically that intangibles, ideas, and innovations have little value when not paired with the business assets that can convert them into something a customer will purchase.

Over the next decade, the Gathering would return frequently to the topic of complementary business assets. The discussions that ensued were rich with examples of each company's efforts to extract value through its CBAs. This appendix is extrapolated from what the Gathering learned about CBAs since 1995.

IDEAS ALONE ARE NOT ENOUGH

It is generally agreed that intellectual capital (IC) by itself is of little value. Firms must provide supporting resources or assets to complement their employees' ideas and innovations. These resources and infrastructure assets are both direct and indirect and comprise both physical and intangible elements. Direct support, which touches the human capital directly, includes tangibles such as computers,

---

[5]P. H. Sullivan, *Profiting from Intellectual Capital* (New York: John Wiley & Sons, Inc., 1998), 293.
[6]P. H. Sullivan, *Value-Driven Intellectual Capital* (New York: John Wiley & Sons, Inc., 2000), 103–106, 116, 118, 121–22, 232–38.

desks, and telephones and intangibles such as information systems, computer software, work procedures, marketing plans, and company know-how. Indirect support includes buildings, lights, electricity, and plumbing, as well as strategic plans, payroll systems, costing structures, and supplier relationships. This company infrastructure provides the environment that encourages the human capital to create and leverage its knowledge.

Complementary Business Assets

CBAs are a unique subset of the firm's assets that are used to create additional value in the commercialization process. CBAs typically include manufacturing facilities, distribution networks, customer lists, supplier networks, service forces, and organization capabilities. CBAs may be thought of as the string of assets through which innovations must be processed in order to reach the customer. CBAs may also be technologies, customer lists, trademarks, or customer relationships. No matter how exciting an intellectual asset itself may be, it will have little commercial value unless it is paired with the appropriate CBAs.

There are two kinds of CBAs: *generic* and *specific*. *Generic* CBAs are widely available. They can be bought or contracted for on the open market and may be used in commercializing a wide range of technology applications. *Specific* CBAs are less common and offer more leverage.

Suppose an inventor has devised a unique product with a large market appeal. If this product could be made using manufacturing equipment readily available in the marketplace, then its manufacture would involve the use of generic assets. If, on the other hand, the product required a manufacturing process or technique that was unique to the technology or the product's design, so that generic manufacturing equipment was not capable of producing it, then that manufacturing capability would be a *specific* CBA. A specific CBA can be used strategically: It can be used as a barrier to competition; it can be licensed out as a source of income; it can be sold; and it can be used to attract joint venture partners. Most important, it can be used to protect a technology from competitors when legal protection is either not desired or not available.

Specific CBAs are usually created in conjunction with the commercialization of a specific application of an intellectual asset. They are therefore unique and are often themselves protectable. In effect, controlling the specific CBAs may be equivalent to controlling the underlying intellectual asset and the ultimate commercial value of an intellectual asset. This has the advantage of protecting a technology without having to reveal the technology itself. Patenting does not provide this advantage.

What a CBA Isn't

Other forms of IC may also be used in the commercialization value chain as if they were CBAs, but these must be considered faux CBAs at best. These pieces of IC—a brand is a good example—add value to an innovation, yet are not operational or active like true CBAs. Because they may increase the probability of success or increase the potential profits from an innovation, they are desirable, but they are neither necessary nor sufficient in the commercialization value chain.

Characteristics of Complementary Business Assets

CBAs are *required* for converting an innovation into value. Their presence in the commercialization chain of activities is absolutely necessary. CBAs are operational and active components of the firm. Because of their roles in converting intangibles into items that can be purchased, CBAs are in continuous operation.

Teece originally opined that a firm needed to own its CBAs in order to extract the greatest amount of value from them. Since then, experience has shown that ownership is not necessary, although when a firm does not own the necessary CBAs, gaining access to them requires a pricing mechanism that allows the firm to reap more of the profits from their use than a simple contractual relationship would allow. Furthermore, outsourcing CBAs does not fundamentally alter the firm's identity (although it may lead a firm to alter its business plan).

Another significant characteristic of complementary business assets is that they are "sticky":

> From the resource-based perspective, firms are heterogeneous with respect to their resources/capabilities/endowments. Further, resource endowments are "sticky": at least in the short run, firms are to some degree stuck with what they have and may have to live with what they lack. This stickiness arises for three reasons. First, business development is viewed as an extremely complex process. Quite simply, firms lack the organizational capacity to develop new competencies quickly. Secondly, some assets are simply not readily tradable, for example, tacit know-how and reputation.[7]

Also, each CBA increases the value of an innovation by converting it in either form or location into something a user will pay for. As a corollary, each CBA

---

[7]Teece et al., "Dynamic Capabilities," 514.

EXHIBIT C.1   Simplified Model of a Knowledge Company Showing the Lens Effect of Complementary Business Assets

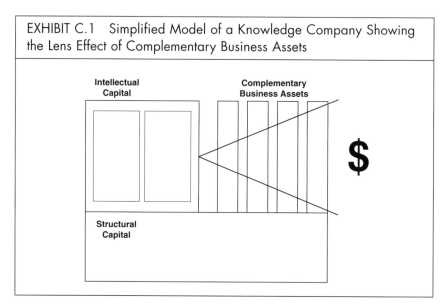

provides a degree of revenue to the firm in direct relation to the amount of increased value it embeds in the innovation on its way to the purchaser. Our initial graphic depiction of a knowledge company, displaying CBAs as a series of lenses, was a good representation of the "magnifying" effect of CBAs (see Exhibit C.1).

Generic versus Differentiable Effect of CBA

The Gathering discovered that CBAs could have both generic and differentiable elements *at the same time*. For this reason, the Gathering modified its graphic model to show that each CBA contains these two elements (see Exhibit C.2)

In the early stages of a product's life cycle, the string of CBAs (the CBA value chain) may comprise generic capabilities. This makes sense because, in the early stages of a product's life, customers find it attractive for one or more of its attributes or features. As the cycle continues, and more sales are realized, competitors begin offering their own version of the product. Typically, the new competitors have a better cost structure and begin to compete with the original product on both features and price. As the cycle continues and the price continues to drop, cost control becomes more important. The original innovator may begin to differentiate his or her CBAs to lower cost, to provide more service, or to enhance the product's appeal in another way. So, initially, the knowledge company model for a new innovator might look like Exhibit C.1. In the later stages of the product life cycle it might look like Exhibit C.3.

EXHIBIT C.2   A Simple Model of a Complementary Business Asset Showing Both Generic and Differentiable Components

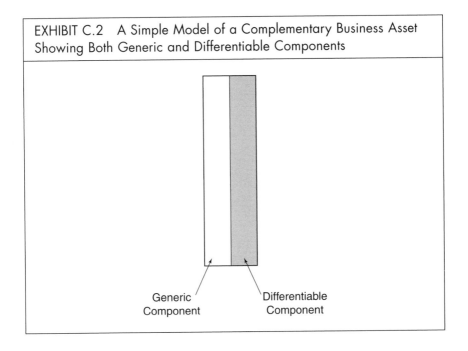

Generic Component   Differentiable Component

EXHIBIT C.3   Model of a Knowledge Company Showing Complementary Business Assets as Partially Generic (Left) and Partially Differentiated (Right)

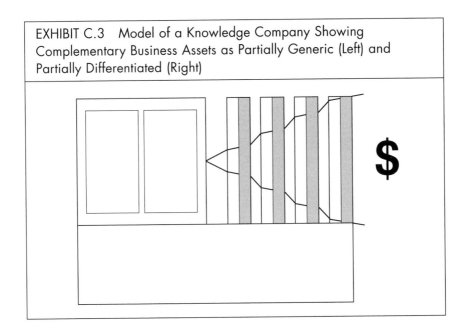

EXHIBIT C.4   The Generic (Left) and Differentiable (Right) Portions of a CBA and the Lens Effect of Each

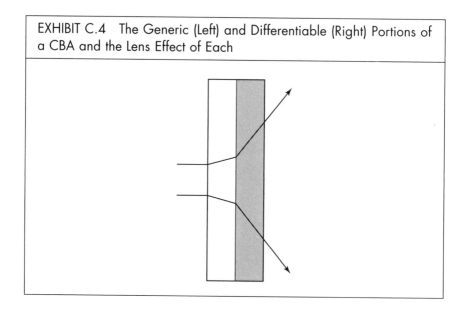

The importance of this is that companies can initiate a new product (i.e., new to a market, not just to the company's offerings) with purely generic CBAs until they see how the market responds to the product. Then they can modify specific CBAs over time, adding to or minimizing the differentiable portion of each CBA as necessary.

The Gathering suspects that the differentiable portion of a CBA does more to magnify value than does the nondifferentiated portion (see Exhibit C.4). This perspective explains why and how companies may dynamically tailor their CBAs as they gain experience in the marketplace.

The lens effect is magnified the more a company differentiates its complementary business assets. Exhibit C.5 shows graphically the kind of effect that can be expected when a company differentiates several of its CBAs.

IC Directly Associated with Individual CBAs

In the basic model of a knowledge firm, IC is viewed as a whole. Another view of a company's IC is that some portion of it may be uniquely tied to individual CBAs. The reason for this is simply that many CBAs require their own IC, both to improve the capabilities of innovations and to contribute to the firm's operational activities. A graphical view of this might look like Exhibit C.6.

EXHIBIT C.5   The Knowledge Company Model Showing the Lens Effect of Differentiable and Generic Assets

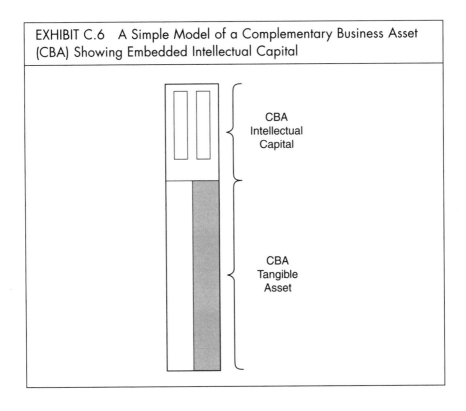

EXHIBIT C.6   A Simple Model of a Complementary Business Asset (CBA) Showing Embedded Intellectual Capital

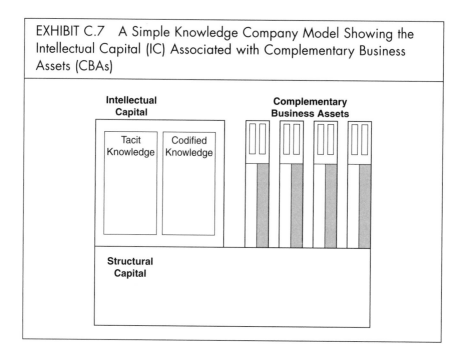

EXHIBIT C.7   A Simple Knowledge Company Model Showing the Intellectual Capital (IC) Associated with Complementary Business Assets (CBAs)

In addition, if one wishes to view this additional bit of sophistication graphically, Exhibit C.7 is an example of how it might be perceived. In this illustration, we see "distributed intelligence" throughout the model of the organization.

Conclusions

CBAs are strategic to firms that subscribe to the asset-based theory of the firm. This theory holds that firms may create strategic advantages by putting together unique combinations of tangible and intangible assets that provide some unique strategic capability in their marketplace. In this context, CBAs are fundamental to the success of the firm.

Resource allocation. Every company is resource constrained. At some time or another, all face shortages of financial capital, other structural capital, IC, and CBAs. How resources and revenues are allocated makes a profound difference in the continuing success of each business. Careful analysis and monitoring of a company's CBAs can aid rational resource management. If one has $3 and the discretion to spend it within the company, what is the wisest allocation? Should it go, in whole or in part, to structural capital, IC, CBAs, or one of the many subsets of each of them? The obvious answer to all these questions is "It depends." It is firm specific in each of the variables we noted previously.

Value extraction. Many Gathering companies have embarked on value extraction programs. These efforts are usually based on the creation of an IP vending (i.e., licensing) relationship or partnership (i.e., alliance). The preferred form of relationship is context specific but typically is fashioned to address well-defined market sectors or opportunities. Field-of-use licensing based on market segmentation guards against waste.

Adequacy of CBAs. Sometimes an owner of IC cannot extract its value, either fully or in part. This usually results from a lack of adequate CBAs. One cure for this ailment is to license the IC to or establish an alliance with a company that has the requisite CBAs already in place.

Intended use of CBAs. Because many CBAs are market or sector specific, realizing the full value of a technology may require a detailed understanding of how the licensee or alliance intends to address the available market and what CBAs are helpful or necessary to do so. Whatever the situation, knowing more about one's own as well as another party's CBAs, and knowing more about the ones that are core and essential, aids in extracting the most value from each IC opportunity.

Efficiency of use. At least theoretically, a firm may have a sound CBA base but employ it inefficiently. This might be because of insufficiently robust intellectual capital to power the CBAs. A better understanding of CBAs in general, as well as a more thorough knowledge of the capability of a firm's own CBAs, allows a company to take a more analytical approach to in-licensing.

Changing value over time. The strategic value of a CBA changes over time as a function of one or more variables. The most influential factors include the nature of and changes in (1) the company and its maturity in its markets, (2) the markets in which it competes, (3) the company's value web, and (4) its product line. As changes occur in the strategic value of its CBAs, the company is well advised to outsource, form alliances, or perhaps emphasize certain CBAs, either to conserve or to enhance its resources.

Seeking the best CBA match. As companies become more knowledgeable about how to extract value from their intangibles, they may realize that their own CBAs are not adequate to extract full value from an innovation. Out-licensing with an appropriate partner can maximize the innovation's value to both parties.

UPDATING THE CONCEPT
OF A BUSINESS MODEL

INTRODUCTION

The term "business model" came into relatively common use during the dot.com era, when the need arose to differentiate between various kinds of e-businesses (e.g., portals, aggregators, destination sites). Businesses continue to use the term "business model" frequently, yet there is no common definition or understanding of what a business model is (or isn't).

The ideas presented in this appendix are a compilation of the ideas of ICM Gathering members as well as the ideas of a range of business and academic thought leaders. Although one must view these concepts as work in progress, nevertheless the authors find the thrust of the emerging definition and description of the term "business model" and its working components to be compelling. They provide a framework that is useful to describe and define what we observe in business operations.

Finally, this appendix suggests a working definition of the term "business model" and develops a framework within which current and potential business models may be defined, tested, and refined.

THE ACADEMIC LITERATURE

In an extensive interview, Professor Henry Chesbrough, Director of the Center for Business Innovation at the Haas School of Business of the University of California at Berkeley, discussed his own research,[1] including the several

---

[1]We are indebted to Professor Chesbrough for his work on business models and his willingness to share. We are further indebted to him for his insights into new ways of looking at the emerging dimensions of business models.

in-depth reviews he has made of the academic literature on the topic of business models.[2]

He found that the literature divided itself into three groupings:

1. *Literature concerning e-business models.* The early literature on business models was concerned with e-business models, their definitions and classifications (such as "portals," "aggregators," "destination sites," and so on). Unfortunately, most of the e-businesses forming the basis for the early studies are now defunct or have been absorbed into other more traditional businesses.

2. *Literature on business models as a theoretical construct.* This grouping of papers takes the idea of a "business model" literally. It deals with "business model" as a theoretical construct, with causal linkages between the model's components. The thrust of this area of research is to identify relationships between business models and IT. It seeks to identify theoretical business models and the information flows needed to support them.

3. *Business models as an organizational mechanism.* This stream of literature analyzes the concept of "business model" as an organizational mechanism that aids in decision making. To date, the papers in this grouping describe what a business model should accomplish, or what functions it should fulfill for the firm.

The third of the three groupings seems most promising in terms of enlightenment for operational managers. The researchers who produced writings in the first grouping have seen the businesses they focused on decline in number and interest. The second grouping, although potentially useful for information technology enthusiasts, does not appear to offer much promise for operational managers.

In summary, the academic literature, still in its infancy, may produce useful insights in the future but has not yet provided much in the way of practical insights.

THE BUSINESS LITERATURE

The business literature comprises books and articles that are not refereed or published in journals or magazines generally viewed as "academic." This literature

---

[2]We would like to acknowledge the Scottish Enterprise, which, in conjunction with Professor Chesbrough and Patrick H. Sullivan, investigated new concepts in business models, including Chesbrough's literature search activities.

is published in quasi-popular business magazines or in books found in airport bookstores or in the "Business" section of major bookstores. Like the academic literature, writings on "business models" in this category are limited.

In the mid-1990s, Charles Stabell and Oystein Fjeldstad introduced the value shop and value network as two competing organizing principles to the value chain associated with Michael Porter.[3]

Another paper, written for Accenture and entitled "A New Paradigm for Managing Shareholder Value," discussed the two new kinds of business models: "In the past 10 years they have only grown more important. Value shop and value network companies (for example, Microsoft, Cisco, PeopleSoft, Comverse Technology, eBay, Amgen, Priceline, Sun Microsystems, amazon, and Yahoo!) now have some of the largest market capitalizations in the U.S. economy."[4]

The authors of the Accenture paper argue that each of the two new business models as well as the traditional value chain model has a different focus and a different set of requirements for obtaining value from its I-stuff:

	Value Chain	**Value Shop**	**Value Network**
Focus	Transforming inputs to product or service outputs	Solving a problem or exploiting an opportunity	Mediating or causing transactions between customers
How obtains value	Finds innovative ways to optimize cost, time, and quality of the company's processes; finds customers for the products; makes the chain more responsive to changes in supply or demand	Captures and exploits knowledge about problems and their solutions; solves problems; and identifies ways to exploit the solution, knowledge of problems, or opportunities	Identifies new clusters or customers or customer usage patterns that enable the firm to multiply exchanges between customers; identifies who to bring into the network, who to kick out, and to whom to sell excess capacity

---

[3]C. B. Stabell and O. D. Fjelstad, "Configuring Value for Competitive Advantage: On Chains, Shops and Networks," *Strategic Management Journal* 19 (1998): 413–437.

[4]J. Ballow, R. Burgman, G. Roos, and M. Molnar, "A New Paradigm for Managing Shareholder Value," www.accenture.com, July 2004, 11.

THE ICM GATHERING VIEW

In reviewing the minutes of ICM Gathering meetings over the years, and highlighting discussions relating to what we now understand to be the concept of business models, it was noticed that companies tend to talk about several things: the focus of a company business, how it differentiates itself from its competitors, the kinds of innovation it features, its relationship with customers and other key external groups, the architecture of its profit streams, and any key internal resources required. Examples of these include:

- *Kinds of innovation.* In Gathering discussions about current or new businesses, companies often discuss the kind of innovation the organization under discussion brings out. For many current or new businesses, their main differentiable feature is some sort of innovation. These innovations may fall into a number of areas, but their existence is often a key to how they intend to compete in the marketplace. Examples of different kinds of differentiable innovations include:
  - Technology
  - Product or service
  - Marketing
  - Sales
  - Product or service support
  - Production
- *Customers.* One of the major elements of a business model is the definition of the target customer. Many companies take this element of a business model for granted, but Gathering discussions and thought leader writings reveal that this is a more complex topic than was perhaps earlier thought. A business model needs to identify several elements about what kind of customer is the target, as well as some defining information about that customer type. A preliminary listing of key information about the kinds of customers a business model targets includes the following:
  - *Kinds of customer.* Customers are of many kinds. Some companies target industrial customers, and some target retail consumers. The kind of customer targeted is a key element in describing a company's current or desired business model. The kinds of customers include, but are not limited to, the following:
    - Intermediaries
    - Industrial customer (as opposed to a retail customer)
    - Consumers

○ *Relationship with customers.* In a presentation to the ICM Gathering in 2004, Hubert St. Onge defined four different levels of relationship that companies may target. In defining these as "target" relationships with the organization's customers, St. Onge believes that both the company and the customer must be in agreement with the relationship and actively seek to create and maintain it. The four levels of relationship with customers are:

○ *Transaction relationship:* a one-time sale of a product or service

○ *Product solution relationship:* selecting or proposing an "augmented" product or service in response to an expressed customers need or concern

○ *Business solution relationship:* shaping or configuring an array of benefits and features or services to provide the value-creating functionality required by the customer

○ *Partnering:* working with the customer to craft business opportunities jointly that would not have been possible without a deep mutual understanding and trust.

• *Architecture of the profit streams.* This element of a business model often represents an innovation in an industry and might more appropriately fall under the heading "Kind of innovation," discussed previously. Nevertheless, because of the degree of its potential impact on an organization's business model, it is identified separately here. Certain companies have found ways of manipulating their revenue or cost streams in order to maximize the firm's profits. For example, Ryan Air is an airline operating in northern Europe. It caters to the economy-conscious passenger. Ryan Air eschews major airports and only flies into and out of outlying airports, many of which have languished in this era of hub and spoke airline networking. Ryan has been able to negotiate contracts with these airports whereby Ryan guarantees a minimum number of passengers for the airports' shops and services per week or month. In return, the airport pays Ryan to land there. In other words, Ryan has not only eliminated landing fees as a cost stream, it has converted them into a revenue stream!

Profit stream areas of focus include both revenue streams and cost streams:

○ *Revenue streams* may include the company's traditional revenue streams (typically for value chain activities) as well as modifications to existing revenue streams, new revenue streams, or revenue streams moved forward so their impact reaches the organization's bottom line earlier than otherwise planned.

○ *Cost streams* may include the elimination of traditional costs, the reduction of such costs, the sharing of costs with another organization, and moving costs backward so that their impact affects the organization's bottom line later than had been planned.

BUSINESS MODELS: A WORKING DEFINITION

The foregoing review of literature and business practice describes some key attributes of what is being called a business model. In general, these attributes describe a business's focus and fundamental intent. Experience and daily usage of the term suggests that a business model is about the conceptual structure of the business. With this in mind, we suggest the following as a working definition of the term "business model": *A business model is a description of the business and its intended areas of focus.* Business models define major descriptors of the business and how it differentiates itself from competitors.

What a Business Model Is Not

A business model is not a strategy. Whereas strategies are action oriented and contain the activities and directions the management intends to take in order to achieve its business objectives, the business model is a static description of business and its intended areas of focus.

A business model is not a plan. Plans identify the issues that must be resolved in order to achieve the short-term business objectives of a firm. They identify specific activities, assign responsibilities and authority, and define timelines and milestones.

A business model is not a marketing strategy or plan. It is not a financial strategy or plan. It is not developed to support funding or fund-raising. It is not contained on a spreadsheet

A BUSINESS MODEL ENGINE

The foregoing suggests that there could be at least five different "dimensions" to a business model. Describing a company's business model could be done by selecting one or more of the alternative courses of action found under each of the six (or perhaps more) dimension headings. Using this process (very much like a business model–generating engine), one could describe a business model by identifying its unique or differentiable elements.

EXHIBIT D.1 Graphic of a
Business Model Decision Showing
the Alternative Choices Available

Kind of Value-Creating Organization

Value Shop

Value Chain

Value Network

For example, suppose the first dimension of choice for defining the business model for a new enterprise were to decide which kind of value-creating organization it expected to be. There would be three alternatives available (see Exhibit D.1).

The second decision one might make in designing the business model for a new enterprise might be to identify the kind(s) of innovation on which it would focus. In this case, there would be six possible alternatives (see Exhibit D.2).

Continuing this process, one might finally produce a Business Model Engine looking something like Exhibit D.3. To use the engine, one selects an alternative for the first decision to be made—the kind of value-generating organization. Then, one selects an alternative for the kind of innovation the company intends to focus on, and so forth. By connecting the alternatives chosen for each of the six decisions made, one can define the basics of a business model (see Exhibit D.4).

EXHIBIT D.2 Two Business Model Decisions and Their Alternative Choices

Kind of Value-Creating Organization	Kind(s) of Innovation
Value Shop	Technology
	Product or Service
Value Chain	Marketing
	Sales
Value Network	Support
	Production

EXHIBIT D.3   A Business Model Engine

Kind of Value Company	Customers		Architecture of Profit Streams	
	Kind of Customer	Relationship with Customer	Revenue	Cost
Value Shop	Intermediary	Transaction	Greenfield Revenue	No Cost Implications
		Product Solution	New Revenue Streams	Eliminate Costs
Value Chain	Consumer	Business Solution	Modify Existing Streams	Share Costs
			Move Streams Forward	Reduce Costs
Value Network		Partnering		Move Costs Backward

EXHIBIT D.4 Graphic of a Business Model Decision Showing the Alternative Choices Available

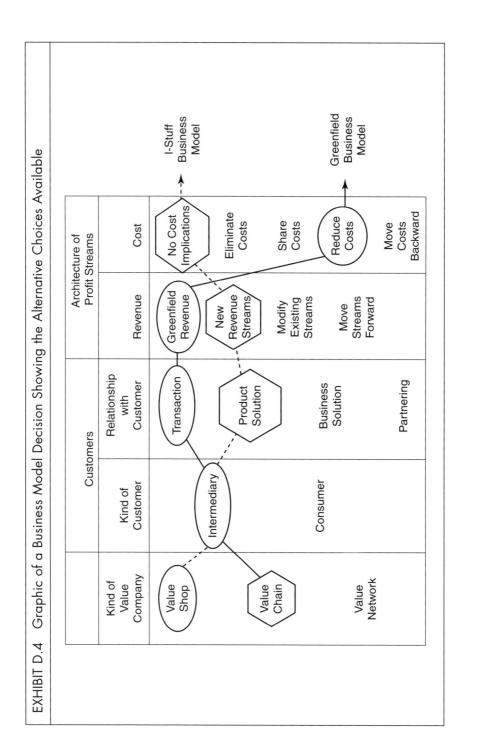

CREATING A BUSINESS MODEL

Companies wishing to describe their own current (or an intended) business model using the ideas in this appendix will find that there is a step preceding the Business Model Engine described above. That step involves the creation of a one-page outline of the company's business. Such an outline must contain a brief overview of the company's business model. Most importantly, the outline must contain a description of what the company is selling, what the pricing structure will be, who the target customers are, and what kind of value organization the company intends to be.

For example, suppose there were a commodity chemical company, whose traditional business involved the selling of commodity chemicals to companies. The commodity chemicals business is a value chain, price-sensitive business, in which purchasers often change from one supplier to another based on who offers the lowest price for the day. In Exhibit D.4, this business model is shown with a solid line connecting the alternative selections. If this commodity chemicals business wanted to start up a new business (in this example, let us use DuPont's new business in Safety Consulting as an example), the new business would be a value shop business. The value shop business model, shown in Exhibit D.4 with a dotted line connecting the alternative selections, is a very different model from the company's traditional business.

Using the Business Model Engine, one can describe different business models and subsequently evaluate and more fully articulate each one.

BUSINESS MODEL IMPLICATIONS FOR I-STUFF

As already noted in the text of this book, the business model necessary for commercializing I-stuff (particularly for value chain companies) may be very different from the company's traditional model. Equally, for value shop and value network companies, business models for different or new I-stuff commercialization opportunities may differ from one another. It is important to determine what these differences are and what the implications of these differences may be for required complementary business assets, for needed I-Stuff, and for focusing the business strategy on what needs to be accomplished to achieve the business objectives set for I-stuff value extraction successfully.

APPENDIX E

NEW CONCEPTS IN MEASURING VALUE

By Rob McLean

Rob McLean is author and co-author of several papers on value measurement and measuring the value of intangibles, and consults with the Value Measurement and Reporting Collaborative. His credentials may be reviewed at *www.matrixlinks.com*.

THIS APPENDIX IS a shorter version of "Rediscovering Measurement," a discussion paper prepared by Rob McLean, with contributions from Pat Sullivan and Rod Anderson. It is revised and printed here with the kind permission of the Value Measurement and Reporting Collaborative (VMRC). The full version can be found on the Web site of VMRC's New Paradigm Initiative, at http://npi.valuemeasurement.net.

Over the past 15 years, a consensus has emerged in the business community about the importance of intellectual capital and intangibles and the need for broader measures of corporate performance than are provided through traditional accounting.

In response, innovators have developed more than 85 new approaches, ranging from highly specialized techniques for valuing specific classes of intangibles to broad frameworks for reporting on corporate performance. These approaches can be classified into five categories, based on whether they are primarily concerned with: Intangibles; indicators; market capitalization; the "capitals"; or value streams. Some of these approaches have been widely adopted and have stimulated a desire in the business community for enhanced disclosure of information useful for evaluating corporate performance and value potential.

Traditional accounting has evolved over hundreds of years. Over the past 40 years or so, this evolution has been guided by rigorous formalized standard-setting processes operating both at the national level in a large number of countries around the world and increasingly at a global level through the activities of organizations such as the International Accounting Standards Board (IASB).

By contrast, innovators who have developed the alternative measurement approaches that have appeared over the past 15 years have focused on responding to the needs of users for new insights and perspectives. Although "best practices" are emerging, the alternative measurement approaches have not so far been subjected to formalized standards processes.

The new measurement approaches differ widely in their objectives, inputs and outputs, and methods, both from traditional accounting—and from each other. Given these differences, it has until now been difficult to assess individual approaches or to compare one approach with another, relative to such characteristics as: The user needs each approach is designed to address; what objects and properties each approach actually measures; the overall validity of the approach; and other technical attributes.

The situation of traditional accounting is much like that of physics a century ago. At that time, it was clear that although Newton's equations could be used to explain the movement of objects and planets, scientists were increasingly aware of phenomena that could not be explained by Newtonian physics. Einstein's work on relativity, published in 1905, presented an alternative way of understanding some of the workings of the universe.

Similarly, traditional accounting still works well to measure the performance of organizations, as long as what we want to measure is measurable as a real (historical) or hypothetical (fair-value) transaction. The transaction-centric nature of accounting is arguably its greatest strength but is also the source of its inherent limitations. If what business decision-makers want to know about cannot be measured by a transaction—such as the future value creation potential of the enterprise, or the contribution to that value potential of knowledge and ideas—then traditional accounting will not be able to help. However, there has as yet been no accounting Einstein to point us toward a new paradigm. We are beginning to understand the problem, but we do not yet have a comprehensive solution.

When viewed through the lens of measurement concepts and criteria, it becomes easier to understand what the boundaries of the traditional accounting paradigm are and to begin imagining what might lie beyond those boundaries. It can be argued that accountants take measurement for granted. The key questions that arise in measurement theory—such as, what are the properties of the objects we want to measure, and what scale and units of measure do we need to measure them?—are not matters of debate in accounting. Answers to these questions are implicitly embedded in accounting concepts such as "the lower of cost or market value" and in accounting standards that build on those concepts.

Even if it were appropriate to take measurement for granted with respect to traditional accounting, it is not appropriate to do so when it comes to the alternative measurement approaches that are the stimulus for the New Paradigm Initiative. It is clear, for example, that performance indicators, such as those used in a Balanced Scorecard, measure different properties of a variety of different objects, using a variety of different units of measure and measurement scales—all this in complete contrast to traditional accounting. Whether users are in a position to appreciate the significance of these differences—when, for instance, performance indicators are presented alongside traditional accounting information in a corporate annual report—has not yet been thoroughly debated.

THE INHERENT LIMITATIONS OF TRADITIONAL ACCOUNTING MEASUREMENT

What Is the Problem?

"Accountants can't count Intellectual capital," declared Tom Stewart, formerly with *Fortune* magazine and now the editor of the *Harvard Business Review*. "Armies of clerks and banks of computers track physical and financial assets, but those accounting systems cannot cope with brainpower."[1]

Over the past decade, Stewart and many others have convinced a large proportion of the business community that the reason why intellectual capital is not on the balance sheet is because accountants do not know how to measure intangibles. This view is not technically correct. Accountants are perfectly capable of measuring intangibles, just as they are capable of measuring tangibles, so long as there is a transaction. The issue that arises with attempting to expand recognition of intangibles in financial statements is not their intangibility, but rather that most intangibles are internally generated and do not therefore result from a discrete third-party transaction. So far, corporate executives are not convinced that it would be worth the effort to implement systems to accrue internal development costs and allocate them to specific intangibles.

This example illustrates that the bedrock of traditional accounting is transactions with third parties. This reliance on transactions is both the greatest strength of traditional accounting and the source of its inherent limitations. The fact that most of the numbers are based on transactions with third parties is the most important reason why financial statements are considered by many to be "reliable." However, the transaction-based, inherently backward-looking nature of the traditional accounting paradigm is also arguably its greatest weakness. It is the most important reason why more and more people question the relevance of performance measurement based on past transactions.

A transaction is, by definition, something that has happened in the past. When people characterize traditional accounting as "backward-looking," they are only being factually correct. Traditional accounting is inherently backward-looking, because transactions, by definition, happen in the past. Yes, on occasion, in the preparation of financial statements, we anticipate transactions that might

---

[1]Thomas A. Stewart, *Intellectual Capital: The New Wealth of Organizations* (New York: Doubleday, 1997), 56–58.

happen in the future. On occasion, we may restate certain assets at "fair market value," in effect substituting a value based on a hypothetical current transaction for that derived from a past transaction. However, in most jurisdictions, the vast majority of the numbers in financial statements are based on past transactions.

It is still *necessary* and *useful* for anyone interested in the performance of an enterprise to know what has happened in the past. However, it is not *sufficient* for anyone—management, investors, shareholders, regulators, or other stakeholders—to know only about what has happened in the past. Most people are at least as interested, if not more interested, in what will happen in the future.

What has happened in the past can often provide some insight into what may happen in the future. However, in a world of accelerating change (a premise that in today's context is hard to dispute), what has happened in the past is increasingly less relevant to understanding what may happen in the future.

A Biopharmaceutical Example

To illustrate the problem further, consider the following fictional example. Assume that BioPharm is a well-financed startup biopharmaceutical company focused on developing genetic therapies that will ultimately be licensed to and distributed through major pharmaceutical corporations. BioPharm's business plan calls for it to conduct research and development over a ten-year period, during which it does not anticipate it will have *any* licensing revenue.

Using traditional accounting measurement, BioPharm's financial statements will show a string of increasing losses, year by year, as the R&D is expensed. However, could one reasonably conclude that during this ten-year period BioPharm as an enterprise is creating *absolutely no value* for its owners or stakeholders?

Whatever value BioPharm creates over that period will not be revealed by a transaction-centric accounting system. This is true regardless of how the transactions are accounted for: Whether or not R&D is written off, intangible assets are capitalized, or assets are restated at fair values. BioPharm's progress in creating value is a function of the creativity of its people, the effectiveness of its research processes, the strength of the intellectual property it develops, the activities of competitors, and so on. None of this can be measured through its recent financial transactions.

BioPharm is an admittedly extreme example, since it has no current revenue, and since its product development cycle is so long. However, even if it had current revenue, or a shorter product development cycle, all the above points are still valid. *The fact is that there is no necessary connection between progress in creating value in an enterprise and the organization's recent financial transactions with third parties.*

One could argue that this is as true in the manufacturing enterprises of the past as it is with the knowledge-based enterprises of the present and future. However, with the manufacturing enterprises of the past, measuring recent transactions appeared to be a satisfactory proxy for measuring progress in creating value. When value creation was closely followed by value realization through a transaction (the mouse trap was manufactured in March and sold in April), concentrating on just value realization alone was good enough. This is no longer true today.

This train of logic leads to two fundamental conclusions:

- What transaction-centric accounting actually measures is the *realization* of value created at some earlier time. Measuring value realization is still necessary and useful, but not a sufficient basis for understanding organizational performance.
- If we wish to provide relevant information to decision-makers, we need measurement that goes beyond the value realization transaction-centric paradigm.

This last point is the main stumbling block. Given that traditional accounting is transaction-centric, how could it be possible to discover a basis for measurement other than transactions?

A Scientific Analogy

The situation of financial accounting today is analogous to that of physics a century ago. At that time, leading scientists knew that Newton's laws could not be used as the basis for explaining gravity, the behavior of the components of the atom, or the mechanics of light. To explain these and other phenomena, scientists had to progress beyond the inherent limitations of Newtonian physics.

In 1962, Thomas Kuhn wrote a landmark work on *The Structure of Scientific Revolutions* that popularized the concept of the "paradigm shift."[2] Using a series of historical examples, Kuhn showed that scientific progress is not characterized by a steady stream of discoveries, each building on the previous one, rather, we see a relatively small number of scientific *revolutions*, in which our understanding of the world shifted dramatically from one paradigm to another.

---

[2]Thomas Kuhn, *The Structure of Scientific Revolutions*, Chicago: University of Chicago Press, 1996.

A scientific paradigm consists of a set of accepted laws, theories, applications, and instrumentation. The research activities of the vast majority of scientists are characterized by Kuhn as "mopping-up operations" within the confines of a particular paradigm. Each scientific paradigm has fundamental limitations, revealed by the problems that cannot be explained within the boundaries of the paradigm. Hence, it was necessary for Einstein to develop a new paradigm—built around the theory of relativity—to account for phenomena that could not be explained by Newtonian physics (see Exhibit E.1).

In accounting as in physics, the issue is one of relevance. The need to transcend the limitations of the traditional transaction-based accounting paradigm arises because we need to be able to measure value creation in the modern economy, just as the scientists of a century ago needed to explain phenomena at the stellar and atomic levels that could not be modeled through Newton's equations.

Traditional accounting is also depicted in Exhibit E.1, recognizing that there is some debate about precisely where to locate the boundaries of the tradition-

EXHIBIT E.1   New and Traditional Paradigms

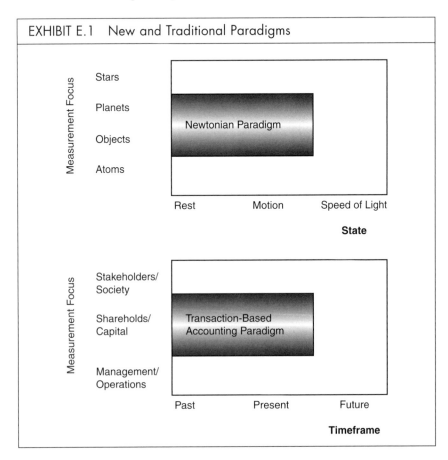

al accounting paradigm, which are determined mainly by the degree to which values other than historical cost, such as fair market values, are used to portray certain classes of assets.

Does the need for a new accounting paradigm mean abandoning transaction-based accounting? Not at all. Although we talk of paradigm *shifts*, the fact is that in physics, multiple paradigms coexist. Newtonian physics is still useful, and it is perfectly adequate for predicting the behavior of objects in motion as we drive to work in the morning. However, it does not provide an adequate basis for modern medical diagnostics or operating a nuclear power station.

Similarly, tracking an organization's performance based on historical financial transactions with third parties is still useful. However, it does not provide an adequate basis for measuring the value creation potential of knowledge-intensive organizations or for tracking progress in achieving that potential.

Accounting standard-setters have been and continue to be engaged in Kuhnian "mopping-up operations" within the traditional accounting paradigm, as they introduce new standards for accounting for acquired intangibles, or methods for accounting for financial derivatives. These, and similar incremental improvements to traditional accounting, are necessary and useful. However, they do not provide a way for traditional accounting to overcome its inherent limitations, which is that it cannot measure using transactions things that cannot be measured using transactions. Traditional accounting is inherently unable to provide insights into future value creation potential; it can only measure the ultimate realization of that value as transactions ultimately occur.

The idea that we might need a new value measurement paradigm in accounting is and will continue to be controversial. This too is perfectly predictable, based on Kuhn. We no longer physically burn scientific revolutionaries at the stake, but anyone who has followed an intense scientific debate, such as the one that rages on about climate change, will understand that we still do so metaphorically.

Kuhn observes that the transition from one scientific paradigm to another does not occur because leading scientists change their minds. He quotes Max Planck, "surveying his own career in his *Scientific Autobiography*, sadly remarking that 'a new scientific truth does not triumph by convincing its opponents and making them see the light, but rather because its opponents eventually die, and a new generation grows up that is familiar with it.' "

Hopefully, we would not need quite so drastic a solution as this in the world of accounting. However, we could not expect that any proposed nontransactional accounting paradigm would be easy for the accounting profession or for corporate reporting standard-setters to accept or grasp, in part because the conceptual frameworks that accountants and standard-setters use are located entirely within the boundaries of the transaction-centric accounting paradigm. We can expect that any proposals for a nontransaction-based approach will be attacked, as they have been already, by some adherents of the traditional paradigm. Such attacks will continue to take place despite the fact, to emphasize the point again, that there is no need to leave the transaction-centric accounting paradigm behind.

Within the context of its own paradigm—that is, within the boundaries of its inherent limitations—there is nothing wrong with transaction-centric accounting. It is what it is, and performs as advertised. Just as Newtonian physics and Einsteinian physics coexist in the real world, so too could the traditional value realization measurement paradigm and a new value measurement paradigm, as *parallel systems*.

Innovations in Value and Performance Measurement

Five Categories

Over the past decade, there has been an astonishing amount of activity by innovators attempting to measure value and performance beyond the boundaries of traditional accounting. Dozens of value measurement approaches have emerged, many of which are identified in Technical Appendix E.1. For purposes of this discussion, we can group these new measurement approaches into five categories: Intangibles, indicators, market capitalization, the "capitals," and value streams (see Exhibit E.2).

People who advocate approaches in the "Intangibles" category tend to focus on extending traditional techniques for measuring the value of tangible assets to the world of intangibles.

Those working on "Indicators" tend to focus on constructing a framework of metrics that extends beyond traditional accounting measurement.

The proponents of "Market Capitalization" approaches base their analysis on decomposing and/or influencing the market price of a company's shares.

The adherents of approaches in the "Capitals" category argue that the best way to build the financial capital of an enterprise is to focus attention on the interrelationships among customer capital, structural capital, intellectual capital, and the other "capitals."

The "Value Streamers" argue that rather than focus on the traditional concept of an "asset," we can directly model the value creation potential of value streams, and the interactions among them, to create a forward-looking system of value creation measurement.

EXHIBIT E.2 Value and Performance Measurement Innovations

Focus	Intangibles	Indicators	Market Capitalization	The "Capitals"	Value Streams
Selected examples	FASB's Intangibles Project Value dynamics Brookings Report	Balanced Scorecard KPIs	Market cap-book value gap analysis Economic value-based analysis	Intellectual capital Human capital Societal capital	Intangibles value streams Event-based enterprise value streams
How the innovators define the problem	Intangibles not fully reflected in financial statements Gap between market and book value	Accounting measurement is not sufficient basis for strategic management of enterprise	Enterprises are not managing gap between book (current operation) and market value	Enterprise are not managing major components of "capital" that account for the majority of enterprise value	Traditional transaction-based (value realization) accounting provides no insight into performance of organization in creating value
How the innovators describe the solution	Measure and disclose fair value of intangible assets	Set goals and track performance using a broad framework of metrics	Decompose market cap into current and future growth value components and create system for tracking drivers of future growth	Frameworks and systems for measuring customer, human, structural, and other "capitals"	Parallel value creation measurement system that models the potential of future value streams and tracks performance in realizing it

Measurement versus Disclosure

It is important to note that in compiling the list of innovations just catego-rized, the focus was solely on *measurement*, and not on corporate reporting or disclosure in general. Work is under way within and beyond the global account-ing profession focused on enhanced disclosure or reporting frameworks. To cite only a few examples, relevant projects include:

- The proposed Enhanced Business Reporting Consortium (EBRC) led by the American Institute of Certified Public Accountants (AICPA)
- The "Information for Better Markets" campaign of the Institute of Char-tered Accountants of England and Wales (ICAEW)
- Work by the Canadian Institute of Chartered Accountants (CICA) on MD&A Guidelines, and an earlier project on Total Value Creation
- Publications sponsored by major firms, such as PricewaterhouseCoopers's book *Value Reporting*
- Exploration by various European institutes, the Global Reporting Initia-tive, and other international bodies of ways to report on intellectual, human, societal, and other forms of capital, and on various dimensions of sustainability

In the context of these initiatives, what is meant by the term "reporting framework"? The Enhanced Business Reporting Consortium defines a report-ing framework as: "A framework to enhance information relevance and consis-tency. This information includes information about opportunities, risks, strategies, and plans, and about the quality, sustainability, and variability of cash flows and earnings, as well as industry-specific, process-oriented value drivers and key performance indicators."[3]

A reporting or disclosure framework is evidently meant to convey something much broader than "measurement." A reporting framework is intended to pro-vide comprehensive guidelines concerning information of all kinds that a com-pany should make available to its stakeholders, addressing both what should be disclosed and how. Only a subset of those disclosures consitute "measures."

---

[3]The Enhanced Business Reporting Consortium.

Comparing Measurement Approaches: Systems and Frameworks

In considering how alternative measurement approaches compare with each other and to traditional accounting, we are confronted with the need to differentiate between measurement approaches that are systemic and those that are not.

Compare, for example, a traditional balance sheet and income statement, and a set of key performance indicators. Both include quantitative measures and to that extent are similar. There are crucial differences, however. The numbers in the balance sheet and income statement emerge from an accounting measurement *system*, in which the debits must match the credits. Any change to any number in a set of financial statements requires a corresponding change in some other number.

By contrast, a set of key performance indicators is generally not systemic, but rather, constitutes what can be referred to as a measurement *framework*. In a framework of key performance indicators, there is normally a logical relationship among the elements of the framework. However, the elements of a framework of key performance indicators are not related to each other in the same systemic manner as are the elements in a set of financial statements. See Exhibit E.3 for the criteria that differentiate a *measurement system* from a *measurement framework*.

Planetary mechanics is a good example of a *measurement system*. The motions of the planets can be modeled with sufficient precision that it is possible to predict eclipses centuries into the future. Weather forecasting is a good example of a discipline that formerly was not a system but has become so. The

---

EXHIBIT E.3 Differences between a Measurement System and a Measurement Framework

Measurement System	Measurement Framework
Backed by an internally consistent integrated "model" (a representation of reality)	Discrete, stand-alone (but may be organized in a logical framework)
To link inputs and outputs through causal linkages	May indicate correlations (but not causal linkages)
Constituent elements of model are non-arbitrary	Selection of framework elements may be arbitrary
Examples: Astronomical calculations Traditional double-entry accounting	Examples: Political risk assessment Key performance indicators

first weather instruments were invented about the same time as double-entry bookkeeping: The hygrometer was invented around 1450, the thermometer in 1592 by Galileo, and the barometer in 1643. The effort to make weather forecasting reliable began in the late 1800s. Vilhelm Bjerknes, a Norwegian, and Lewis Fry Richardson of Britain are credited as pioneers in the attempt to model future weather through a system of mathematical equations. In his first full-scale attempt in the early 1900s, it took Richardson several months to do the calculations to support a six-hour forecast for an area near Munich—a forecast that was not only somewhat late to be a forecast but was also wildly inaccurate even in hindsight.

Despite its lack of immediate success, Richardson's attempt set the course for innovation in weather prediction. Now, a century later, satellites ring the globe providing thousands of real-time weather observations, complex computer models produce detailed forecasts of weather at multiple levels in the atmosphere, covering virtually all the earth's surface, and aviators and sailors can download "grid charts" from the Internet providing an extraordinary amount of forecast data. Weather forecasting is not perfect, but it is a system.

This line of thinking leads to the question: Are any of the alternative value measurement approaches in any of the five categories referred to previously "a system," or do any have the potential to become so with further development? This and other criteria are discussed later.

This line of thinking also leads to the observation that the relationships among disclosure, measurement, and systemic measurement can be depicted as shown in Exhibit E.4.

It is evident that any enhanced reporting or disclosure framework will include a combination of measurement information that is systemic, as well as measurement information that is not systemic.

This leads to the following question: What are the implications for users, producers, and auditors of measurement information of combining systemic and nonsystemic approaches within a broader reporting or disclosure framework? This question is not specifically addressed in this appendix, but the later analysis provides an initial foundation for addressing it.

A New Value Measurement Paradigm?

Virtually all the approaches in each of the categories described previously were developed to meet the specific needs of decision-makers. In most cases, their practical utility for these purposes has been demonstrated in many successful implementations.

However, there is a higher-level issue here. Many, if not most, of these approaches were explicitly developed in an attempt to overcome the limitations

EXHIBIT E.4   An Enhanced Reporting Framework

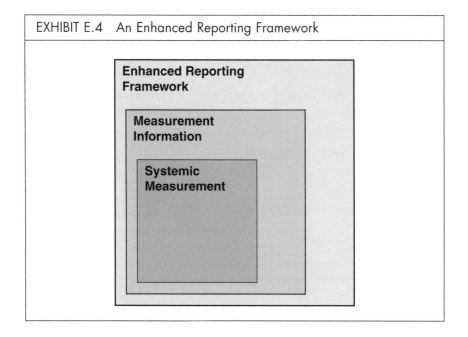

of traditional accounting. In the context of the argument given previously, it is logical to ask: To what extent did they succeed? In other words, do any of the approaches in the five categories represent the equivalent, in relation to value and performance measurement, of Einstein's breakthrough on relativity? Or do they simply represent incremental improvement on the status quo, but not a fundamental breakthrough? How would we recognize the difference? By what criteria could we assess the degree to which any of these value measurement approaches is, or points toward, a new paradigm in value measurement? The next sections attempt to lay some of the necessary groundwork for addressing these questions.

Measurement Concepts

Some Basic Definitions

Let us begin by considering what we mean by "measurement." The Oxford Dictionary of English (OED) defines "measure" as follows:

> As a verb:
>
> - "Ascertain the amount or degree of something by using an instrument or device marked in standard units"

- "Take an exact quantity of something"
- "Judge someone or something by comparison with a certain standard"

The OED defines the noun as:

- "The size, length, or amount of something as established by measuring"

Measurement is defined as "the action of measuring something." A related concept is "unit of measure," defined as "a quantity chosen as a standard in terms of which other quantities may be expressed." It is evident that in order to measure something in a way that provides insight to others, there needs to be some level of agreement about the unit(s) of measure.

Measurement Fundamentals

This analysis draws heavily on the summary of measurement theory, information theory, and accounting theory included in the April 2003 Issue Paper published by the Fédération des Experts Comptables Européens (FEE): "Principles of Assurance: Fundamental Theoretical Issues related to Assurance in Assurance Engagements," referred to henceforth as the "FEE Paper." (See Technical Appendix E.2 for URLs to sections of the FEE paper relating to information, measurement, and accounting theory.)

In its review of measurement theory, the FEE paper reminds us of some measurement fundamentals.

- Measurement relates to objects; or more precisely, properties of objects; or even more precisely, properties of "systems"; or even more precisely still, indicants of properties of systems. (For our purposes here, it will in most cases be sufficiently precise to refer to measuring "properties of objects.")
- To measure something involves quantification of properties, based on some mathematical model. Quantification does not necessarily mean numerical; valid measurement scales can be:
  - Nominal (determining whether something does or does not meet some criterion)
  - Ordinal (a scale in which things are arranged in rank order)
  - Interval (a scale on which equal intervals between objects represent equal differences)
  - Ratio (a scale on which the ratios of the numbers assigned accurately reflect ratios of the magnitudes of the objects being measured).

Financial measures represent a ratio scale.

Measuring Value

According to the Oxford Dictionary of English, "value" or "values" have several connotations:

- "The regard that something is held to deserve; the importance, worth, or usefulness of something"
- "The material or monetary worth of something"
- "The worth of something compared to the price paid or asked for it"
- "Principles of standards of behavior; one's judgment of what is important in life"
- "The numerical amount denoted by an algebraic term: A magnitude, quantity or number"

A "valuation" is defined as "an estimation of the worth of something, especially one carried out by a professional valuer." Related concepts include: Value added, value analysis, value engineering, value-free, value judgment, value-laden, valueless, value received, valuable, and valuable consideration.

These definitions lead to the following observations and questions:

- Is value ever "absolute," or is it always relative? For practical purposes, it is almost always true that value is "in the eye of the beholder."
- Values expressed in currency (e.g., this car is worth $10,000) seem more absolute than "moral" values, but even in everyday life we differentiate between monetary cost and value to a potential buyer.
- Transaction value is in fact an amount that sits somewhere between the perceived value of something to a buyer and the perceived value to the seller: Normally, a buyer will complete a transaction only if the acquisition cost is less than the value perceived by the buyer.
- This logic suggests that "perspective" or "context" is relevant to any value measurement. In other words, every value measure inherently reflects a specific perspective, even if that perspective is not explicitly referenced or recognized as such.

If we reassemble the term "value measurement" or "quantification of value," the following observations emerge:

- Like all measures, one would assume that the "value" we want to measure or quantify is a property of an object or system.
- The difficulty that arises is that if all value is relative or contextual, this would suggest that value is not strictly a property of an object or

system, since we also need to take into account the perspective of the "beholder."

This would suggest that value might be a property of a *relationship* that includes the object or system and the beholder, not of the object or system per se. If we don't want to go this far, at a minimum, we need to associate the idea of a "perspective" or "context" with the value-related property of the object or system. To comprehend the significance of any quantification of value, it is therefore essential to:

- Be aware of the object and properties being measured
- Be aware of the perspective
- Understand the underlying mathematical system

Measuring Performance

According to the OED, to perform is to "carry out, accomplish, or fulfill" an action, task, or function. "Performance" has several connotations:

- "The act of presenting a play, concert, or other form of entertainment"
- "The action or process of performing a task or function"
- "A task or operation seen in terms of how successfully it is performed"
- "The capabilities of a machine, product, or vehicle"

Related concepts include "performance art" and "performance bond." These definitions lead to the following observations and questions:

- Is performance absolute or relative? To the extent that we wish to differentiate between different levels of performance, it can be argued that performance is always measured in relation to some point of reference, such as an objective (e.g., performance targets), a standard (e.g., 9s sigma), or precedent (e.g., last year's performance).
- Do we need to take "perspective" into account, as in the case of value? In other words, is performance in the eye of the beholder? Logic would suggest that perspective is a factor not so much in the interpretation of the reference point as in the selection of the reference point. That is, different beholders might choose difference reference points for evaluating performance, but performance could be objectively determined in rela-

tion to each of those reference points without taking perspective into account.

- Any organization with multiple stakeholders faces the possibility that different stakeholders may adopt different reference points for differentiating between satisfactory and unsatisfactory performance.
- If we reassemble the term "performance measurement," or "quantification of performance," the following observations emerge:
  - Is the "performance" we want to measure or quantify a property of an object or system, or a property of an object or system in some sort of relationship with the reference point?

It seems likely that performance can be a property of an object or system, but that it has no real meaning apart from one or more reference points, whether or not those reference points are defined implicitly or explicitly. To comprehend the significance of any quantification of performance, it is therefore essential to:

- Be aware of the object and properties being measured
- Be aware of the reference point
- Understand the underlying mathematical system

Summary

In sum, as we develop criteria for differentiating among different measurement approaches, we must keep in mind:

- That measurement pertains to a "property" of an object or system, not to the object or system itself. To understand the meaning of a measure, it is important to be clear about what it is, and is not, measuring.
- That all *value* measures are "relative" to a particular perspective, whether or not that perspective is explicit. To comprehend the significance of any quantification of value, it is essential to:
  - Be aware of the object and properties being measured
  - Be aware of the perspective
  - Understand the underlying mathematical system
- That all *performance* measures are "relative" to one or more reference points, whether or not these are explicit

Measurement Criteria

Principal Source of Criteria

The criteria analysis in this appendix builds on the analysis of measurement theory, information theory, and accounting theory included in the FEE paper referred to previously. Although the FEE paper had different objectives than this appendix, it provides a highly relevant overview and synthesis of fundamental theoretical concepts.

One can think of information, measurement, and accounting theory as being related, as in Exhibit E.5.

The FEE paper includes an extensive analysis of, and ultimately a synthesis of, criteria emerging from information, measurement and accounting theory. In order to adapt the analysis in the FEE paper to profiling measurement approaches, some relevant distinctions must be made.

The first is to differentiate between criteria for assessing measures and criteria for assessing measurement systems or approaches. A measurement system may incorporate various types of measures: Necessarily, then, the criteria used to profile a measurement approach or system will be somewhat more general, or operate at a higher level, than the criteria that would be applied to specific individual measures.

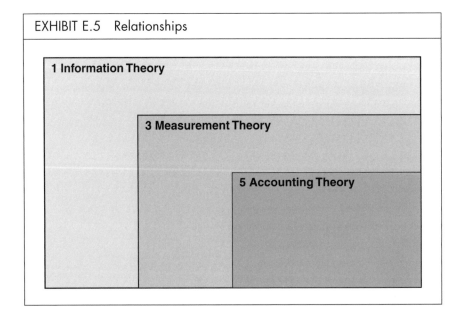

EXHIBIT E.5   Relationships

1 Information Theory

3 Measurement Theory

5 Accounting Theory

A second distinction is to differentiate between criteria that would be applied to assess a specific instance of a measure or measurement approach and criteria that would be applied to assess the measurement approach as an approach. In this appendix, we refer to the former as "evaluation criteria" and the latter as "profiling criteria."

In an assurance engagement, an auditor applies "evaluation criteria" to assess the specific subject matter of the engagement. The auditor provides an opinion on a specific instance of financial statements—for example, the financial statements of XYZ Corporation for the year ended December 31, 200X—not on the general class of financial statements as a measurement approach. By contrast, the focus of this appendix is to suggest criteria that could be applied to profile a measurement approach as an approach, in comparison with other approaches. To illustrate further, the issue that concerns us here is not whether a particular instance of a measurement approach demonstrates a certain "bias" (to cite one criterion of interest), but rather whether all instances of a specific measurement approach are biased because of something inherent in the approach itself.

As a result of these two distinctions, the approach followed here is not to attempt to incorporate all of the criteria described in the FEE paper, but rather to select from and adapt those criteria that could be usefully applied to profile measurement approaches, as well as to suggest additional criteria that may be relevant.

Building on this background material, this section sets out to answer the following questions:

1. What is the minimum set of "profiling criteria" that can be used to describe authoritatively the similarities and differences between one measurement approach and another?
2. How can such criteria be organized into an overall model that can be applied to generate a "profile" for a measurement approach in relation to the criteria.

Context

To begin with, there are three contextual overarching criteria that should be considered at the outset in classifying a measurement approach:

- Who are the users?
- Why do they want to use the measurement approach—in other words, what purpose does it serve?
- What does the approach actually measure?

Let us consider each in more detail.

Who are the users of the measurement approach? Users can potentially be classified first by differentiating among those who are internal to the organization (e.g., employees), versus those who are outside the organization (e.g., external stakeholders), versus those who sit at the interface between external and internal (e.g., Board of Directors).

Internal users can subdivided into:

- Operational staff
- Operational management
- Executive management

External users can be subdivided into:

- Those who have an existing relationship with the organization as:
  - Owners or members
  - Customers or the equivalent
  - Suppliers or business partners

- Those who are affected by the organization's actions (members of society)
- Those who may use measurement information in the process of deciding whether to enter into a relationship with the organization in the future

A further differentiation can be made among:

- Users who simply are the recipients of measurement information
- Users who provide key inputs
- Users who plan and manage the administration of a measurement approach

What are the purposes of the measurement approach: In other words, why do users use it, or why should the want to use it? The purposes of a measurement approach may classified by determining:

- Whether the measurement approach plays a role in the day-to-day operations or transactions of the organization, or whether its function is related more to management
- Whether the measurement approach influences decisions, and if so, what sorts of decisions:
  - Decisions of internal users (management decisions) versus external users (e.g., investment decisions)
  - In the case of management decisions, one can differentiate among day-to-day routine decisions, versus routine decisions that are made routinely, versus strategic decisions that are made infrequently; one can also

differentiate among decisions that are normally made by operational staff, operational management, or executive management

- Whether the emphasis is on quantifying value or quantifying performance

What does the measurement approach measure: In other words, what are the objects and properties that are the "subject matter" of the measurement approach? The subject matter of a measurement approach can be classified with respect to:

- Whether the principal objects/properties being measured relate to:
  - Financial transactions of the organization
  - Things owned by the organization (such as tangible and some intangible assets)
  - Processes taking place inside or outside the organization
  - People and entities that are internal to the organization and/or their relationships to the organization
  - Value streams in which the organization participates
  - People and entities that are external to the organization and/or their relationships to the organization
  - Attributes of the organization itself
  - Transactions of external parties that relate to the organization (such as those that influence stock price)
  - Events that relate to the organization

- Whether the units of measure are primarily financial or nonfinancial
- Whether the scale of the measurement is primarily numeric or non-numeric
- Whether the timeframe to which the measures relate is primarily the past or the future

Utility of a Measurement Approach

With the foregoing criteria defining the overall context at a high level, let us move on to criteria that can help analyze in more detail the "utility" of a measurement approach, which broadly relates to what it can be used to measure.

The "utility" criteria are derived from information, measurement, and accounting criteria, as summarized in Technical Appendix E.2, related to such matters as:

- User information needs
- Valuable information

- Relevance/decision-usefulness (making a difference in a decision)
- User benefits

Does the main focus of the approach involve quantification related to value, quantification related to performance, or both? For example, a Balanced Scorecard provides insights into performance, but normally it does not measure value. Traditional financial statements measure both value and performance, based, however, principally on financial transactions.

To the extent an approach quantifies value, what are the principal parameters of the approach? What are the objects that are or can be measured using this approach:

- Financial transactions of the organization
- Assets or the organization, tangible and intangible
- Entities or units of the organization
- Value streams in which the organization participates
- Relationships between people or entities and the organization
- Transactions of external parties that relate to the organization

What are the principal perspectives from which value is quantified?

- People or entities inside the organization
- The organization itself
- The owners of the organization
- The market in general
- Specific potential buyers or sellers
- Other external stakeholders

What are the attributes of the underlying mathematical system used to quantify value?

- Systemic or nonsystemic
- Standards-based or ad hoc
- What value concepts are relied on, for example:
  - Historical cost accounting
  - Market comparables as used in valuation
  - Discounting of potential future cash flows
  - Strategic value based on market or competitive analysis

To the extent an approach quantifies performance, what are the principal parameters of the approach? What objects/properties can be measured using this approach?

- Processes internal to the organization
- People internal to the organization
- Entities internal to the organization
- The organization itself
- External processes in which the organization participates
- External relationships of the organization

What is or are the principal reference point(s) in relation to which performance is quantified?

- Previous performance
- Performance goals or targets
- Performance of peer organizations or competitors
- Performance related to stakeholder expectations
- Performance related to defined standards

What are the attributes of the underlying mathematical system used to quantify performance?

- Systemic or nonsystemic
- Standards-based or ad hoc
- Absolute or relative
- Measurement scale

Comparability: To what extent is it possible to use measures generated by the approach to do value or performance comparisons? What types of comparisons does the approach enable?

- Internal comparisons
- Prior periods
- Targets
- External comparisons with peers or competitors
- Benchmarking

Extensibility: To what extent can the measurement approach be adapted for broader purposes? Extensibility can be assessed based on the following factors:

- Does the approach have the potential to serve broader purposes than at present? How much development would be required to support this?
- Could the approach be adapted to measure different objects/properties than at present?
- What are the existing inherent limitations of the approach and to what extent could these be overcome through further development?

- Does the approach have an existing or potential role in external corporate reporting?
- Is there an existing or potential linkage to emerging standards such as XBRL?

Validity of a Measurement Approach

The validity of a measurement approach is another key area for comparisons among different approaches. For purposes of this analysis, key aspects of validity that build on the criteria summarized in Appendix D.2 include:

- Construct, content, and criterion-related validity
- Reliability

Validity in use: From a user perspective, what is the relative validity of the value or performance measures related to the objects/properties being measured?

At a pragmatic level, a user of a measurement approach may make a number of intuitive "judgment calls" with respect to whether a measurement approach is sufficiently valid for measuring specific categories of objects/properties. For instance, a user might intuitively perceive that a measurement approach offers sufficient validity for valuing tangible but not intangible assets; or is sufficiently valid to measure the performance of business entities but not valid if applied to business processes.

Reliability in use: To what extent are users prepared to trust the results of the measurement approach sufficiently so as to make decisions based on the measures?

A user may also make a judgment call with respect to the types of decisions he or she is prepared to make based on the measurement approach, also taking into account the extent of corroborating evidence that is available.

Technical validity. At a technical level, there are three key aspects of validity for any measure:

1. Does a measure accurately reflect the underlying concepts of theory (if any) on which it is based? (This is referred to as "construct validity.")
2. Does a measure actually measure what it purports to measure? (This is referred to as "content validity.")
3. Does a measure provide a satisfactory amount of feedback information (looking backward) or predictive information (looking ahead), and what is the shelf-life of the measure. In other words, for how long is the

information still valid or useful? (This is referred to as "criterion-related validity.)

Technical reliability. At a technical reliability level, there are two major aspects:

1. Accuracy: Does the measure offer a satisfactory level of accuracy, free from systemic error or bias?
2. Precision: Does the measure offer a satisfactory level of precision, free from random error or bias?

The units of measure and scale are related to both accuracy and precision. For instance, if the measurement scale is not sufficiently granular, this may limit accuracy or precision, or both.

Practicality of a Measurement Approach

Building on relevant criteria outlined in Technical Appendix E.2, the practicality of a measurement can be assessed in relation to criteria such as the following:

- Absolute and relative benefits as perceived by users
- Absolute and relative costs
- Short- and long-term resource requirements
- Availability of inputs
- Appropriateness of outputs
- Characteristics of users that are essential to make effective use of the measures
- Inherent characteristics of the information on which the measures are based

VMRC has developed an online system that enables users to apply these and other criteria in evaluating alternative measurement approaches. For additional information, please visit: http://npi.valuemeasurement.net

VALUE AND PERFORMANCE MEASUREMENT INNOVATIONS

THE FOLLOWING IS an initial compilation of value and performance innovations.

Method	Category	Innovator(s)
Accounting for the Future (AFTF)	Value streams	Nash
APQC Performance Measurement	Indicators	ACPQ
Balanced Scoreboard	Indicators	Kaplan, Nortron
Brand Valuation	Market Cap	Brand Finance
Business IQ	Capitals	Sandvik
Calculated Intangible Value	Intangibles	NCI Research (see Andriessen)
Celemi Monitor	Capitals	Celemi
Citation-Weighted patents	Intangibles	B. H. Hall, et al.
Cognos Scorecards/ Dashboards	Indicators	Cognos
Customer Value Management	Capitals	SMS
Customer Value Measurement	Capitals	NTF Group (AU)
Dolphin Navigator	Indicators	IC Community
Economic Value Added	Market Cap	Stern Stewart
Enhanced Business Reporting	Indicators	AICPA

Method	Category	Innovator(s)
Enterprise Capital Model	Capitals	St. Onge, Armstrong
Future Value Management	Market Cap	Burgmann, Accenture
Global Reporting Initiative	Indicators	GRI
Hermes Principles	Market Cap, Value Streams	Hermes Pensions Management Limited
Holistic Value Approach	Capitals	Roos
Human Resource Accounting	Capitals	Various
Human Capital Index	Capitals	Watson Wyett
Inclusive Value Methodology	Intangibles	M'Pherson
Inside Out	Intangibles	ICAEW
Intangible Assets Monitor	Intangibles	Sveiby
Intangibles Scoreboard	Intangibles	Lev
Intangibles Valuation	Intangibles	Sullivan
Intangible Value Framework	Intangibles	Allee
Intangibles Value Stream Modeling	Value Streams	Sullivan, McLean
IC Evaluation	Capitals	Celemi
IC Monitor	Capitals	Nordic Industrial Fund
IC Rating	Capitals	Intellectual Capital Sweden
IC Reporting	Capitals	Denmark Ministry of Industry
Intellectual Capital Audit	Capitals	Brookings
Intellectual Capital Benchmarking System	Capitals	Viedma
Intellectual Capital Dynamic Value	Intangibles	Bounfour
Intellectual Capital Monitor	Capitals	Stam

Method	Category	Innovator(s)
Intellectual Capital Report	Capitals	MERITUM project
Intellectual Capital Statement	Capitals	Mouritsen
IPM Benchmarking	Capitals	Sullivan, McLean, McCullough
IP Score	Intangibles	Danish Patent Office
Investor Assigned Market Value	Market Cap	Standfield
Invisible Balance Sheet	Capitals	Sveiby
iValuing Factor	Intangibles	Standfield
Intellectual Capital Index	Capitals	Roos et al.
Jenkins Report	Indicators	AICPA
Key Performance Indicators	Indicators	KPMG (Bray)
Konrad Group	Indicators, Capitals	Konrad Group
Knowledge Audit Cycle	Capitals	Marr, Schiuma
Knowledge Capital	Market Cap	Lev
Market to book ratio	Market Cap	Various
Market Value of Intangibles	Market Cap	Sveiby
MD&A Guidelines	Indicators	CICA
Measures that Matter	Indicators	EYI, Low
Measuring and Accounting Intellectual Capital (MAGIC)	Capitals	EU
MeyerMonitor	Indicators	Meyer Monitor
Patent Assets Monitor	Indicators	Siemens
Patent Value Predictor	Intangibles	Patent Value Predictor
Performance Prism	Indicators	Cranfield School of Management, Accenture
PBViews	Indicators	PerformanceSoft
QRP Scorecard	Indicators	QRP

Method	Category	Innovator(s)
Real Options	Value Streams	PL-X Systems (and others)
SAP Value Measurements	Indicators	SAP
Shareholder Value Measurement	Market Cap	Various (see CICA)
Skandia Navigator	Capitals	Edvinsson
Social Responsibility Reporting	Capitals	Various
Stakeholder Accounts	Indicators	Denmark
Sustainability Reporting	Indicators	Various
Sustainability Value Measurement	Indicators	Ekos
Technology Factor	Intangibles	Dow, A.D. Little
Tobin's Q	Market cap	Tobin
Tomorrow's Company	Indicators	RSA London
Total Value Creation	Value Streams	Anderson, McLean
21st Century Annual Report	Indicators	ICAEW
Unseen Wealth	Intangibles	Brookings Institution
Value-Added Intellectual Coefficient	Intangibles	Pulic
Value Chain Scoreboard	Indicators	Lev
Value Creation Index	Value Streams	E&Y
Value Dynamics	Intangibles	Libert, Boulton, Samek
Value Explorer	Indicators	KPMG (Andreissen)
Value Extraction	Capitals	ICM Gathering
Value Networks	Capitals	Verna Allee
Value Reporting	Indicators	PWC
Weightless Wealth Toolkit	Intangibles	Andreissen

Technical Appendix E.2
Resources

http://npi.valuemeasurement.net/concepts.html provides access to electronic versions of this document, the extract of the FEE Paper, and additional relevant information.

http://npi.valuemeasurement.net/profiles.html provides access to VRMC's measurement profiling system, along with instructions and sample reports.

http://npi.valuemeasurement.net/participate.html provides information about how to participate in the New Paradigm Initiative.

http://npi.valuemeasurement.net/documents/html provides access to additional relevant documents, Web site links, and other information.

APPENDIX F

CREATING AN I-STUFF STRATEGY

A STRATEGY MAY be thought of as the set of focused activities a firm engages in to achieve its major objectives. (The realization of the firm's strategic vision is, of course, a primary long-term objective.) A firm's strategy may be selected in a number of ways: *inspiration*, or the brilliant vision of the leader; *accommodation* among competing political factions; *rational choice* after careful study; or *default* (the path of least resistance). These and many other general categorizations describe the ways organizations arrive at their business strategy. The rational-choice style, espoused by many but practiced by few, is the most difficult and complex approach, yet it offers the greatest reward. This appendix discusses the rational-choice approach as it relates it to the development of an I-stuff strategy. The rational-choice approach is built on two closely linked descriptions of what the firm wishes to become. The first of these, the corporate mission, defines the value the firm wishes to create for its customers or for society. The second, the corporate vision, describes what the company expects to look like in the future as it continues to create and provide the defined value.

There are good reasons given by companies for the strategy development approach they adopt. For example, companies arriving at their strategic direction by default find themselves on a trajectory that seems to produce results and then stay with it. "After all," the argument goes, "it's working well for us so far." Still other companies turn to their CEO for that inspiring view of the future that will define what the firm will become. Unfortunately, most CEOs are mortal and not gifted with the ability to see the future clearly. Nor are they necessarily able to divine a successful strategy that will carry the firm toward the achievement of the vision. Still other companies, probably organizations that are more people oriented, go through major internal debates, with strong positions becoming established and win-lose positions being developed between the leaders of what often become warring camps. Companies such as these usually end up with a no-decision strategy (default) or an accommodation strategy that suboptimizes the firm's capabilities and future.

As part of I-stuff strategy development, it will be helpful to describe the steps in the rational choice approach that precede I-stuff strategy development.

EXHIBIT F.1   The I-Stuff Strategy Development Process

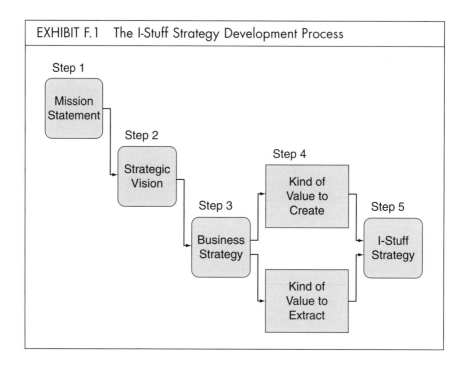

Exhibit F.1 displays the steps involved in the rational-choice approach to I-stuff strategy development.

The activities required for each of the steps identified in Exhibit F.1 are briefly described in the following discussion.

STEP ONE: CREATE A STATEMENT OF MISSION

The mission statement is the first entry in the string of ever-more-detailed descriptions that allow the company to know clearly where it is going in the long term, what value it is providing, and how it intends to provide that value. Under the rational-choice approach, the corporate mission statement contains the value the company expects to provide or the organization's *raison d'être*.

Mission statements should contain one or two different kinds of information. First, the mission statement should identify the value the organization expects to create for their customers or for society. When appropriate, a mission statement may also define for whom it expects to make its contribution and geographically where this will take place.

Many corporate mission statements fall just short of being as helpful as they otherwise might be. For example, the actual corporate mission statement for McDonald's is: "To be the world's best quick service restaurant experience." This mission statement might become more helpful if it were more explicit, for example: *To provide tasty, consistent quality, reasonably priced quick service foods world-wide, delivered consistently, and in a friendly atmosphere.* Whereas the *actual* statement highlights the desire to provide the "best" quick service food experience, "best" is not as well defined as in the *rewritten version.* Here the elements comprising "best" are delineated (taste, consistent quality, price, consistency of delivery, friendliness of atmosphere), as is the geography (world-wide). In the rewritten version of McDonald's mission statement, "how" the company expects to differentiate itself from its competitors is defined by the sum of all the elements the statement contains.

Good corporate mission statements are rarely more than one sentence long.

Step Two: What Is a Strategic Vision?

Whereas the corporate mission describes *what value* a company seeks to provide, a strategic vision describes *what the organization will look like in the future.* As an operational statement describing the future organization, it is more specific than a mission statement. It differs from a strategic plan in that the latter describes specific steps leading to the achievement of long-term goals. The strategic vision focuses on describing the organization as "what it wishes to become." A strategic vision does not concern itself with "how" it will be achieved. The "how" is left to later planning or to individual initiative.

Another way to understand strategic vision is to focus on the reasons for creating one. Here are some observations about what a well-conceived and broadly accepted strategic vision can do for an organization:

1. *The vision provides strategic meaning for the organization.* Vision permits the organization to focus its energies—for if everything is important, nothing is important. Vision differentiates foreground from background. Because the foreground acquires meaning only in relation to the background, an important part of vision development is to say what is excluded from the vision.

2. *The vision provides a common definition of subjective social reality for the organization's members.* It defines a vocabulary and a framework for discussing alternative plans, actions, and potential outcomes. It symbolizes an infrastructure of values, culture, and context that helps individual actors relate to one another and to the more abstract organization of which they are a part.

3. *The vision provides a reference point for managing the organization's beforemath.* It pulls people toward the desired future, reducing the need for formal directives.

4. *The vision is most important when dimensions of the proposed change are quite large, the change involves organizational values, culture, or structure, and the time to adjust is long.* It provides a continuing focal point as people and conditions change during the implementation of the strategic plan.

The importance of a well-conceived and well-articulated vision of the future is perhaps the most important piece of intellectual capital a firm can develop. Once known and widely acknowledged, such a view of the future allows employees at all levels of the firm to know whether an idea or an activity makes sense to pursue. It helps people know which path to take.

> "Said Alice to the Cheshire Cat:
>> 'Would you tell me, please, which way I ought to go from here?'
>> 'That depends a good deal on where you want to get to,' said the Cat.
>> 'I don't much care where—,' said Alice.
>> 'Then it doesn't matter which way you go,' said the Cat.[1]"

A final word on "visioning." Many organizations believe they have a vision for the future, but few have visions that are strategically helpful. In order to be helpful, a vision must state what the company wishes to become in operational terms, not how it intends to get there. It is also very important that visions describe the future state in a way that allows progress toward it to be measured. (Otherwise, the use of terms such as "best" or "preferred" or "number one" is meaningless.) With a well-articulated vision for the future, and a firm grasp on where the company is now, any firm is in a position to make the strategic decisions that will help it achieve its vision.

STEP THREE: OUTLINE THE CORPORATE BUSINESS STRATEGY

Once it is clear what value the organization exists to provide and also what the organization wishes to become, the business strategy for how the company intends to achieve these ends may now be determined. There is no simple formula describing what a business strategy contains because each business is unique; each has its own values, mission, and vision. Suffice it to say here that whatever business strategy the firm chooses to define, it must be articulated in

---

[1] L Carroll, Alice's Adventures in Wonderland and Through the Looking Glass, Penguin Books, London and New York, 1998, p. 56.

ways that make progress toward the strategy measurable. For example, statements like "becoming the provider of choice for the widget market" are not nearly as useful as saying "becoming number one in terms of market share in the widget market." Progress toward becoming number one in market share may be measured, whereas there is no obvious measure of progress toward becoming the "provider of choice."

When the business strategy is developed, defined, and promulgated by the organization, I-stuff managers are able to initiate Step Four of the I-stuff strategy development process.

Step Four: Identify the Kinds of Value the Organization's I-Stuff Can Provide

With the corporate mission and business strategy in hand, I-stuff managers can now ask themselves: How can the organization's I-stuff support the business strategy and the achievement of the strategic mission?

To answer this question, I-stuff managers must review each element of the corporate business strategy and decide what kind of value the company's I-stuff might provide to each. Appendix B contains a listing of the kinds of value that ICM Gathering companies have identified as being provided by their intangibles. (Although the listing in Appendix B is by no means a comprehensive one, it is representative enough that firms should be able to identify any additional kinds of value they wish to seek from their intangibles.)

Step Four of the I-stuff strategy development process is completed with the listing of the kinds of value that the organization's I-stuff could provide to identified elements of the firm's business strategy or to elements of its strategic vision.

Step Five: Outline, Discuss, and Finalize the Organization's I-Stuff Strategy

After completing Steps Three and Four, the firm is in a good position to identify the kinds of I-stuff that are important to support its business strategy or strategic vision.

1. First, create an inventory of the firm's significant I-stuff. By significant, we mean the firm's I-stuff when there is an anticipation that it will provide value for the organization.

2. Next, identify the kind of value the company wishes to extract from each piece of I-stuff in the inventory (see Appendix B).

3. With the value desired in mind, as well as the need to create and upgrade the company's I-stuff and its value continually, the firm should be able to define the kinds of I-stuff the firm wishes to *continue* to create or develop.

4. Then, define for each identified piece of I-stuff how the firm intends to extract the identified value. In simple terms, one could create an Excel spreadsheet listing each piece of I-stuff from which value is to be extracted. The first column on the spreadsheet might list the pieces of I-stuff, whereas the second column might identify the kind of value the firm expects to extract from each. In the third column one might find a brief description of how the value is to be extracted (e.g., for value to be extracted in the form of revenue, one might identify the value conversion mechanism to be used: sell, license, joint venture, strategic alliance, integration, and so on).

5. Finally, on completion of Steps One through Four, and mindful that a strategy has been defined in this appendix as *the set of focused activities organizations engage in to achieve their major objectives*, I-stuff managers should be in a position to identify the I-stuff management activities necessary for the company's I-stuff to provide the best potential support to its business.

As to the creation of a strategy document that collects and collates the information developed above, it might contain information such as the following:

- Overview of Company Business Strategy
- Elements of the Business Strategy Supportable with I-Stuff
- Kinds of Value That I-Stuff Can Provide to Each Element of Business Strategy Listed
- Significant I-Stuff Activities
- I-Stuff Value to be Created
- I-Stuff Value to be Extracted
- How the Value is to be Extracted
- Major I-Stuff Management Activities

The creation of an I-stuff strategy, as outlined here, is a "new" process for doing something that many firms have been doing for quite some time. For firms new to the management of I-stuff, there may be a few new or different ideas about how an I-stuff strategy is developed or what one contains. Nevertheless, the authors believe that the process outlined in this appendix is, as is often the case with intangibles management, little more than organized common sense!

INDEX